Against All Enemies

Inside America's War on Terror

Richard A. Clarke

FREE PRESS
NEW YORK • LONDON • TORONTO • SYDNEY

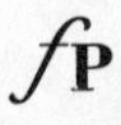

FREE PRESS
A Division of Simon & Schuster, Inc.
1230 Avenue of the Americas
New York, NY 10020

For information about special discounts for bulk purchases,
please contact Simon & Schuster Special Sales:
1-800-456-6798 or business@simonandschuster.com

DESIGNED BY LISA CHOVNICK
Manufactured in the United States of America

1 3 5 7 9 10 8 6 4 2

ISBN 0-7432-6024-4

*f*P

To those who were murdered on
September 11, 2001, including those who
tried to stop it, among them John O'Neill and the
extraordinarily brave passengers on United flight 93;
and to all those they left behind.

Contents

Preface

From inside the White House, the State Department, and the Pentagon for thirty years, I disdained those who departed government and quickly rushed out to write about it. It seemed somehow inappropriate to expose, as Bismarck put it, "the making of sausage." Yet I became aware after my departure from federal service that much that I thought was well known was actually obscure to many who wanted to know.

I was frequently asked "exactly how did things work on 9/11, what happened?" In looking at the available material, I found that there was no good source, no retelling of that day which history will long mark as a pivot point. Then, as I began to think about teaching graduate students at Georgetown and Harvard, I realized that there was no single inside account of the flow of recent history that had brought us to September 11, 2001, and the events that followed from it.

As the events of 2003 played out in Iraq and elsewhere, I grew increasingly concerned that too many of my fellow citizens were being misled. The vast majority of Americans believed, because the Bush administration had implied it, that Saddam Hussein had something to do with the al Qaeda attacks on America. Many thought that the Bush administration was doing a good job of fighting terrorism when, actually, the administration had squandered the opportunity to eliminate al Qaeda and instead strengthened our enemies by going off on a completely unnecessary tangent, the invasion of Iraq. A new al Qaeda has emerged and is growing stronger, in part because of our own actions and inactions. It is in many ways a tougher opponent than the original threat we faced before September 11 and we are not doing what is necessary to make America safer from that threat.

This is the story, from my perspective, of how al Qaeda developed and attacked the United States on September 11. It is a story of the

CIA and FBI, who came late to realize that there was a threat to the United States and who were unable to stop it even after they agreed that the threat was real and significant. It is also the story of four presidents:

- Ronald Reagan, who did not retaliate for the murder of 278 United States Marines in Beirut and who violated his own terrorism policy by trading arms for hostages in what came to be called the Iran-Contra scandal;
- George H. W. Bush, who did not retaliate for the Libyan murder of 259 passengers on Pan Am 103; who did not have an official counterterrorism policy; and who left Saddam Hussein in place, requiring the United States to leave a large military presence in Saudi Arabia;
- Bill Clinton, who identified terrorism as the major post–Cold War threat and acted to improve our counterterrorism capabilities; who (little known to the public) quelled anti-American terrorism by Iraq and Iran and defeated an al Qaeda attempt to dominate Bosnia; but who, weakened by continued political attack, could not get the CIA, the Pentagon, and FBI to act sufficiently to deal with the threat;
- George W. Bush, who failed to act prior to September 11 on the threat from al Qaeda despite repeated warnings and then harvested a political windfall for taking obvious yet insufficient steps after the attacks; and who launched an unnecessary and costly war in Iraq that strengthened the fundamentalist, radical Islamic terrorist movement worldwide.

This is, unfortunately, also the story of how America was unable to develop a consensus that the threat was significant and was unable to do all that was necessary to deal with a new threat until that threat actually killed thousands of Americans.

Even worse, it is the story of how even after the attacks, America did not eliminate the al Qaeda movement, which morphed into a distributed and elusive threat, how instead we launched the counterproductive Iraq fiasco; how the Bush administration politicized counterterrorism as a way of insuring electoral victories; how critical homeland security vulnerabilities remain; and how little is being done to address the ideological challenge from terrorists distorting Islam into a new ideology of hate.

Chance had placed me inside key parts of the U.S. government throughout a period when an era was ending and another was born. The Cold War that had begun before my birth was ending as I turned forty. As the new era began I started what turned into an unprecedented decade of continuous service at the White House, working for the last three presidents.

As the events of 2003 unfolded, I began to feel an obligation to write what I knew for my fellow citizens and for those who may want to examine this period in the future. This book is the fulfillment of that obligation. It is, however, flawed. It is a first-person account, not an academic history. The book, therefore, tells what one participant saw, thought, and believed from one perspective. Others who were involved in some of these events will, no doubt, recall them differently. I do not say they are wrong, only that this account is what my memory reveals to me. I want to apologize in advance to the reader for the frequent use of the first-person singular and the egocentric nature of the story, but it was difficult to avoid those features and still do a first-person, participant's account.

The account is also necessarily incomplete. Many events and key participants are not mentioned, others who deserve rich description are only briefly introduced. Great issues such as the need to reform the intelligence community, secure cyberspace, or balance liberty and security are not fully analyzed. There will be other places for a more analytical reflection on those and other related issues of technical detail and policy import. Much that is still classified as secret by the U.S. government is omitted in this book. I have tried, wherever possible, to respect the confidences and privacy of those about whom I write. Nonetheless, there are some conversations that must be recalled because the citizenry and history have a justifiable need to know.

I recognize there is a great risk in writing a book such as this that many friends and former associates who disagree with me will be offended. The Bush White House leadership in particular have a reputation for taking great offense at criticism by former associates, considering it a violation of loyalty. They are also reportedly adept at revenge, as my friend Joe Wilson discovered and as former Secretary of the Treasury Paul O'Neill now knows. Nonetheless, friends should be able to disagree and, for me, loyalty to the citizens of the United States must take precedence over loyalty to any political machine.

Some will say this account is a justification or apology, a defense of some and an attack on others. It is meant to be factual, not polemical. In a decade of managing national security, many made mistakes, definitely including me. Many important steps were also taken in that decade as the result of the selfless sacrifice of thousands of those who serve the superpower and try daily to keep it on the path of principle and progress. I have tried to be fair in recounting what I know of both the mistakes and the service. I leave bottom-line assessments of blame and credit to the reader, with a caution that accurate assignments of responsibility are not easily done.

The close reader will note that many names recur throughout the book over a period of not just a decade, but more than two decades. That fact reflects the often unnoticed phenomenon that during the last five presidencies, many of the behind-the-scenes national security midlevel managers have been constant, people such as Charlie Allen, Randy Beers, Wendy Chamberlin, Michael Sheehan, Robert Gelbard, Elizabeth Verville, Steven Simon, Lisa Gordon-Hagerty, and Roger Cressey. When things worked, it was because they were listened to and allowed to implement their sound advice. Working closely with them were an even less noticed cadre of administrative assistants, such as the stalwart Beverly Roundtree, who has kept me in line and on time for the last fifteen years of our twenty-five-year association and friendship.

No one has a thirty-year run in national security in Washington, including ten years in the White House, without a great deal of help and support. In my case that help has come from Republicans, Democrats, and independents, from Members of Congress, journalists, partners in foreign governments, extraordinary colleagues, mentors and mentees, and a long list of very tolerant and long-suffering bosses. Since some will not want to be named, I will spare them all specific mention here. They know who they are, and so do I. Many thanks. Thanks too to Bruce Nichols of Free Press and to Len Sherman, without whom I would not have been able to produce a readable book.

In the 1700s a small group of extraordinary Americans created the Constitution that governs this country. In it, they dictated an oath that the President of the United States should swear. Forty-three Americans have done so since. Scores of millions of Americans have sworn a very similar oath upon becoming citizens, or joining the armed forces, becoming FBI agents, CIA officers, or federal bureaucrats.

All of the above-mentioned groups have sworn to protect that very Constitution "against all enemies." In this era of threat and change, we must all renew our pledge to protect that Constitution against the foreign enemies that would inflict terrorism against our nation and its people. That mission should be our first calling, not unnecessary wars to test personal theories or expiate personal guilt or revenge. We must also defend the Constitution against those who would use the terrorist threat to assault the liberties the Constitution enshrines. Those liberties are under assault and, if there is another major, successful terrorist attack in this country there will be further assaults on our rights and civil liberties. Thus, it is essential that we prevent further attacks and that we protect the Constitution . . . against all enemies.

Chapter 1

EVACUATE THE WHITE HOUSE

I RAN THROUGH THE WEST WING to the Vice President's office, oblivious to the stares and concern that brought. I had been at a conference in the Ronald Reagan Building three blocks away when Lisa Gordon-Hagerty called to say an aircraft had struck the World Trade Center: "Until we know what this is, Dick, we should assume the worst." Lisa had been in the center of crisis coordination many times in exercises and all too often in the real world.

"Right. Activate the CSG on secure video. I'll be there in less than five," I told her as I ran to my car. The CSG was the Counterterrorism Security Group, the leaders of each of the federal government's counterterrorism and security organizations. I had chaired it since 1992. It was on a five-minute tether during business hours, twenty minutes at all other times. I looked at the clock on the dashboard. It was 9:03 a.m., September 11, 2001.

As I drove up to the first White House gate Lisa called again: "The other tower was just hit." "Well, now we know who we're dealing with. I want the highest-level person in Washington from each agency on-screen now, especially FAA," the Federal Aviation Administration.

As I pulled the car up to the West Wing door, Paul Kurtz, one of the White House counterterrorism team, ran up to me. "We were in the Morning Staff Meeting when we heard. Condi told me to find you fast and broke up the meeting. She's with Cheney."

Bursting in on the Vice President and Condi—Condoleezza Rice, the President's National Security Advisor—alone in Cheney's office, I caught my breath. Cheney was famously implacable, but I thought I saw a reflection of horror on his face. "What do you think?" he asked.

"It's an al Qaeda attack and they like simultaneous attacks. This may not be over."

"Okay, Dick," Condi said, "you're the crisis manager, what do you recommend?" She and I had discussed what we would do if and when another terrorist attack hit. In June I had given her a checklist of things to do after an attack, in part to underline my belief that something big was coming and that we needed to go on the offensive.

"We're putting together a secure teleconference to manage the crisis," I replied. "I'd like to get the highest-ranking official from each department." My mind was already racing, developing a new list of what had to be done and done now.

"Do it," the Vice President ordered.

"Secret Service wants us to go to the bomb shelter," Condi added.

I nodded. "I would and . . . I would evacuate the White House."

Cheney began to gather up his papers. In his outer office the normal Secret Service presence was two agents. As I left, I counted eight, ready to move to the PEOC, the Presidential Emergency Operations Center, a bunker in the East Wing.

Just off the main floor of the Situation Room on the ground level of the West Wing is a Secure Video Conferencing Center, a clone of the Situation Room conference room except for the bank of monitors in the far wall opposite the chairman's seat. Like the conference room the Video Center is small and paneled with dark wood. The presidential seal hangs on the wall over the chair at the head of the table.

On my way through the Operations Center of the Situation Room, Ralph Seigler, the longtime Situation Room deputy director, grabbed me. "We're on the line with NORAD, on an air threat conference call." That was a procedure instituted by the North American Aerospace Defense Command during the Cold War to alert the White House when Soviet bombers got too close to U.S. airspace.

"Where's POTUS? Who have we got with him?" I asked, as we moved quickly together through the center, using the White House staff jargon for the President.

"He's in a kindergarten in Florida. Deb's with him." Deb was

Navy Captain Deborah Lower, the director of the White House Situation Room. "We have a line open to her cell."

As I entered the Video Center, Lisa Gordon-Hagerty was taking the roll and I could see people rushing into studios around the city: Donald Rumsfeld at Defense and George Tenet at CIA. But at many of the sites the Principal was traveling. The Attorney General was in Milwaukee, so Larry Thompson, the Deputy, was at Justice. Rich Armitage, the number two at State, was filling in for Colin Powell, who was in Peru. Air Force four-star General Dick Myers was filling in for the Chairman of the Joint Chiefs, Hugh Shelton, who was over the Atlantic. Bob Mueller was at the FBI, but he had just started that job.

Each Principal was supported by his or her member of the CSG and behind them staffs could be seen frantically yelling on telephones and grabbing papers. Condi Rice walked in behind me with her Deputy, Steve Hadley. "Do you want to chair this as a Principals meeting?" I asked. Rice, as National Security Advisor, chaired the Principals Committee, which consisted of the Secretaries of State and Defense, the CIA Director, the Chairman of the Joint Chiefs, and often now the Vice President.

"No. You run it." I pushed aside the chair at the head of the table and stood there, Condi visibly by my side.

"Let's begin. Calmly. We will do this in crisis mode, which means keep your microphones off unless you're speaking. If you want to speak, wave at the camera. If it's something you don't want everyone to hear, call me on the red phone."

Rice would later be criticized in the press by unnamed participants of the meeting for "just standing around." From my obviously partial perspective, she had shown courage by standing back. She knew it looked odd, but she also had enough self-confidence to feel no need to be in the chair. She did not want to waste time. I thought back to the scene in this room when the Oklahoma City bombing took place. President Clinton had walked in and sat down, chairing the CSG video conference for a few minutes. While it showed high-level concern and we were glad to have him there, it would have slowed down our response if he had stayed.

"You're going to need some decisions quickly," Rice said off camera. "I'm going to the PEOC to be with the Vice President. Tell us what you need."

"What I need is an open line to Cheney and you." I turned to my White House Fellow, Army Major Mike Fenzel. The highly competitive process that selected White House fellows had turned out some extraordinary people over the years, such as another army major named Colin Powell. "Mike," I said, "go with Condi to the PEOC and open a secure line to me. I'll relay the decisions we need to you."

Fenzel was used to pressure. As a lieutenant, he had driven his Bradley Fighting Vehicle down the runway of an Iraqi air base shooting up MiGs and taking return fire. As a captain, he had led a company of infantry into war-torn Liberia and faced down a mob outside the U.S. embassy. (Eighteen months after 9/11, Fenzel would be the first man to parachute out of his C-17 in a nighttime combat jump into Iraq.)

"Okay," I began. "Let's start with the facts. FAA, FAA, go." I fell in to using the style of communication on tactical radio so that those listening in the other studios around town could hear who was being called on over the din in their own rooms.

Jane Garvey, the administrator of the Federal Aviation Administration, was in the chair. "The two aircraft that went in were American flight 11, a 767, and United 175, also a 767. Hijacked."

"Jane, where's Norm?" I asked. They were frantically looking for Norman Mineta, the Secretary of Transportation, and, like me, a rare holdover from the Clinton administration. At first, FAA could not find him. "Well, Jane, can you order aircraft down? We're going to have to clear the airspace around Washington and New York."

"We may have to do a lot more than that, Dick. I already put a hold on all takeoffs and landings in New York and Washington, but we have reports of eleven aircraft off course or out of communications, maybe hijacked."

Lisa slowly whispered, "Oh shit." All conversation had stopped in the studios on the screens. Everyone was listening.

"Eleven," I repeated. "Okay, Jane, how long will it take to get all aircraft now aloft onto the ground somewhere?" My mind flashed back to 1995 when I asked FAA to ground all U.S. flights over the Pacific because of a terrorist threat, causing chaos for days. It had taken hours then to find the Secretary of Transportation, Federico Peña.

"The air traffic manager," Jane went on, "says there are 4,400 birds up now. We can cancel all takeoffs quickly, but grounding them all that are already up . . . Nobody's ever done this before. Don't know how long it will take. By the way, its Ben's first day on the job." Garvey was referring to Ben Sliney, the very new National Operations Manager at FAA.

"Jane, if you haven't found the Secretary yet, are you prepared to order a national ground stop and no fly zone?"

"Yes, but it will take a while." Shortly thereafter, Mineta called in from his car and I asked him to come directly to the Situation Room. He had two sons who were pilots for United. He did not know where they were that day. I suggested he join the Vice President.

Roger Cressey, my deputy and a marathoner, had run eight blocks from his doctor's office. Convincing the Uniformed Secret Service guards to let him back into the compound, Roger pressed through to the Situation Room. I was relieved to see him.

I turned to the Pentagon screen. "JCS, JCS. I assume NORAD has scrambled fighters and AWACS. How many? Where?"

"Not a pretty picture, Dick." Dick Myers, himself a fighter pilot, knew that the days when we had scores of fighters on strip alert had ended with the Cold War. "We are in the middle of Vigilant Warrior, a NORAD exercise, but . . . Otis has launched two birds toward New York. Langley is trying to get two up now. The AWACS are at Tinker and not on alert." Otis was an Air National Guard base on Cape Cod. Langley Air Force Base was outside Norfolk, Virginia. Tinker AFB, home to all of America's flying radar stations, was in Oklahoma.

"Okay, how long to CAP over D.C.?" Combat Air Patrol, CAP, was something we were used to placing over Iraq, not over our nation's capital.

"Fast as we can. Fifteen minutes?" Myers asked, looking at the generals and colonels around him. It was now 9:28.

I thought about the 1998 simultaneous attacks on the American embassies in Kenya and Tanzania. There was the possibility now of multiple simultaneous attacks in several countries. "State, State. DOD, DOD. We have to assume there will be simultaneous attacks on us overseas. We need to close the embassies. Move DOD bases to combat Threatcon."

The television screen in the upper left was running CNN on mute. Noticing the President coming on, Lisa turned on the volume and the crisis conference halted to listen. ". . . into the World Trade Center in an apparent terrorist attack on our country."

During the pause, I noticed that Brian Stafford, Director of the Secret Service, was now in the room. He pulled me aside. "We gotta get him out of there to someplace safe . . . and secret. I've stashed FLOTUS." FLOTUS was White House speak for Mrs. Bush, First Lady of the United States, now in a heavily guarded, unmarked building in Washington. Stafford had been President Clinton's bodyguard, led the presidential protection detail. Everyone knew that, despite the Elvis hairstyle, Stafford was solid and serious. He told presidents what to do, politely and in a soft Southern drawl, but in a way that left little room for discussion.

Franklin Miller, my colleague and Special Assistant to the President for Defense Affairs, joined Stafford. Frank squeezed my bicep. "Guess I'm working for you today. What can I do?" With him was a member of his staff, Marine Corps Colonel Tom Greenwood.

"Can you work with Brian," I told Miller. "Figure out where to move the President? He can't come back here till we know what the shit is happening." I knew that would not go down well with the Commander in Chief. "And Tom," I directed at Colonel Greenwood, "work with Roger—Cressey—on getting some CAP here—fast."

Stafford had another request. "When Air Force One takes off, can it have fighter escorts?"

"Sure, we can ask," Miller replied, "but you guys know that CAP, fighter escorts, they can't just shoot down planes inside the United States. We'll need an order." Miller had spent two decades working in the Pentagon and knew that the military would want clear instructions before they used force.

I picked up the open line to the PEOC. I got a dial tone. Someone had hung up on the other end. I punched the PEOC button on the large, white secure phone that had twenty speed dial buttons. When Major Fenzel got on the line I gave him the first three decisions we needed. "Mike, somebody has to tell the President he can't come right back here. Cheney, Condi, somebody. Secret Service concurs. We do not want them saying where they are going when they take off. Second, when they take off, they should have fighter escort. Three, we need to authorize the Air Force to shoot down any aircraft—including a hijacked passenger flight—that looks like it is threatening to attack and cause large-scale death on the ground. Got it?"

"Roger that, Dick, get right back to you." Fenzel was, I thought, optimistic about how long decisions like that would take.

I resumed the video conference. "FAA, FAA, go. Status report. How many aircraft do you still carry as hijacked?"

Garvey read from a list: "All aircraft have been ordered to land at the nearest field. Here's what we have as potential hijacks: Delta 1989 over West Virginia, United 93 over Pennsylvania . . ."

Stafford slipped me a note. "Radar shows aircraft headed this way." Secret Service had a system that allowed them to see what FAA's radar was seeing. "I'm going to empty out the complex." He was ordering the evacuation of the White House.

Ralph Seigler stuck his head into the room, "There has been an explosion in the Pentagon parking lot, maybe a car bomb!"

"If we evacuate the White House, what about the rest of Washington?" Paul Kurtz asked me. "What about COG?" Continuity of Government was another program left over from the Cold War. It was designed to relocate administration officials to alternate sites during periods of national emergency. COG was also planned to devolve power in case the President or key Cabinet members were killed.

Roger Cressey stepped back in to the video conference and announced: "A plane just hit the Pentagon." I was still talking with FAA, taking down a list of possibly hijacked aircraft. "Did you hear me?" Cressey was on loan to the White House from the Pentagon. He had friends there; we all did.

"I can still see Rumsfeld on the screen," I replied, "so the whole building didn't get hit. No emotion in here. We are going to stay focused. Roger, find out where the fighter planes are. I want Combat Air Patrol over every major city in this country. Now."

Stafford's order to evacuate was going into effect. As the staff poured out of the White House compound, the Residence, the West Wing, and the Executive Office Building, the Uniformed Secret Service guards yelled at the women, "If you're in high heels, take off your shoes and run—run!" My secretary, Beverly Roundtree, was on the line to Lisa, telling her that she and the rest of my staff were still in our vault in the Executive Office Building. "Okay, okay," Lisa was saying, knowing she could not persuade her to leave, "then bring over the chem-bio gear."

Our coordinator for Continuity of Government (we will call him Fred here to protect his identity at the request of the government) joined us.

"How do I activate COG?" I asked him. In the exercises we had done, the person playing the President had always given that order.

"You tell me to do it," Fred replied.

At that moment, Paul handed me the white phone to the PEOC. It was Fenzel. "Air Force One is getting ready to take off, with some press still on board. He'll divert to an air base. Fighter escort is authorized. And . . ." He paused. "Tell the Pentagon they have authority from the President to shoot down hostile aircraft, repeat, they have authority to shoot down hostile aircraft."

"Roger that." I was amazed at the speed of the decisions coming from Cheney and, through him, from Bush. "Tell them I am instituting COG." I turned back to Fred: "Go."

"DOD, DOD." I tried to get the attention of those still on the screen in the Pentagon. "Three decisions: One, the President has ordered the use of force against aircraft deemed to be hostile. Two, the White House is also requesting fighter escort of Air Force One. Three, and this applies to all agencies, we are initiating COG. Please activate your alternate command centers and move staff to them immediately."

Rumsfeld said that smoke was getting into the Pentagon secure teleconferencing studio. Franklin Miller urged him to helicopter to

DOD's alternate site. "I am too goddamn old to go to an alternate site," the Secretary answered. Rumsfeld moved to another studio in the Pentagon and sent his deputy, Paul Wolfowitz, to the remote site.

General Myers asked, "Okay, shoot down aircraft, but what are the ROE?" ROE were Rules of Engagement. It was one thing to say it's okay to shoot down a hijacked aircraft threatening to kill people on the ground, but we needed to give pilots more specific guidelines than that. I asked Miller and Greenwood to make sure DOD had an answer to that question quickly. "I don't want them delaying while they lawyer that to death."

Lisa slipped a note in front of me: "CNN says car bomb at the State Department. Fire on the Mall near the Capitol."

Ralph Seigler stuck his head around the door: "Secret Service reports a hostile aircraft ten minutes out."

Beverly Roundtree arrived and distributed gas masks. Cressey suggested we activate the Emergency Broadcast System.

"And have them say what?" I asked.

"State, State . . ." I called to get Rich Armitage's attention.

The Deputy Secretary of State had been a Navy SEAL and looked it. He responded in tactical radio style: "State, here, go."

"Rich, has your building just been bombed?" I asked.

"Does it fucking look like I've been bombed, Dick?"

"Well, no, but the building covers about four blocks and you're behind a big vault door. And you need to activate your COG site."

"All right, goddamn it, I'll go look for myself," Armitage said, lifting himself out of the chair and disappearing off camera. "Where the hell is our COG site . . ."

Fred returned. "We have a chopper on the way to extract the Speaker from the Capitol. Did you want all departments to go to COG or just the national security agencies?" The Speaker of the House, Dennis Hastert, was next in line to the presidency if Bush and Cheney were killed or incapacitated. Soon, he would be skimming across the backed-up traffic and on his way to a cave.

"Everybody, Fred, all departments. And check with the Capitol Police to see if there is a fire."

"Already did," Fred replied. "It's bogus. No fires, no bombs, but the streets and Metro are jammed with people trying to get out of town. It's going to be hard to get people to alternate sites."

Seigler was back: "Hostile aircraft eight minutes out."

Franklin Miller pulled me aside. Miller and I had been staff officers together at the State Department in 1979. Ever since then we had been friendly, but competitive. Miller went to the Pentagon, while I stayed at State. We had both become office directors, then Deputy Assistant Secretaries, then Assistant Secretaries, now Special Assistants to the President. "We gotta get these people out of here," Frank said and then looked me in the eyes. "But I'll stay here with you, if you're staying."

The White House compound was now empty except for the group with Cheney in the East Wing bomb shelter and the team with me in the West Wing Situation Room: Roger, Lisa, and Paul from my counterterrorist staff, Frank Miller and Marine Colonel Tom Greenwood and a half dozen Situation Room staff.

Roger Cressey, sitting on my right, was a career national security practitioner. I had hired him as a civil service employee at the State Department ten years earlier. To give him some real-world experience, I had sent him on assignment to the embassy in Tel Aviv. Later, in 1993, I asked him to go to Mogadishu as an aide to Admiral Jonathan T. Howe, who had left the White House job as Deputy National Security Advisor to be, in effect, the U.N.'s governor in Somalia. Cressey drove the darkened streets of Mogadishu at night in a pickup truck with a 9mm strapped to his hip, listening to the gunfire rippling around town. Two years later when another American, General Jacques Klein, was appointed by the U.N. to run bombed-out Eastern Slavonia, Cressey had gone into the rubble with him. Together they dealt with warring Croatians and Serbs, including war criminals, refugees, and organized crime thugs. From there, he had gone to the civilian office in the Pentagon that reviewed the military's war plans. Cressey had joined me at the White House in November 1999 just as we placed security forces on the first nationwide terrorist alert. Now thirty-five years old, he was married to a State Department expert on weapons of mass destruction and had a beautiful two-year-old daughter. He thought his father-in-law was on American 77. (Later Cressey would learn that Bob Sepucha was safe.)

Lisa Gordon-Hagerty, sitting behind me, had started her career at the Lawrence Livermore National Laboratory as an expert on nuclear weapons and the health effects of radiation. Blonde and stylish, she stood out among the White House staff. Lisa had helped to create and organize NEST, the Nuclear Emergency Support Team. The support that NEST was supposed to give was to U.S. military Special Forces trained to seize and disarm nuclear weapons in the hands of terrorists. Lisa had trained with Delta Force and SEAL Team Six. I was impressed by her understanding of weapons of mass destruction, including chemical and biological devices, especially during the Tokyo subway attack in 1995 when terrorists had sprayed sarin nerve gas. In 1998 I asked her to join me in the White House to design and implement a new national plan to defend against terrorist attacks using chemical and biological weapons. Three weeks after her arrival, al Qaeda attacked the two U.S. embassies in Africa. Lisa had stayed up for three days straight coordinating the flow of FBI, State, Marine, and disaster response teams to Kenya and Tanzania.

Paul Kurtz, on my left, was another career civil servant. I had first hired him in 1987 in the Intelligence Bureau at State. There he became an expert on nuclear weapons and ballistic missiles. Following the first Gulf War, he went into Iraq repeatedly for both the International Atomic Energy Agency (IAEA) and the U.N. Special Commission to hunt down hidden Iraqi weapons. Kurtz then became the Political Advisor to the U.S. Commander of Operation Northern Watch, based in Turkey and taking a Blackhawk flight every week into the Kurdish areas of Iraq. The week after he left that job, his successor died when the U.S. Air Force mistakenly shot down the U.S. Army Blackhawk. Kurtz then went on to North Korea, inspecting for a nuclear weapons program. On his first inspection, Kurtz and his team were forced into a concrete block building and surrounded by loudly jeering Korean troops who thrust bayonets in the windows at them. He joined the White House terrorism team in December 1999 and spent Christmas Day that year accompanying the National Security Advisor to the terrorism centers at CIA and FBI as part of the Millennium Terrorist Alert. Like Cressey, he had run marathons and he was the kind of guy that no one disliked.

These people did not flap. They were like family to me, but suddenly I realized that I wanted them to leave for their own safety. I checked again with FAA to see if they still thought there were hijacked aircraft aloft. There were 3,900 aircraft still in the air and at least four of those were believed to be in the hands of the terrorists.

I huddled everyone together just outside the Video Conferencing Center and asked them to leave. Lisa spoke for the group: "Right, Dick. None of us are leaving you, so let's just go back in there."

"Hold on. We will be the next target. It's no shame to relocate. Some of you have kids too—think about them," I said, looking at Roger, whose second child was due in a few months.

Roger did not hesitate. He said, "If we don't hold this thing together, no one will and we don't have time for this." Then he brushed by me and walked back into the Video Conferencing Center. Frank Miller grabbed a legal pad and said, "All right. If you're staying, sign your name here."

"What the hell's the point of that?" Paul Kurtz asked.

Frank slowly scanned the group, "I'm going to e-mail the list out of the compound so the rescue teams will know how many bodies to look for."

Everyone signed and walked back in. We resumed the video conference. "DOD, DOD, go." I asked the Pentagon for an update on the fighter cover.

Dick Myers had a status report. "We have three F-16s from Langley over the Pentagon. Andrews is launching fighters from the D.C. Air National Guard. We have fighters aloft from the Michigan Air National Guard, moving east toward a potential hostile over Pennsylvania. Six fighters from Tyndall and Ellington are en route to rendezvous with Air Force One over Florida. They will escort it to Barksdale. NORAD says that it will have AWACS over New York and Washington later this morning."

DOD Deputy Secretary Paul Wolfowitz had relocated to the Alternate National Military Command Center outside Washington and had now rejoined the conference. "We have to think of a message to the public. Tell them not to clog up the roads. Let them know we are in control of the airways. Tell them what is happening. Have somebody go out from the White House."

"Paul, there is nobody in the White House but us and no press on the grounds. I think the President will have something to say when he lands in Barksdale, but we have to be careful . . . we really don't know what is going on, are attacks still under way . . . anybody?"

Dale Watson, counterterrorism chief at FBI, was waving at the camera indicating he had an update. "Go ahead, Dale."

"Dick, got a few things here. Our New York office reports that the Port Authority is closing all bridge and tunnel connections into Manhattan. We have a report of a large jet crashed in Kentucky, near the Ohio line.

"We think we ought to order all landmark buildings around the country to evacuate, like the Sears Tower, Disney World, the Liberty Bell, the TransAmerica Building in San Francisco. This thing is still going on. And Dick, call me in SIOC when you can." SIOC—the Strategic Information and Operations Center—is FBI's command center. Dale had something he did not want to share with everyone in the conference.

Frank Miller took over the video conference and I stepped out and called Watson on a secure line. "We got the passenger manifests from the airlines. We recognize some names, Dick. They're al Qaeda." I was stunned, not that the attack was al Qaeda but that there were al Qaeda operatives on board aircraft using names that FBI knew were al Qaeda.

"How the fuck did they get on board then?" I demanded.

"Hey, don't shoot the messenger, friend. CIA forgot to tell us about them." Dale Watson was one of the good guys at FBI. He had been trying hard to get the Bureau to go after al Qaeda in the United States with limited success. "Dick, we need to make sure none of this gang escapes out of the country, like they did in '93." In 1993 many of the World Trade Center bombers had quickly flown abroad just before and after the attack.

"Okay, I've got that." As we talked, we both saw on the monitors that WTC 2 was collapsing in a cloud of dust. "Oh dear God," Dale whispered over the line.

"Dale, find out how many people were still inside." I had often been in the World Trade Center and the number that popped into my head was 10,000. This was going from catastrophe to complete and total calamity.

"I'll try, but you know one of them. John just called the New York Office from there." John was John O'Neill, my closest friend in the Bureau and a man determined to destroy al Qaeda until the Bureau had driven him out because he was too obsessed with al Qaeda and didn't mind breaking crockery in his drive to get Usama bin Laden. O'Neill did not fit the narrow little mold that Director Louis Freeh wanted for his agents. He was too aggressive, thought outside the box. O'Neill's struggle with Freeh was a case study in why the FBI could not do the homeland protection mission. So, O'Neill retired from the FBI and had just become director of security for the World Trade Center complex the week before.

We were silent for a moment. "Dale, get the word out to evacuate the landmarks and all federal buildings across the country."

"You got it . . . and Dick . . . hang in there, we need you."

I walked over to the communications desk where one of the longest-serving Situation Room staff was still there. Gary Breshnahan had come to the White House as an Army sergeant during the Reagan administration. To insure communications back to the Situation Room, Gary had accompanied National Security Advisor Bud McFarlane on the secret mission to Tehran that became the central act of the Iran-Contra fiasco. Later Gary had videotaped Bill Clinton's deposition during the impeachment process. He was a single father of three.

"You shouldn't still be here, Gare," I tried.

"You want this fuckin' video to work, don't you?"

"Okay, well if you're staying . . . can you pull up Coast Guard and Treasury?"

"Coast Guard, no problem. But I'll bet the mortgage nobody is home at Treasury."

When I walked back to the Video Conferencing Center Cressey

told me what had happened to one of the aircraft we thought was headed toward us. "United 93 is down, crashed outside of Pittsburgh. It's odd. Appears not to have hit anything much on the ground."

A new site was appearing on a wall monitor, a row of men in light blue, Coast Guard Commandant Jim Loy in the middle of them. He was one of the most competent people in federal service, quiet and effective. (Loy would later run the new Transportation Security Administration and then be promoted to run the new Department of Homeland Security as its Deputy Secretary.)

"Dick," the commandant informed me, "we have a dozen cutters steaming at flank speed to New York. What more can we do to help?"

"Jim, you have a Captain of the Port in every harbor, right?" He nodded. "Can they close the harbors? I don't want anything leaving till we know what's on them. And I don't want anything coming in and blowing up, like the LNG in Boston." After the Millennium Terrorist Alert we had learned that al Qaeda operatives had been infiltrating Boston by coming in on liquid natural gas tankers from Algeria. We had also learned that had one of the giant tankers blown up in the harbor, it would have wiped out downtown Boston.

"I have that authority." Loy turned and pointed at another admiral. "And I have just exercised it."

"Justice, Justice, over." I signaled to Larry Thompson, the DAG, Deputy Attorney General. "Larry, can you have Immigration get together with Customs and close the land borders?"

"Consider it done, but you know what the borders are like. You can just walk across in a lot of places, especially along the Canadian border. By the way, we need some help getting the AG back. Can we get approval for an aircraft out of Milwaukee?" All flights were now banned, except for the fighters and AWACS.

Frank Miller reported that DOD had gone on a global alert, DEFCON 3: "That hasn't happened since the '73 Arab-Israeli War." I remembered it. It was the first time I had worked a crisis. I was a young staffer in the National Military Command Center when Soviet nuclear warheads were discovered en route to Egypt. Secretary of Defense James Schlesinger had ordered DEFCON 3 and sent U.S. forces racing all over Europe without telling our NATO allies.

"State, State, go." Armitage acknowledged the call. "Rich, DOD has gone to DEFCON 3 and you know what that means." Armitage knew; he had been an Assistant Secretary of Defense in the first Bush administration.

"It means I better go tell the Ruskies before they shit a brick." Armitage activated the Nuclear Risk Reduction Center, down the hall from the State Department Operations Center. The NRRC was connected directly to the Russian Ministry of Defense just outside the Kremlin. It was designed to exchange information in crises to prevent misunderstanding and miscalculation.

Armitage reappeared. "Damn good thing I did that. Guess who was about to start an exercise of all their strategic nuclear forces?" He had persuaded his Russian counterpart to defer the operation. "By the way, we are taking calls here from countries all over the world who want to help. We are going to close all our embassies to the public and skinny down the staffs, step up security."

Jane Garvey was waving her arms at the camera. "We're down to 934 aircraft aloft, but we have a problem in Alaska." A Korean Airlines 747 looked like it had been hijacked. "KAL 85, NORAD is scrambling."

"Has Alaska Center got comms with it?" I wanted to know if FAA could talk to the 747. Garvey indicated a thumbs-up, yes. "Okay, tell KAL it will obey orders from the F-15s or we will blow it up. We are not about to have them fly into Prudhoe Bay." I had an image of the 747 taking out the port that exported all the oil from the North Slope.

President Bush had landed at Barksdale Air Force Base in Louisiana, escorted by fighter aircraft. He called Cheney on a secure landline. On the basis of Frank Miller's recommendations, Cheney pressed the president to proceed to a bunker, either Strategic Command headquarters in Omaha or NORAD in Cheyenne Mountain, Colorado. The press corps on board were told not to report where they were.

Before lifting off again, Bush taped a statement to be broadcast only after he was airborne. "Make no mistake. The United States will hunt down and punish those responsible for these cowardly acts." At this point, they hardly seemed cowardly. "Freedom itself was attacked this morning by a faceless coward. And freedom will be defended." He seemed tentative.

Cressey told me that Fenzel was looking for me. I picked up the open line to the Presidential Emergency Operations Center, only to find that once again it was a dial tone. When I punched the PEOC button, the person answering the line grunted and passed the phone to Major Fenzel. "Who is the asshole answering the phone for you, Mike?" I asked.

"That would be the Vice President, Dick. And he'd like you to come over." Frank Miller again took over the chair of the video conference, becoming, as I was most of the day, the nation's crisis manager.

I had walked from the Situation Room in the West Wing through the Residence to the East Wing many times before, flashing my badge at the many guard posts along the way. Now, as I walked through the West Wing and the Residence, there was no one there. No sound. The guards had been ordered by Brian Stafford to assume a perimeter a block outside the White House fence. They had cordoned off streets and set up machine guns. Inside the fence, the White House itself was eerily empty.

In the quiet of that walk, I caught my breath for the first time that day:

- This was the "Big al Qaeda Attack" we had warned was coming and it was bigger than almost anything we had imagined, short of a nuclear weapon. With the towers collapsed, the death toll could be anywhere from 10,000 to maybe as high as 50,000. No one knew. And it wasn't over. I kept hearing in my mind Marlon Brando's whispered words from *Apocalypse Now,* "The horror, the horror."
- Now we would finally bomb the camps, probably invade Afghanistan. Of course, now bin Laden and his deputies would not be at the camps. Indeed, by now the camps were probably as empty as the White House. We would begin a long fight against al Qaeda, with no holds barred. But it was too late.

They had proven the superpower was vulnerable, that they were smarter, they had killed thousands.

- The recriminations would flow like water from a fire hose. There was no time for thinking like that. Not now. We had to move fast. Other attacks were probably in the works and had to be stopped. The country was in shock. The government had largely fled Washington. The nation needed reassurance. We needed to find our dead.

As I made it to the bottom of the stairs in the East Wing, I turned the corner and found a machine gun in my face. Cheney's security detail had set up outside the vault doors, with body armor, shotguns, and MP5 machine guns. Although they knew me, they were not about to open the vault door.

"Hey guys, it's me. The Veep called me over here. At least call inside and let him know I'm here." While they did that, they frisked me. Condi Rice's deputy, Steve Hadley, came to the vault door to identify me and escort me in. Inside the vault there were more MP5s and shotguns in the narrow corridor lined with bunk beds.

In the Presidential Emergency Operations Center the cast was decidedly more political. In addition to the Vice President and Condi Rice, there was the Vice President's wife, Lynne; his political advisor Mary Matalin; his security advisor, Scooter Libby; Deputy White House Chief of Staff Josh Bolten; and White House communications director Karen Hughes. The monitors were simultaneously blaring the coverage from five networks.

On one screen, I could see the Situation Room. I grabbed Mike Fenzel. "How's it going over here?" I asked.

"It's fine," Major Fenzel whispered, "but I can't hear the crisis conference because Mrs. Cheney keeps turning down the volume on you so she can hear CNN . . . and the Vice President keeps hanging up the open line to you." Mrs. Cheney was more than just a family member who had to be protected. Like her husband, she was a right-wing ideologue and she was offering her advice and opinions in the bunker.

I moved in and squatted between Cheney and Rice. "The President agreed to go to Offutt," Cheney informed me. His manner implied that it had been a hard sell.

"He can't come back here yet," I insisted. "Do you need anything?" I asked the Vice President.

"The comms in this place are terrible," he replied. His calls to the President were dropping off.

"Now you know why I wanted the money for a new bunker?" I could not resist. The President had canceled my plans for a replacement facility.

"It'll happen," Cheney promised. "Are you getting everything you need, everybody doing what you want?" Cheney asked, placing his hand on my shoulder. I had known Dick Cheney for a dozen years and for that long been fascinated at how complex a person he was. On the surface, he was quiet and soft-spoken. Below that surface calm ran strong, almost extreme beliefs. He had been one of the five most radical conservatives in the Congress. The quiet often hid views that would seem out of place if aired more broadly. It had been speculated in the press that he would really be the president for national security affairs, not the inexperienced Governor from Texas. Yet now he was wanting to make sure that the President knew what we had been doing in his absence. "I want you to prepare a briefing for him when he lands in Omaha. And I need a timeline of everything that you have done."

I retraced my route through the abandoned Executive Mansion. It was 12:30 p.m.

Back in the West Wing, I discovered that Gary Breshnahan had been right: no one was able to get to the Treasury video conferencing site. I grabbed Paul Kurtz. He and I had spent two days literally crawling around Wall Street a few weeks before. We had gone on the floor of the New York Stock Exchange, but we had also gone through the tunnels carrying the fiber optic cable to the Verizon and AT&T switches. We had identified several buildings that were they taken out, would disconnect Wall Street from the world. "Paul, get Treasury, get the Fed, activate the National Communications System. We have to make sure the markets can close their books and we're going to have to protect the comms centers and SIAC."

SIAC is the Securities Industry Automation Corporation, the mainframes, fiber, and data backup that made the American and New York Stock Exchanges work. Kurtz and I had been in their computer rooms. The National Communications System was yet another Cold War relic, housed in DOD but working for the White House. NCS was mandated to insure that critical telephony and data flowed even under attack. In their Arlington center, all the major telephone companies sat together around the table. Kurtz called the manager there, Brent Greene and said, "Tell them all they need to support Verizon." A Verizon switching center for Wall Street was next to the World Trade Center and we could see from the television coverage that the building, filled with routers and switches, was punctured.

Kurtz reached out for the market makers. In 1993 when the World Trade Center was bombed, President Clinton was called directly by Wall Street firm CEOs who had been prevented from reentering the towers. Unable to close their transaction accounts for the day, billions of dollars were up in the air, unassigned. That day eight years earlier, at the President's direction, I had called the Fire Commissioner and gotten agreement to let key staffers back into the towers. That wasn't an option now, both towers had dropped. Kurtz called the people on Wall Street we had met earlier in the year. He learned that they had off-site backup and had avoided the 1993 problem. He also learned that it would be hard to reopen the markets because of the infrastructure damage.

I walked back into the Video Conferencing Center and took the chair. "FEMA, FEMA go." The Federal Emergency Management Agency was responsible for disasters and there had never been one as big as this. Mike Brown, the Deputy Director, appeared on-screen.

"The Mayor has called for the evacuation of Manhattan south of Canal Street. Governor Pataki has called up the National Guard. We have eight FEMA-sponsored teams en route to Manhattan and four rolling to Arlington. Both New York and D.C. have declared a state of emergency."

"How many dead?" I asked.

"They have no idea, thousands," he said, shaking his head.

Cressey had been preparing a PowerPoint briefing for Bush's arrival in Omaha and Kurtz had done a timeline on what had happened when, and what we had done. The deck looked good, simple, straightforward. I asked Kurtz to walk it over to the PEOC. Then, remembering the difficulty I had in getting in, I asked my Secret Service liaison officer, Agent Pete McCauley, to escort and vouch for Kurtz.

Kurtz and McCauley walked incredulously through the empty White House, past the abandoned interior guard posts. Pete gave the documents to an agent he knew at the vault door in the East Wing for handoff to the Vice President. Together they climbed back up, into the open air of the Colonnade along the Rose Garden. Halfway to the West Wing, they heard a sudden crashing roar and looked up to see two F-15 Eagles screech across the South Lawn at three hundred feet, shaking the two-hundred-year-old Executive Mansion. McCauley pressed his back against the wall, "Holy Mary, Mother of God!"

Kurtz, a Holy Cross graduate, completed the prayer: "Blessed art thou among women and blessed is the fruit of thy womb, Jesus." The Combat Air Patrol had arrived. The White House was a war zone.

Back in the Situation Room, I was looking for Breshnahan. "POTUS is inbound Offutt. I need video connectivity to STRATCOM and I need them to have this PowerPoint." Gary indicated that would not be a problem, but he would need to disconnect the Coast Guard. Just before 3:00 p.m., we saw Bush stride into the underground bunker at Strategic Command, Offutt Air Force Base, Nebraska. Everyone stepped out of the West Wing Video Conferencing Center, except Frank Miller and me.

The last item on the agenda was supposed to be where the President should be. Instead, we began there. "I'm coming back to the White House as soon as the plane is fueled," the President said. "No discussion. Item two, briefing by Dick Clarke."

I walked through "What Happened," from 08:50 to 10:06, four aircraft impacting the earth. Next, the "Response Actions," the nationwide grounding of aircraft, the borders closed, the ports sealed, the forces on DEFCON 3, the government moved to caves, FEMA mortuary units en route to Manhattan.

Next was "Issues for the Next 24–48 hours." Given that the President had decided to return to the White House, I suggested that a constitutional successor be deployed with a support team outside the city. (Commerce Secretary Don Evans was found and moved to a secret location outside the city.) We would need another public statement by the President, from the Oval Office, after his return. Also to be decided was the continued grounding of the air transportation system, military deployments to guard critical infrastructure here and abroad, and the schedule for reopening the markets. We needed to order the federal workforce to stay home. Basically, we needed the country to go on hold for a day or two until we learned whether there were more attacks coming, until we organized improved security, until we began to pick up the pieces.

CIA Director George Tenet was up next. He left no doubt that al Qaeda had committed these atrocities. He had already been on the telephone to key counterparts around the world, lining up the forces for the counterstrike.

Defense Secretary Don Rumsfeld briefed on the status of forces. The Atlantic Fleet had departed Norfolk and was steaming with aircraft carriers and cruisers toward New York. He omitted the fact that no one had ordered the Atlantic Commander to do that. At times like these, initiative was a good thing. About 120 fighters were finally circling America's metropolitan areas. Forces worldwide were on battle status.

FEMA talked of the Urban Search and Rescue Teams driving up the turnpike to Manhattan. A blood drive was under way. Emergencies were in effect in New York State, Virginia, and the District of Columbia. Then the President was up, out, and in the air, escorted by F-15s and racing for Andrews Air Force Base. His was the only passenger aircraft in the air over America. The skies were clear. Somehow FAA had landed over four thousand aircraft, diverting flights from Europe to tiny Canadian fields with few if any hotels. Canadian citizens were opening their homes to strangers, who were slowly piecing together what had happened to them, what had happened to America.

After Bush left Omaha, World Trade Center tower Number 7 collapsed and with it the mayor's command post and the Secret Service field office.

In the Situation Room, the talk turned to next steps. "Okay," I began, "we all know this was al Qaeda. FBI and CIA will develop the case and see if I'm right. We want the truth, but, in the meantime, let's go with the assumption it's al Qaeda.What's next?" I asked the video conference.

"Look," Rich Armitage responded, "we told the Taliban in no uncertain terms that if this happened, it's their ass. No difference between the Taliban and al Qaeda now. They both go down." The Taliban was the radical Muslim group controlling Afghanistan.

"And Pakistan?" I asked.

"Tell them to get out of the way. We have to eliminate the sanctuary." Armitage was on a roll. If Pakistan did not cooperate, we would have a major problem with a nuclear-armed Islamic state.

"We'll need presidential pressure on Yemen and Saudi Arabia too," said John McLaughlin, Tenet's deputy. "And a major covert action program for three to five years, support to the Northern Alliance." It was too late, however, for Massoud, the leader of the Afghan Northern Alliance. He had been assassinated by al Qaeda twenty-four hours earlier.

"There are forty-two major Taliban bombing targets," General Myers said, reviewing a briefing handed to him.

Just before 7:00, the 747 known as Air Force One touched down at Andrews AFB and the President moved quickly to Marine One, which was parked close by. The helicopter, accompanied by two decoys, took a circuitous path over the city before diving onto the South Lawn of the White House. Above them, AWACS watched the skies and vectored F-15s and F-16s on Combat Air Patrol. They were tracking a smaller USAF aircraft with Secretary of State Colin Powell. Upon his landing at Andrews, a heavily armed convoy whisked him directly to the White House.

At 8:30 the President addressed the nation from the Oval Office. Karen Hughes had built the consensus of the video conference into the message. "We will make no distinction between the terrorists who committed these acts and those who harbor them." Immediately following the address, the President met with us in the PEOC, a place he had never seen. Unlike in his three television appearances that day, Bush was confident, determined, forceful.

"I want you all to understand that we are at war and we will stay at war until this is done. Nothing else matters. Everything is available for the pursuit of this war. Any barriers in your way, they're gone. Any money you need, you have it. This is our only agenda." The President asked me to focus on identifying what the next attack might be and preventing it.

When, later in the discussion, Secretary Rumsfeld noted that international law allowed the use of force only to prevent future attacks and not for retribution, Bush nearly bit his head off. "No," the President yelled in the narrow conference room, "I don't care what the international lawyers say, we are going to kick some ass."

Bush had already learned that some of the hijackers were people that the CIA had known were al Qaeda and were in the United States. Now he wanted to know when the CIA had told the FBI and what the FBI had done about it. The answers were imprecise, but it became clear that CIA had taken months to tell FBI that the terrorists were in the country. When FBI did learn, they failed to find them. Had FBI put them on the television show *America's Most Wanted* or alerted the FAA about them, perhaps the entire cell could have been rounded up. Bush's look said he would want to come back to this issue later.

For now, however, the President shifted to the economic damage. Somehow he had learned that four shopping malls in Omaha had closed after the attacks. "I want the economy back, open for business right away, banks, the stock market, everything tomorrow." Ken Dam, the Deputy Secretary of the Treasury, filling in for the traveling Paul O'Neill, pointed out that there was physical damage to the Wall Street infrastructure. "As soon as we get the rescue operations done up there, shift everything to fixing that damage so we can reopen," Bush urged. Turning to Secretary of Transportation Norm Mineta, he pressed for resumption of air travel. Mineta suggested that flights could begin at noon the next day.

Brian Stafford urged the President to spend the night in the bunker, but he would have none of it. Following the meeting, he went to the Oval Office and began working the telephones. I returned to the Situation Room and found my team hard at it.

Cressey was on the telephone to New York City Mayor Rudolph

Giuliani's chief of staff. "Anything he wants, troops, equipment. And if FEMA or any agency is slow, call us directly."

Kurtz was talking to Verizon about the Stock Exchange. I asked him to put them on hold for a minute so I could give him what in the White House we called guidance: "From the President for you . . . two priorities. First, search and rescue. Second, reopen the markets. Let me know what you need to do that." Paul looked up, a bit of fatigue appearing for the first time. "How about five miles of fiber optic cable and a dozen switches and routers . . . installed?"

"That should not be a problem. We can get that." I pressed him, remembering the President's determination. "So you can have the markets open Thursday?" I knew as soon as I said it that was too ambitious, even though we were already getting calls from CEOs at Cisco, AT&T, and others offering personnel and equipment no questions asked. "Try Monday," Kurtz shot back and went on with the call.

Lisa was in dialogue with Governor George Pataki. "Well, don't you have even an estimate of the dead?"

I took her aside. "You know those chemical and bio detectors you're developing? I want some, now, here and at the Capitol."

"Well, there are only three small problems with that, Dick," Lisa began. "A) they're experimental, and B) they're in California, and C) nothing is flying."

"Right, so here at the White House, Wednesday, up and running . . . ?" I asked.

"Okay, okay," she said, adding it to her list.

The Navy staff of the White House Mess had reappeared and were distributing sandwiches. "We're going to stay open all night." I realized I hadn't eaten since the night before when I had gone to a new seafood restaurant near the White House with Rich Bonin of *60 Minutes*. Bonin was obsessed with al Qaeda, had done a story about terrorism with me and Lesley Stahl in October. They had taped three hours of interviews with me for a seventeen-minute segment. Now, without my knowing it, CBS was running much of the unused interview, including me explaining the concept of Continuity of Government.

The night before, Bonin had asked if it was true that I had asked for a transfer. As of October 1, I would be starting a new national program on cyber security. Bonin wanted to run the story that I was quitting the terrorism job in frustration with the new administration's lack of focus on al Qaeda. I asked him not to, but admitted that I had sought the transfer. It seemed like ages ago.

I grabbed a sandwich from the Mess and walked outside with Cressey to the parking lot that had once been a public street known as West Executive Avenue. My car was still parked askew in front of the West Wing. It was the only vehicle left. The night was clear and quiet. We were in the middle of Washington and there was hardly a sound. I debriefed Roger on the Principals meeting with the President.

I realized then that until today I had not ever briefed the President on terrorism, only Cheney, Rice, and Powell. We had finally had our first Principals meeting on terrorism only a week earlier. The next step was to have been a briefing to walk the President through our proposed National Security Presidential Directive (NSPD). The *Washington Post* later reported (January 20, 2002) that the NSPD had as its goal to "eliminate al Qaeda." The plan called for arming the Northern Alliance in Afghanistan to go on the offensive against the Taliban, pressing CIA to use the lethal authorities it had been given to go after bin Laden and the al Qaeda leadership. Bush had never seen the plan, the pieces of which had first been briefed to Cheney, Rice, Powell, and others on his team in January. I had not been allowed to brief the President on terrorism in January or since, not until today, September 11. It had taken since January to get the Cabinet-level meeting that I had requested "urgently" within days of the inauguration to approve an aggressive plan to go after al Qaeda. The meeting had finally happened exactly one week earlier, on September 4. Now, as I was telling Cressey, I thought the aggressive plan would be implemented.

"Well, that's fuckin' great. Sounds like they're finally going to do everything we wanted. Where the hell were they for the last eight months?" Cressey asked.

"Debating the fine points of the ABM Treaty?" I answered, looking up at the sky for the fighter cover.

"They'll probably deploy the armed Predator now too," Cressey said, referring to his project to kill bin Laden with an unmanned aircraft. CIA had been blocking the deployment, refusing to be involved in running an armed version of the unmanned aircraft, to hunt and kill bin Laden. Roger Cressey was still fuming at their refusal. "If they had deployed an armed Predator when it was ready, we could have killed bin Laden before this happened."

"Yeah, well, this attack would have happened anyway, Rog. In fact, if we had killed bin Laden in June with the Predator and this still happened, our friends at CIA would have blamed us, said the attack on New York was retribution, talked again about the overly zealous White House counterterrorism guys." I tried to think ahead, of what we could best do now. "From here on in it's a self-implementing policy, or as you guys from the Pentagon would say, a self-licking ice cream cone . . . but it's too late, way too late. The best thing you and I can do now is figure out how to block any follow-on attacks."

We walked back in. The next task was securing the air transport system so flights could resume. U.S. aviation had long been insecure and the 1997 Commission on Aviation Safety and Security had avoided the tough decisions, like federalizing airport security. The FBI had even attempted to eliminate the Federal Air Marshal program in 1998, arguing that armed FAA agents on hijacked aircraft could be killed by FBI's commandos storming a hijacked aircraft. Now, we had thousands of aircraft scattered at airfields all over the United States and Canada, and probably a quarter of a million passengers sleeping on airport floors. We also had a continuing threat. Had all of the al Qaeda teams struck? We resumed our video conference and I put the question to FAA: how could we resume flight?

"We can't just put everybody back on the planes and go back to business as usual," Mike Canavan was insistent. Canavan was an Army three-star general, a former commander of Delta Force, who had only recently retired and taken over the job of Director of Security at FAA. He had been in Puerto Rico doing a personnel shake-up of his San Juan operation when the attacks hit. Using his military contacts, he had grabbed a DOD aircraft to get back. Using his FAA contacts, he had been given F-16 escorts so that he would not be shot down by mistake.

"We need to search all the aircraft and airports for hidden

weapons. I think some of the knives or box cutters they used had already been put on the aircraft for them." Canavan had a report of box cutters found hidden away on one of the aircraft that had been grounded.

"Mineta told the President that the system would reopen at noon Wednesday. That would just give us about twelve hours, Mike." I was looking for a reality check from FAA because my team did not see how the airports could reopen for days.

"Open tomorrow? That ain't gonna happen, Dick." Canavan had already had this conversation with his boss, following Mineta's return from the White House. "We have been on to the airlines. They could not open at noon even if we wanted to. And we don't. I want FAMs on every flight."

"Well that means thousands of Federal Air Marshals and last time I checked you had a few dozen," I said, knowing where Canavan was going. The FAA had flown armed agents on only a few flights on overseas routes. I made Canavan a proposal I knew he would like. "After the bombing at the Atlanta Olympics we threw hundreds of federal agents into security in Atlanta, Border Patrol, Customs, Secret Service, U.S. Marshals. We can do that again, but it will take days to brief them and position them."

Canavan agreed. "That's what I need for now, but we are going to have to have a dedicated and large FAM program quickly, and it's going to cost."

"Mike, I told the President about the minimum-wage rent-a-cops doing screening of passengers and carry-on. He understands that will have to end." We would have to screen every passenger closely before we resumed flights and then put in place a permanent system.

"FAA needs to take that over, too," Canavan pushed, "but for this week we are going to have to supplement the rent-a-cops with the real thing, local police, National Guard, federal agents."

"What about everything else?" Paul Kurtz asked. "Are we letting everything resume flying this week? How do we check private planes? I look out my window every day and see private jets taking off from National flying right at the White House before they veer off." Large passenger aircraft were only a piece of what had been grounded that day. Cargo aircraft, executive jets, personal aircraft, traffic helicopters, crop dusters, Goodyear blimps, and hot air balloons also filled America's skies on a normal day. Dealing with them would have to come later. I asked Kurtz to work with FAA to phase those other aircraft back in after we had a security plan for them. For weeks thereafter, I would catch snippets of Paul's conversations. "I don't care if there is no aerial camera shot of the game, no blimps over stadiums . . ." and "What do you mean *I* still have all the traffic helicopters grounded?"

Condi Rice joined us again in the Situation Room. The President now wanted to be sure we were all going to get some sleep. "I need you bright and fresh in the morning. Go home." Rice made sure we understood it was an order. I worried about her security if she planned to go back to her apartment in the nearby Watergate. So had the President; she was going to spend the night in the Residence.

After 1:00 a.m., I agreed to go home briefly to shower and change. Lisa and Mike Fenzel would stay, supported by Margie Gilbert of the National Security Agency. Before I left, I called Pete McCauley to get a ride through the Secret Service positions around the building and to put us on a list to get out . . . and get back in. We drove through their barricades, down the empty streets. A Humvee with a .50 caliber machine gun was on the corner of 17th and Pennsylvania. We stopped on the Roosevelt Bridge over the Potomac and watched the smoke still rising from the Pentagon, lit by the floodlights that had been brought in. It gave me a chill. As we pulled up to my house in Arlington and shut off the car, we heard the drone of a heavy four-engine aircraft. AWACS circling.

An hour later, as I dressed to go back in, I wondered again how many al Qaeda sleeper cells there were in the United States. I had long believed they existed. So had John O'Neill, who was now dead under tons of steel. So had Dale Watson, who had tried to get the FBI to look for the sleepers. Were there still cells planning more attacks? Thousands had died; we in the West Wing had almost been among them. Now we had the full attention of the bureaucracies and the full support of the President. I had to get back to the White House and begin planning to prevent follow-on attacks. I found my Secret Service–

issued .357 sidearm, thrust it in my belt, and went back out into the night, back to the West Wing.

I expected to go back to a round of meetings examining what the next attacks could be, what our vulnerabilities were, what we could do about them in the short term. Instead, I walked into a series of discussions about Iraq. At first I was incredulous that we were talking about something other than getting al Qaeda. Then I realized with almost a sharp physical pain that Rumsfeld and Wolfowitz were going to try to take advantage of this national tragedy to promote their agenda about Iraq. Since the beginning of the administration, indeed well before, they had been pressing for a war with Iraq. My friends in the Pentagon had been telling me that the word was we would be invading Iraq sometime in 2002.

On the morning of the 12th DOD's focus was already beginning to shift from al Qaeda. CIA was explicit now that al Qaeda was guilty of the attacks, but Paul Wolfowitz, Rumsfeld's deputy, was not persuaded. It was too sophisticated and complicated an operation, he said, for a terrorist group to have pulled off by itself, without a state sponsor—Iraq must have been helping them.

I had a flashback to Wolfowitz saying the very same thing in April when the administration had finally held its first deputy secretary–level meeting on terrorism. When I had urged action on al Qaeda then, Wolfowitz had harked back to the 1993 attack on the World Trade Center, saying al Qaeda could not have done that alone and must have had help from Iraq. The focus on al Qaeda was wrong, he had said in April, we must go after Iraqi-sponsored terrorism. He had rejected my assertion and CIA's that there had been no Iraqi-sponsored terrorism against the United States since 1993. Now this line of thinking was coming back.

By the afternoon on Wednesday, Secretary Rumsfeld was talking about broadening the objectives of our response and "getting Iraq." Secretary Powell pushed back, urging a focus on al Qaeda. Relieved to have some support, I thanked Colin Powell and his deputy, Rich Armitage. "I thought I was missing something here," I vented. "Having been attacked by al Qaeda, for us now to go bombing Iraq in response would be like our invading Mexico after the Japanese attacked us at Pearl Harbor."

Powell shook his head. "It's not over yet."

Indeed, it was not. Later in the day, Secretary Rumsfeld complained that there were no decent targets for bombing in Afghanistan and that we should consider bombing Iraq, which, he said, had better targets. At first I thought Rumsfeld was joking. But he was serious and the President did not reject out of hand the idea of attacking Iraq. Instead, he noted that what we needed to do with Iraq was to change the government, not just hit it with more cruise missiles, as Rumsfeld had implied.

Joint Chiefs Chairman Hugh Shelton's reaction to the idea of changing the Iraqi government was guarded. He noted that could only be done with an invasion by a large force, one that would take months to assemble.

On the 12th and 13th the discussions wandered: what was our objective, who was the enemy, was our reaction to be a war on terrorism in general or al Qaeda in specific? If it was all terrorism we would fight, did we have to attack the anti-government forces in Colombia's jungles too? Gradually, the obvious prevailed: we would go to war with al Qaeda and the Taliban. The compromise consensus, however, was that the struggle against al Qaeda and the Taliban would be the first stage in a broader war on terrorism. It was also clear that there would be a second stage.

Most Americans had never heard of al Qaeda. Indeed, most senior officials in the administration did not know the term when we briefed them in January 2001. I found a moment without meetings and sat at my computer and began: "Who did this? Why do they hate us? How will we respond? What can you as an American do to help?" It all came out, in a stream of pages. I wrote of al Qaeda's hatred of freedom, of its perversion of a beautiful religion, of the need to avoid religious or ethnic prejudice. Thinking it might be helpful, I sent it to John Gibson in Speech Writing.

Meanwhile, Roger Cressey and I dusted off the draft National Security Presidential Directive on al Qaeda, authorizing aid to the

Northern Alliance in Afghanistan. Joined by Lisa Gordon-Hagerty, we also began to list the major domestic vulnerabilities to further terrorist attacks and to task the departments to start plugging the holes. Trains with HAZMAT—hazardous materials—were diverted from major cities. Crop dusters were grounded until they could be tracked and we could be sure terrorists were not filling them with biological agents. Special security teams were sent to protect telecommunications hubs, chemical plants, and nuclear reactors.

George Tenet and Cofer Black (the counterterrorism chief at CIA) were off and running now, demanding action from friendly intelligence services and preparing at last to send CIA officers into Afghanistan. Colin Powell and Rich Armitage were turning Pakistan around, from halfhearted support of the U.S. campaign against al Qaeda to full cooperation.

Later, on the evening of the 12th, I left the Video Conferencing Center and there, wandering alone around the Situation Room, was the President. He looked like he wanted something to do. He grabbed a few of us and closed the door to the conference room. "Look," he told us, "I know you have a lot to do and all . . . but I want you, as soon as you can, to go back over everything, everything. See if Saddam did this. See if he's linked in any way . . ."

I was once again taken aback, incredulous, and it showed. "But, Mr. President, al Qaeda did this."

"I know, I know, but . . . see if Saddam was involved. Just look. I want to know any shred . . ."

"Absolutely, we will look . . . again." I was trying to be more respectful, more responsive. "But, you know, we have looked several times for state sponsorship of al Qaeda and not found any real linkages to Iraq. Iran plays a little, as does Pakistan, and Saudi Arabia, Yemen."

"Look into Iraq, Saddam," the President said testily and left us. Lisa Gordon-Hagerty stared after him with her mouth hanging open.

Paul Kurtz walked in, passing the President on the way out. Seeing our expressions, he asked, "Geez, what just happened here?"

"Wolfowitz got to him," Lisa said, shaking her head.

"No," I said. "Look, he's the President. He has not spent years on terrorism. He has every right to ask us to look again, and we will, Paul."

Paul was the most open-minded person on the staff, so I asked him to lead the special project to get the departments and agencies to once again look for a bin Laden link to Saddam Hussein. He chaired a meeting the next day to develop an official position on the relationship between Iraq and al Qaeda. All agencies and departments agreed, there was no cooperation between the two. A memorandum to that effect was sent up to the President, but there was never any indication that it reached him.

The next week President Bush addressed a Joint Session of Congress in the most eloquent speech of his career. Gone was any tentativeness or awkwardness as a speaker. Karen Hughes had drafted the text personally on her old typewriter. It included my questions and some of my answers: who is the enemy, why do they hate us . . .

The weeks that followed were filled with meetings, back to back. A Campaign Coordination Committee, co-chaired by Franklin Miller and me, developed a game plan for attacking al Qaeda. A Domestic Preparedness Committee, chaired by Deputy Attorney General Larry Thompson, pooled the departments' efforts to identify and remedy vulnerabilities in the U.S. to further attack. The Cabinet and their deputies had their eyes opened. It was a time of jitters. There were clearly bogus reports of commando teams targeting the White House and nuclear bombs on Wall Street, but many of the people now reading such intelligence had never seen it before and could not tell the wheat from the chaff. Reagan National Airport remained closed, but because of concerns about aircraft possibly headed toward the White House, we were on constant alert.

Throughout it all, we thought of the dead, of the horror. Those of us who had stayed in the White House that day now knew why the United flight had crashed in Pennsylvania, that heroic passengers had fought and died, and probably saved our lives in the process. But we tried to stay unemotional, to stay focused on the work that had to be done, the work that kept us in the White House eighteen hours a day and more, every day since 9/11. We were told that parts of my FBI friend, John O'Neill, had been found in the rubble in New York and that there would be a memorial service in his hometown of Atlantic City. I told Condi Rice that we would be taking a half day off. Lisa, Roger, and Bev Roundtree joined me and we drove to New Jersey.

As the Mass ended and John's coffin rolled by, the bagpipes played, and, finally, I wept from my gut. There was so much to grieve about. How did this all happen? Why couldn't we stop it? How do we prevent it from happening again and rid the world of the horror? Someday I would find the time to think through it all and answer those questions.

Now is that time.

Chapter 2

Stumbling into the Islamic World

Little noticed by most Americans, including in its government, a new international movement began growing during the last two decades. It does not just seek terror for its own sake; that international movement's goal is the creation of a network of governments, imposing on their citizens a minority interpretation of Islam. Some in the movement call for the scope of their campaign to be global domination. The "Caliphate" they seek to create would be a severe and repressive fourteenth-century literalist theocracy. They pursue its creation with gruesome violence and fear.

To understand why that movement has chosen America as its target and why America failed to see the effects of its own actions, we need to remind ourselves of some events of the last twenty-five years.

The story, the strands of history that brought us to September 11 and to today's war on terrorism and Iraq, does not start with Bill Clinton or George W. Bush. It goes back to their two predecessors, Ronald Reagan and George H. W. Bush.

First, in this chapter, Ronald Reagan. He had been obsessed with aggressively confronting the Soviet Union, not just by outspending the Red Army, but by inserting U.S. military influence in new regions to put Moscow off balance. His efforts to push the Soviet Union to collapse worked, much to the surprise of most of official Washington. By confronting Moscow in Afghanistan, inserting the U.S. military in the Persian Gulf, and by strengthening Israel as a base for a southern flank against the Soviets, Reagan created new equations. The moves were unquestionably correct strategically, but the details of how they were handled left problems and wrong impressions that grew with time. As a junior officer and then midlevel manager, I played a small role in each of these events, which shaped my perceptions of the U.S. role in the region.

The world that Ronald Reagan inherited as President was freshly reshaped by two crucial changes that happened in 1979, the Iranian Revolution and the Soviet invasion of Afghanistan. Both events rekindled the radical movement in Islam and both drew America further into the realm of Islam. Although a low-level official at the time, I had a ringside seat to these events. No one thought then that, as dramatic as the 1979 changes were, they were America's first steps into a new era when U.S. forces would fight multiple wars in the Middle East and confront Middle Eastern terrorism at home.

I had joined the State Department in 1979 to work on the issue of the Soviet Union's growing military power, particularly its nuclear weapons facing NATO. I had focused on these issues for half a decade at the Pentagon. As 1979 came to an end, however, the White House froze all nuclear arms control talks with Moscow and began to concentrate on the Persian Gulf, the Middle East, and South Asia.

The 1974 Arab Oil Boycott of the United States had made clear to Washington the importance of Persian Gulf resources. In 1979 America's greatest ally in the Gulf was violently overthrown by a radical Islamic group. Then, on Christmas Day, the Soviet Red Army moved south in the direction of the Persian Gulf, by invading and occupying Afghanistan.

The State Department, then and now, was mostly staffed by Foreign Service officers, professional international relations and regional affairs specialists who spend most of their career overseas. In 1979, the Department's Bureau of Politico-Military Affairs (State's "little Pentagon") was not led by a Foreign Service officer, but by a former *New York Times* columnist, Leslie Gelb. To help him deal with the Pentagon's technical arguments on arms control, Gelb created a small office of young, civil service, military analysts. I was part of that team, along with junior staff who would have an increasing and persistent role in the next twenty years: Arnold Kanter, later the Special Assistant to the President for Defense Policy and Under Secretary of State in the George H. W. Bush administration; Randy Beers, who would go on to serve four presidents on the National Security Council staff; Franklin Miller, who would serve twenty years in senior Pentagon positions, then as Special Assistant to the President, in which capacity he would join me in the emptied White House on 9/11.

After the twin shocks of the Iranian Revolution and the Soviet invasion of Afghanistan, our group of politico-military analysts was given a new focus: the Persian Gulf.

In the Persian Gulf, the Shah of Iran had served two useful purposes for Cold War America. First, he had guaranteed a source of oil unaffected by the Arab Oil Boycott. Second, he had offered to use Iran's newfound wealth to create a modern military "as strong as Germany's" on the Soviet Union's southern flank. Cold War America saw all foreign policy issues through the prism of the conflict between the two superpowers, much as we now see the world through the war on terrorism. The Cold War had parallels with the War on Terror. Both conflicts raged globally, with regional wars, secret sleeper cells, and competing ideologies. The two struggles also threatened the horrific destruction of our cities by weapons of mass destruction (although in the Cold War we knew the enemy actually had thousands of nuclear weapons). Our opponents in both vowed to seek the imposition of their form of government and way of life on all nations. In retrospect, some (particularly those born after 1970) believe America overreacted to the Cold War threat. At the time, however, it seemed an existential struggle, the depth of which is now difficult for many to recall or understand.

FOLLOWING THE SOVIET INVASION OF AFGHANISTAN, our little analytical team began fielding questions from the State Department leadership and from the White House. A Soviet strategic bomber base appeared to be under construction in Afghanistan. From it, we were asked, could Soviet bombers attack U.S. naval forces in the Indian Ocean, should the U.S. bomb the Afghan base before it became operational? We determined the construction was actually a Soviet agricultural aid development project.

If the Soviet Union poured troops into Iran, could they get to the Persian Gulf before U.S. forces could stage a D-Day–like landing? Yes, the Soviets could beat us there because we had no forces in the area and no realistic plan or capability to project forces to the Persian Gulf, but then neither did the Soviets. The first part of that answer resonated with both the Carter and Reagan administration leadership; the latter part was ignored. Prior to 1979, the United States had little military presence in the Indian Ocean or Persian Gulf. The exception was a small naval facility in Bahrain, which we had agreed to maintain when the British left.

Thus did the United States embark on a fevered campaign to develop the military capability to project force into the region and to create bases into which those forces could be sent. I was asked to meet with the U.S. military planners who were assigned to this task. Instead of finding them in the bowels of the Pentagon, I found them at the end of a noisy runway on a fighter base in Florida. They were in trailers surrounded by barbed wire and they were wearing field camouflage. Of course, I had to ask why.

"We're called the Rapid Deployment Joint Task Force, RDJTF," General Robert Kingston explained. "So I want it to look like we can deploy rapidly to the region."

"Can you?" I asked.

"No, but that's where you guys come in. You're gonna get us some bases." Kingston smiled. Some of his military colleagues also thought it a little odd that he was behind barbed wire in trailers in Tampa, and began referring to General Kingston as "Barbed Wire Bob." His enthusiasm and sense of urgency were, however, infectious.

My colleagues and I soon found ourselves negotiating in Egypt, Bahrain, Kuwait, Oman, the United Arab Emirates, Qatar, and Saudi Arabia. Unable to procure bases, we asked for "access" agreements and the right to enhance existing facilities. No nation wanted to offend the other superpower by overtly agreeing to facilitate the U.S. military. In most cases, however, we reached understandings that would allow us to improve air bases and pre-positioned war matériel secretly, without any guarantee that we would be able to use it in a crisis. The Saudis were different. They agreed to the creation of the facilities, but they would build them much larger than was necessary for their own small forces, a concept that became known as "Overbuilding, Overstocking." Thousands of American civilian contractors moved into the Kingdom, causing resentment among some Muslims who read the Koran as banning the presence of infidels in the country that hosted the two holiest mosques of Islam.

We negotiated with the British over a long forgotten coaling station on a rock in the Indian Ocean called Diego Garcia. (In later years I and my British counterpart in London were designated "co-mayors" of that distant island neither of us had ever seen.) In 1980 we asked the British, "Could we please use Diego Garcia and maybe add to it a little?" Soon, it was capable of launching B-52s and about to sink from the weight of pre-positioned war matériel.

A year after the shocks of 1979, another unexpected event hit, dragging the United States a bit further into the politics of the region. A new president in Iraq, Saddam Hussein, launched a preemptive attack on Iran in an attempt to seize its oil fields. Saddam may also have been provoked by the Iranian leader Ayatollah Khomeini, who appealed to the Shi'a majority in Iraq to rise up. At first, Washington maintained neutrality. The United States did not have good relations with Iraq, which had been close to the Soviet Union. Our relations with Iran, however, were terrible and getting worse.

The new Iranian government seized the U.S. embassy staff and held them for over a year. Iran then contributed to the turmoil in Lebanon, a nation that the United States had always considered a friendly and stable, pro-Western anchor at the eastern end of the Mediterranean. When the turmoil worsened in 1982, Ronald Reagan was in his second year as President. Seeing the events in Lebanon as linked to the anti-American regime in Iran and threatening to Israel, which Reagan had begun calling an ally, he ordered Marines into Beirut. By so doing, Reagan began what would become a misadventure that gave terrorists the impression they could attack the United States with relative impunity.

Reagan explained to a prime-time audience that we went into

Lebanon in part "because of the oil." Lebanon had no oil. The Iranian-supported Hezbollah faction in Lebanon responded to the new American military presence by staging devastating car bomb attacks on the U.S. Marines barracks and twice on our embassy. In the attack on the Marine barracks alone, 278 Americans died.

There would be no similar loss of American lives in terrorism until the Libyan attack on Pan Am 103 six years later during the first Bush's presidency. Those two acts stood as the most lethal acts of foreign terrorism against Americans until September 11. Nothing occurring during Clinton's tenure approached either attack in terms of the numbers of Americans killed by foreign terrorism. Neither Ronald Reagan nor George H. W. Bush retaliated for these devastating attacks on Americans.

After the Marine barracks was leveled in Beirut, Americans were faced for the first time with what Middle East terrorism could really do, and how a confused multifactional civil war could drag us in. At the State Department, our newly created Middle East politico-military team was pressed into supporting our besieged Beirut embassy. Although Reagan had decided not to attack Syria or Iran (both of which were implicated in the attacks on the Marines and the embassy), he was determined to keep a U.S. diplomatic presence. From the radio room in the Operations Center, we would check on the status of the American diplomats who had relocated to the Ambassador's Residence in the Beirut neighborhood of Yazde.

"Yazde, Yazde, this is State, over. What is your status?"

"State, State, Yazde here. We are taking artillery fire from a ridge across the way," came the voice crackling across thousands of miles. "We could sure use some support from New Jersey." That was not a request for letters from back home, but rather a call for suppressing fire from the U.S. battleship riding off the coast. The Reagan administration had decided to deter further attacks by showing U.S. military muscle. Minutes later, the long guns of a World War II throwback turned east and fired their famous "shells as big as Volkswagens."

"Yazde, Yazde, are you still taking fire from that ridgeline, over."

"State, Yazde: there is no ridgeline there anymore."

Despite our military superiority, however, we were unable to counter the religious fervor of the Iranian-Syrian–supported faction. Lebanon seemed to be going down into a long, bloody death spiral of factional conflict that the United States was ill prepared to affect. After a series of bombings and shellings, Reagan ordered U.S. forces out of Lebanon. Throughout the Middle East, it was noted how easily the superpower could be driven off, how the U.S. was still "shell-shocked" from its defeat in Vietnam. Years later Usama bin Laden would refer to the success of terrorism in driving the United States out of Beirut, a city whose pleasures he had enjoyed before becoming a devout Muslim.

It was against this backdrop of hostile relations with Iran that the Reagan administration began to look anew at the war between Iran and Iraq, which had erupted when Saddam Hussein invaded Iran in 1980, hoping to take advantage of the weakness of the new revolutionary government and its inability to get American spare parts for the weapons the shah had bought. There has been speculation that the United States gave Saddam a green light to attack Iran, perhaps in the hopes that if he seized the oil-rich province of Khuzistan, we would continue to have access to Iranian crude and perhaps because Washington hoped that the new Iranian regime would collapse without its major source of revenue. I tried to find evidence of such a U.S. strategy then, from inside the State Department and from my sources in the Pentagon and the White House. As far as I could tell, Saddam's attack on Iran was a surprise to Washington just as his attack on Kuwait would be almost a decade later.

Shortly after it began, the Iran-Iraq War became a stalemate, with very high casualties on both sides. Our little politico-military team at State was asked to draft options to prevent an Iranian victory or, as we entitled one paper, "Options for Preventing Iraqi Defeat." As time passed and the war continued, many of those options were employed. Although not an ally of Iraq, the Reagan administration had decided that Saddam Hussein should not be allowed to be defeated by a radical Islamist, anti-American regime in Tehran.

In 1982, the Reagan administration removed Iraq from the list of nations that sponsored terrorism. Iraq was thus able to apply for certain types of U.S. government–backed export promotion loans. Then in 1983, a presidential envoy was sent to Baghdad as a sign of support for Saddam Hussein. A man who had been the Defense Secretary seven years earlier in a previous Republican administration was sent carrying a presidential letter. The man was Donald Rumsfeld. He went to Baghdad not to overthrow Saddam Hussein, but to save him from probable defeat by the Iranian onslaught. Shortly thereafter, I saw American intelligence data begin to flow to Baghdad. When Iran was preparing an offensive in a sector, the Iraqis would know from what U.S. satellites saw and Saddam would counter with beefed-up defenses.

In 1984, the United States resumed full diplomatic relations with Iraq. Although the U.S. never sold arms to Iraq, the Saudis and Egyptians did, including U.S. arms. Some of the bombs that the Saudis had bought as part of overstocking now went to Saddam, in violation of U.S. law. I doubt that the Saudis ever asked Washington's permission, but I also doubt that anyone in the Reagan administration wanted to be asked.

After the intelligence flow to Saddam was opened up, our State Department team was then asked to implement the next option in the plan to prevent Iraqi defeat, identifying the foreign sources of Iranian military supplies and pressuring countries to halt the flow. We dubbed the diplomatic-intelligence effort Operation Staunch. I spent long days tracing arms shipment to Iran and firing off instructions to American embassies around the world to threaten governments with sanctions if they did not crack down on the gray market arms shipments to Tehran. The effort was surprisingly successful, raising the price and reducing the supply of what arms Iran could get.

By 1986, the Iran-Iraq War expanded into attacks on oil tankers. To insure its oil made it to market, Iraq shifted its product to neutral Kuwaiti tankers. Undeterred by attacking a "neutral" state's shipping, Iran bombed the Kuwaiti tankers. The Soviet Union then offered to send the Red Navy to the Persian Gulf to protect the Iraqi oil shipments. Horrified at the prospect of the Soviet fleet in the oil lanes, the White House asked our State Department team to come up with an alternative that would satisfy Iraq and Kuwait. We proposed that the Kuwaiti tankers be "reflagged," their registration and names changed so that they became American ships subject to protection by the United States Navy. To defend the American ships carrying Saddam's oil, the U.S. Navy placed large convoys of U.S. warships into the Persian Gulf. On my wall in the State Department, we mapped minefields and locations of ship attacks. For the first time, we examined what to do if things escalated into a U.S.-Iranian war. They didn't, although shots were fired by both sides as the convoys made their way through the Gulf. (Ten years later, terrorism would force me to look again at options for a war with Iran.)

Simultaneously, Ronald Reagan's administration was responding to the threat of the Soviet Union's military involvement in the Middle East by bringing the United States closer militarily to Israel. Prior to this period, it was a given in the State Department that the United States could not expand military relations with Arab states and at the same time do so with Israel. U.S. military relations with Israel were minimal in the 1960s and 1970s. We had greatly expanded arms supplies after the 1973 Arab-Israeli War, but our two militaries hardly knew each other. Looking at the threat the Soviet Union posed to the eastern Mediterranean, the Reagan administration sought to change that. The Administration proposed "Strategic Cooperation" with Israel. It was just short of a military alliance. To operationalize the concept, in 1983 we created something called the Joint Politico-Military Group or JPMG, a U.S.-Israeli planning group. First as a staff member and later as the U.S. head of the JPMG, I sought to find roles for the Israeli military in joint operations with American forces in the event of a war with the Soviet Union. My partner in this effort would be a heroic Israeli fighter pilot turned defense bureaucrat and strategist, David Ivry.

When in 1981 Israeli intelligence had developed irrefutable information that Saddam Hussein was building the Osiraq nuclear reactor to develop a bomb, the Israeli cabinet asked Ivry's reaction to the idea of preemptively bombing the plant. He recommended against it, although he said his air force could do it at considerable risk to the pilots. When the cabinet decided to order the attack anyway, Ivry planned the raid personally. Ivry went on to serve successive Israeli governments of all parties as the permanent civilian head of the Ministry of Defense, national security advisor, and ambassador to Washington.

I met Ivry after the Congress passed the Comprehensive Anti-Apartheid Act of 1987. Although the law was aimed at South Africa, it had a little noticed provision that required the Reagan administration to investigate what nations were sending arms to South Africa in violation of the U.N. embargo. The provision also required that the results of the investigation be sent to the Congress and held open the possibility that the United States would ban military cooperation with any state found in violation of the embargo. No one in the State Department wanted to be involved in implementing that provision, because it was widely assumed the investigation would find that the biggest gunrunner to the apartheid regime would be Israel. Being the youngest Deputy Assistant Secretary of State at the time and having responsibility for intelligence analysis, I was given the hot potato and asked to run the investigation. I booked a flight to Tel Aviv.

Sitting in Ivry's office in the heart of the Kiriat, the walled-off complex in Tel Aviv that serves as Israel's Pentagon, I laid out to the Director General of the Israeli Ministry of Defense what I knew and what I suspected about Israeli–South African cooperation. I omitted any reference to rumors of their cooperation on nuclear weapons, but mentioned joint development of long-range ballistic missiles and fighter aircraft. David was clearly uncomfortable, but I began to think that it was not just because some young American was sitting there accusing him and his government.

"I am not saying we are doing these things, these rumors that you mention," David began. "But we must have a defense industry; we cannot depend on other countries for our defense. A defense industry in a small country like ours has to export to stay alive, to keep costs in check. We do not sell to the Soviets or their allies, never. We have developed our own advanced weapons technologies. We have very smart, very capable engineers. America, however, will not buy our weapons. American defense contractors prevent the Pentagon from buying from us, they spread lies that what we have developed we stole from them. If we stole it from them, how is it they haven't been able to develop some of these technologies that we have working, unmanned aerial vehicles, air-to-ground guided smart bombs, other things."

I had just met General Ivry, but I thought I saw a side to him that was not hinted at in the CIA profile of him as a hard-ass fighter pilot. "General, I have been to South Africa. Have you?"

He hesitated. "Yes, yes I have." Then he added a justification that did not admit to the weapons programs. "We have a very large Jewish community there that we have to insure is protected from the anti-Semitism."

"Anti-Semitism is a terrible, ugly thing, General. I saw a small piece of it growing up. My house was the only non-Jewish family in the neighborhood. I saw what people would do to the temple, I saw the harassment, heard the epithets. But, General, apartheid is the same thing. It's racism. Don't you think a government based on apartheid is a sin?"

Ivry had been looking at his hands. Now he looked up and into my eyes. "Yes. Yes, I do."

The next week Ivry asked to appear before the Israeli cabinet. After the meeting the government of Israel announced that it was terminating any and all defense relations with South Africa and banning the import and export of defense items between the two countries, in keeping with the U.N. embargo.

The U.S.-Israeli Strategic Cooperation had a slow start. The Israeli Defense Forces had been the ultimate loner all of its life, never having operated with another nation's forces.

The talks went slowly at first. Perhaps we could do an anti–submarine warfare exercise, I suggested. "Why would we want you to find our submarine?" came the bemused reply.

Well, perhaps we could do an air-to-air exercise similar to Top Gun. "No, we will beat you and then your pilots will be mad at us." I suggested that the U.S. be allowed to position military supplies in Israel for our forces to use in a crisis with the Soviets. "Certainly. And we will use them when we have a crisis too." Eventually, however, we reached agreements.

My counterpart in the U.S. military was a Navy admiral who, at first, did not seem schooled in diplomacy. When asked at our first social dinner in Tel Aviv whether he had ever been to Israel before, Admiral Jack Darby thought a moment and then replied in a slow Southern drawl, "Well, that would depend on whether you count when I was in my submarine. You know, you can see a lot through a periscope."

Eventually, we agreed on a series of exercises, which became larger with time. We also agreed on the development of war plans in the event the Soviet Union acted militarily in the region. Darby completely ingratiated himself with the Israeli military and built bonds of personal trust. When, later, Jack Darby became head of U.S. Submarine Force Pacific, he collapsed and died while jogging around Pearl Harbor. The Israel Defense Forces flew the Darby family to Israel for the dedication of the Jack Darby Memorial Grove in the desert.

David Ivry had grown concerned at the prospect of Soviet, Syrian, or Iraqi missiles attacking Israel. Together, we successfully proposed the U.S. fund the Israeli development of a missile defense system, as well as the interim deployment of U.S. Patriot missiles. We also managed to get the Pentagon to evaluate the Israeli unmanned aerial vehicle and air-to-ground smart bomb. The Marines bought the former, the Air Force the latter. (A few years later on the Iraqi border with the Marines, I got to "fly" one of the Israeli-made unmanned aerial vehicles over Iraqi troops.) Ivry also became my advocate in the Israeli cabinet, arguing successfully for my personal requests that they agree to international standards on nonproliferation of missiles and chemical and biological weapons.

(At the outset of the first Gulf War, Ivry and I conspired to get our governments to agree to deploy a U.S. Army Patriot unit in Israel. No foreign troops had ever been stationed before in Israel. We also worked together to sell Patriots to Israel, and to tie in the Kiriat with American satellites that detected Iraqi Scud missile launches toward Israel. After the war, CIA circulated unfounded rumors that Israel had sold some of the Patriots to China. Many in the State Department who thought that I was "too close to the Israelis" sought to blame me. Ivry called. "I hear you are in trouble. What can I do?" I jokingly suggested that he invite the U.S. to send an inspection team to Israel to do "anywhere, anytime" checking to see if any of the Patriots were missing or had been tampered with. I knew it was a silly idea. Israel would never give another country that kind of unfettered access. Ivry did not think the idea was silly. Again he went to the Cabinet for me. The ensuing U.S. Army inspection concluded that there was no reason to believe that Israel had tampered with or transferred any Patriot missile, software, designs, or associated material. I was cleared, but not without making enemies at CIA and State.)

Our stronger military relationship with Israel came about only by the Reagan White House imposing it on the Pentagon and State Department. The decision was the right thing to do militarily and morally, but the closer relationship with Tel Aviv did over time inflame some Arab radicals and give them propaganda to help recruit terrorists to their anti-American cause. Thus, between our buildup in the Gulf and our programs with Israel, by the mid-1980s, the United States had a growing military presence in the Middle East. Marines were regularly staging landings in Israel, Air Force and Navy fighters were flying into Israel air bases. Patriot radars scanned the skies. In Egypt, Oman, and Bahrain, the United States had bombs and other war matériel in warehouses and bunkers. A large U.S. Navy squadron plied the Persian Gulf. Reagan had checkmated the Iranians by strengthening Saddam Hussein. He had built new relations with both Israel and key Arab states to allow the U.S. military to operate against any Soviet threat into the Mediterranean or Persian Gulf.

These actions by the Reagan administration were defensive. What they did in Afghanistan, however, was go on the offensive, in a way that drew the United States further into the region.

In the mid-1980s, as the Deputy Assistant Secretary for Intelligence at the State Department, I produced a series of analyses of the cost to the Soviet Union of fighting the proxy wars in El Salvador, Nicaragua, Angola, Mozambique, and Afghanistan. We had only estimates, inferences, of the effect on the Kremlin treasury. Nonetheless, even the low-end guesses would place a serious burden on what was already a badly underperforming Soviet economy. That was, of course, what President Reagan and CIA director Bill Casey had hoped, that by turning the tables, going on the counteroffensive in the proxy wars and by rapidly increasing our own defense spending, America could force the Kremlin to respond in ways that would overtax the Soviet economy.

Afghanistan offered Reagan and Casey their best opportunity to drain the other superpower. Moscow had overcommitted there. Rather than just manipulate the Kabul government and secure the area around the capital, after invading in late 1979, the Red Army had decided to pacify the country. It was a major deployment for which they were not ready, equipped, or trained. The initial fighting showed the weaknesses of the Red Army's conscript divisions, but Moscow had responded with Spetsnaz Special Forces and Airborne troops. They began to employ heavily armed helicopters and new close-support aircraft, which were beginning in 1985 to have devastating effects.

Yet, despite their rhetoric, the Reagan administration had not significantly funded the Afghan resistance. The Afghan war analysts on my staff kept numerical indicators of the fighting, as well as anecdotal information on the spirit of the Afghan fighters. By 1985 the analysts were growing concerned that the tide had shifted in favor of Moscow.

My boss and mentor was a career ambassador, but hardly from central casting. Morton Abramowitz filled his darkened office with cigar smoke, and left ashes in his wake. He was oblivious to the fact that what little hair he had was often standing straight up. He had saved hundreds of thousands of Cambodians when, as U.S. Ambassador to Thailand, he had initiated a cross-border feeding program. Later, as Ambassador to Turkey, he would be responsible for starting a similar effort to save the Kurds in the wake of the First Gulf War. He focused not on appearances, but on getting things done.

"Don't just tell me we're losing, Clarke, tell me what the fuck to do about it." That was how Abramowitz received our analysis of the shifting tide in Afghanistan.

Our analysis had focused on the Hind-D helicopter as being the thing that had worked for the Soviets. Afghan bullets bounced off its armor plate, while the helicopter's rockets ripped apart the hidden mujahedeen camps. "We need to give them Stingers to shoot down the Hinds," I shot back.

"Agh, come up with a new thought. CIA and the Pentagon won't agree to release the missiles." Mort was relighting the stub of a cigar. "You wanna do something? Go see your friend Richard Perle, the Prince of Darkness, get him to release the Stingers."

Perle was Assistant Secretary of Defense and greatly distrustful of the State Department, whom he saw as capitulationists and accommodationists in the Cold War. Following the military coup in Turkey in 1984, Perle had flown to Ankara to counteract the State Department's denunciations of the takeover. His message: deal with the instability, but lay out a roadmap for a return to civilian rule. Perle charmed the Turkish pashas, as the four-star generals were known. He clearly loved their country, insisting on traveling throughout it and buying rugs and copper pots. I had been assigned by State to go along on the trip to keep an eye on Perle. Instead, I too had been charmed by his manner and persuaded by his logic about the strategic importance of Turkey.

Now, at Abramowitz's urging, I used my nascent friendship to have a private meeting with Perle. I confronted him with the Pentagon's refusal to send Stingers to Afghanistan. He at first denied it, but then hit an intercom button and asked an aide whether it was true. "God damn it! Who blocked it? Well, fuck the CIA!" He then hit another intercom button and, more politely, asked, "Can I stick my head in on Cap for a second?"

Perle left me alone in his office for a long time while he went down from the fourth floor to Secretary of Defense Caspar Weinberger's huge office on the Pentagon's third-floor E Ring. When he came back, his explanation was simple: "Cap didn't know about it." I was still wondering whether his knowing about it now meant that he would approve the release of the Stingers to the mujahedeen. "No U.S. Army on the ground in Afghanistan. The muj will have to come out and be trained in Pakistan."

With State, Defense, and the National Security Council in favor of deploying Stingers and with heavy congressional pressure, CIA relented. The training was over and the weapons smuggled in by September 1986. Within weeks of the deployment of the infrared-seeking Stinger antiaircraft missiles and the wire-guided British Javelins, the mujahedeen had figured out a clever strategy to employ them in tandem to deal with the Soviets' countermeasures. The number of Hind and MiG kills started slowly, but then accelerated dramatically. Over 270 Soviet aircraft were shot down. Then the Hind kills stopped. The Soviets were no longer flying their airborne tanks into harm's way.

The overall covert action program expanded greatly in Reagan's second term. Unclassified studies show that it grew from $35 million in 1982 to $600 million in 1987. With few exceptions, the funds bought matériel that was given to Afghan fighters by Pakistan's intelligence service. CIA personnel were not authorized to enter Afghanistan, except rarely.

State's analysts were not cleared to know details about the U.S. covert action program, including the Stingers. They could, however, see the effects in the war and they heard the Afghans talking about the Stinger. By 1987, they told me the tide was shifting back to the Afghans. Soon they predicted that the Soviets would pull back to Kabul. They were wrong. The Soviets agreed in 1988 to pull back all the way out of the country, and did so the following year.

Pakistani military intelligence funded by the U.S. and Saudi governments and "charitable" organizations, had turned groups of nineteenth-century Afghan tribesmen and several thousand Arab volunteers into a force that had crippled the mighty Red Army. The Stinger had been the final element they had needed.

Throughout the war, the Soviets had restrained themselves from bombing the mujahedeen sanctuary and U.S. staging base that was Pakistan. On a few occasions their fighter aircraft had strayed over the border, but they had taken American cautions seriously and not attacked. Following the Geneva agreement that called for a quick Soviet withdrawal, two things happened. First, the major base used by the CIA and Pakistani intelligence to stockpile arms for the Afghans mysteriously blew up in an explosion of immense size. The nearby city of Rawalpindi shook for hours. Second, a few months later, the military ruler of Pakistan died in an unexplained aircraft crash. I could never find the evidence to prove that Soviet KGB had ordered these two acts as payback for their bitter defeat, but in my bones I knew they had.

The word of the death of Pakistan's ruler came to me as

Abramowitz and I stood on the deck of the USS *Theodore Roosevelt* in the Atlantic. A Navy officer tapped on my helmet to get my attention over the roar of F-14s taking off. He signaled for us to step inside the tower so we could talk. "State Ops just radioed us. They want you two back in Washington. There's a COD getting ready to take you direct to Andrews. Seems the Pakistani president died in a plane crash."

I was glad we would have an S-3 Carrier Onboard Delivery aircraft, but puzzled by why the State Department leadership should want us back so fast. I asked him, "What else do you know about it?"

"Oh, yeah," the officer replied, "the American ambassador. He was on board the plane, too." Abramowitz paled. I felt as though I had been kicked in the stomach. The American ambassador was Arnold L. Raphel, Abramowitz's close friend and my mentor. He had risen rapidly through the State Department, demonstrating great understanding of South Asia and the Middle East, cleaning up messes others had made in Lebanon and elsewhere. Despite his successes and responsibilities, Arnie, as everyone called him, found time to encourage and advise younger officers and to fight against sexism in the Foreign Service. In the years that followed, as we stumbled through one Middle East crisis after another, some of us would often wonder what would have happened had Arnie not been on that aircraft. The American government had many highly competent experts on the Soviet Union, but few senior officers who could both speak Urdu and Farsi and make things happen in Washington.

Were we right to have armed the Afghans with Stingers and other weapons? Was it a misjudgment to have involved the Saudis? There are many who believe that these were mistaken Cold War policies that laid the seeds of al Qaeda.

Even with hindsight, I believe the Reagan administration was right to assist the Afghans and to drain the Soviet Union's resolve. We had sought to end the proxy wars by proving to Moscow that these conflicts could be a two-way street. Our security was directly affected by those struggles. The stakes in the Cold War were high. We also sought to help a people who were occupied by an invader who had come to set up a puppet government. The Stinger missiles were largely expended in the war or destroyed in the Rawalpindi blast. Others were bought back. Some were not accounted for, but became inoperative when their unique batteries expired. None were ever used by terrorists, although Stinger became a generic name for shoulder-launched antiaircraft missiles around the world.

The involvement of the Saudis and other Arab states was also prudent. Not only did it reduce the financial cost to the United States, but it also proved to those governments that we had common goals and beliefs, despite our differences about Israel. The U.S. did, however, make four mistakes during the Reagan administration that affect us today.

First, the fact that the CIA became dependent upon the Pakistani intelligence service to aid the Afghans meant that we developed fewer ties and loyalties among the Afghans that we should have been able to generate for our multibillion-dollar effort. (Later in the 1990s, CIA would also make a similar mistake, failing to put U.S. operatives into the country to kill bin Laden and the al Qaeda leadership, relying on hired Afghans instead.)

Second, when the U.S. engaged the Saudis, Egyptians, and other Arab states in the fighting against the Soviets, America sought (or acquiesced in) the importation into Afghanistan and Pakistan of an army of "Arabs" without considering who they were or what would happen to them after the Soviets left. The Saudis took the lead in assembling the group of volunteers. The Saudi intelligence chief, Prince Turki, relied upon a man from a wealthy construction family that was close to the Saudi royal family. Turki empowered a son of that family, one Usama bin Laden, to recruit, move, train, and indoctrinate the Arab volunteers in Afghanistan. Many of those recruited were misfits in their own societies. Many had connections to the Muslim Brotherhood, a longtime fundamentalist group that had threatened Egypt and Syria. Many of these volunteers later became the al Qaeda network of affiliated terrorist groups, staging campaigns in Algeria, Egypt, and elsewhere.

Third, America's quick pull-out of assets and resources following the Soviet defeat left us with little influence over, or understanding of, what happened next. The United States sought to reduce the burden of Afghanistan on our foreign policy and our intelligence budget, largely abandoning the country to its own fate. (Later, after our invasion in 2001, we would also try to influence Afghanistan on the cheap.) Following the Soviet withdrawal in 1989, the Afghan factions eventually defeated the Soviet puppet regime and then set upon each other. Kabul and other cities were destroyed in the civil war, forcing huge refugee flows into Pakistan on top of those who had fled there during the long war with the Soviets. Pakistani intelligence, whom we had empowered in Afghanistan, used its power and influence to bring order out of the chaos through a new religious faction, the Taliban. The Pakistanis also facilitated the Taliban's use of the Arab Afghan War veterans, al Qaeda, to fight for the Taliban.

Fourth, the U.S. did little to help Pakistan understand or deal with the corrosive effects on its society caused by the mix of millions of Afghan refugees and the wealthy, fanatic, misfit Arabs who came and stayed. Instead, concerned with Pakistan's nuclear program, the U.S. cut aid to the country. The aid cutoff did not, of course, end the nuclear program. Rather, it insured that the country that was deploying nuclear weapons was politically unstable and threatened with a takeover by fanatics.

The Red Army and the Soviet Union were greatly changed by the war in Afghanistan. As the body bags and the lies had piled up, the average citizen's faith in the Communist Party had further declined, as had the standard of living. Changes, however, also came in Afghanistan.

The withdrawal of the last Soviet soldier took place in February 1989, the first full month of the administration of George H. W. Bush. It was just a matter of time until the pro-Moscow puppet government fell. In Afghanistan a new power structure was emerging. The new players were the tribal chiefs who had led fighting forces, the Pakistani military intelligence officers who had conveyed the American supplies to them, and the Arab volunteers who had brought money and Korans.

As they sat together in Kabul, Kandahar, and Jalalabad, they mused on what was now happening to the Soviet Union. Among them were the Saudi Usama bin Laden, the Pakistani Khalid Sheik Muhammad, the Indonesian known as Hambali, and others we did not know then. In the wake of their Afghan defeat (and, the Arabs believed, because of that defeat), the Soviet Union was now unraveling. Some Afghans and some Arab fighters pondered what you could do with money, Korans, and a few good weapons. You could overthrow an infidel government. More important, you could destroy a superpower. They just had. It was now 1990.

Chapter 3

Unfinished Mission, Unintended Consequences

CHARLIE ALLEN HAD HIS HAIR ON FIRE. That is the way that Steve Simon, then the head of the State Department politico-military analysis team, put it. "You better talk to him. He thinks Iraq is really going to do it."

By 1990 I had become the Assistant Secretary of State for Politico-Military Affairs, greatly outraging many Foreign Service officers who thought that job and many other good jobs I filled with young civil service experts should have been preserved for their "union" members.

Charlie Allen was widely admired and disliked in CIA, and for the same reason: he was usually right. A legend, always involved in the most important programs, he had narrowly dodged dismissal because he had been dragged to Tehran by Bud McFarlane on the ill-fated secret trip with the cake and the Koran. Now as National Warning Officer, he was dissenting from CIA's corporate view that Iraq was only intimidating Kuwait to affect oil prices. CIA's official analysis given to the White House said that no one would go to war in temperatures hovering around 108 degrees Fahrenheit. It was, after all, late July 1990.

"What makes you think it's real, Charlie. After all it is 108 degrees out there," I teased Charlie Allen on the secure phone, knowing my quoting the CIA analysis would set him off.

"Don't believe those guys. They wouldn't notice if an Iraqi T-72 drew up in the CIA parking lot next to them." Allen's hair was on fire.

"Seriously, why do you think the Iraqis are up to something? Aren't they just trying to scare the Kuwaitis?"

"Emcon," was all Charlie said back.

"They're operating under emcon? No radio transmissions from their units? Hiding their locations, their movements? You don't do that if you are just trying to scare someone."

"You got it, boyo." Allen knew he had made the sale.

"All right. I'll try to get a Deputies Committee, but no one is in town. Scowcroft and Bob Gates are out at NSC. Baker and Eagleburger are out at State. Who will chair it?" Although not 108 degrees in our nation's capital, Washington felt like it and most of the leadership had left town.

Under Secretary Bob Kimmitt chaired the late afternoon meeting. Only Kimmitt, NSC's Richard Haass, and I seemed concerned. CIA Deputy Director Dick Kerr said there was no chance of an Iraqi invasion of Kuwait. Admiral Dave Jeremiah agreed and refused my suggestion to retain U.S. forces that were leaving the area after an exercise. State's own Middle East bureau had a report from our ambassador, April Glaspie, noting Saddam's reassurances to her. The meeting broke up without a sense of urgency. I went home.

Steve Simon met me at my house and we sat on the stoop and began to drain a bottle of Lagavulin. John Tritak, then a leading State Department analyst, joined us. I debriefed them on the meeting and we commiserated about the bureaucracy. As the second round was being poured, the telephone rang. John took it. "You have to go back in. The Deputies Committee is reconvening."

"Why, so we can all agree not to do anything again?" I asked bitterly.

John shook his head and grinned: "No, actually, it seems like there really is an Iraqi T-72 in the parking lot . . . of the U.S. Embassy in Kuwait."

The Principals returned to Washington. President Bush was hesitant about how America should respond. His foreign policy alter ego, Secretary of State Jim Baker, and his Defense Secretary, Dick Cheney, were reluctant to act. National Security Advisor Brent Scowcroft, however, thought that Iraq had just changed the strategic equation in a way that could not be permitted to continue. So did British Prime Minister Margaret Thatcher. The two argued that nothing stood between the advance units of the Iraqi army in Kuwait and the immense Saudi oil fields. If we did nothing in response to Iraq's seizing Kuwait, Saddam Hussein would think that he could get away with seizing the Saudis' eastern oil fields. If that happened, Baghdad would control most of the world's readily available oil. They could dictate to America.

Reluctantly, Bush and his team decided that they needed to defend the Saudi oil fields, and do so quickly. They needed Saudi permission for the defensive deployment, but there were some in the Pentagon and White House who thought that U.S. forces needed to protect the Saudi oil with or without Saudi approval.

The mission to persuade the Saudi King to accept U.S. forces was given to Defense Secretary Dick Cheney. He assembled a small team, including Under Secretary of Defense Paul Wolfowitz, Central Command head Norman Schwarzkopf, Sandy Charles of the NSC, and me, then the Assistant Secretary of State for Politico-Military Affairs.

Our aging aircraft landed on the Azores in the mid-Atlantic to refuel. While the refueling went on, we drove to a hilltop to look down on the small island at night. I chatted with Schwarzkopf, who was a little known figure in Washington. His Central Command in Tampa was generally regarded as a backwater, the least important of the major military commands. Nonetheless, I had spent some time with him in Tampa earlier in the year and gotten to like the big bear of a general. As he asked me how I thought the trip would go we looked down on the lights of the Azores. Suddenly, a power failure plunged the island into darkness. "Well, hopefully the trip will go better than it's starting," Cheney replied.

It was night when we landed in a steamy Jeddah and went to the King's palace. The Saudi princes sat on the opposite side of the wide room; the King was at the head of the U-shaped audience chamber. For a late-night meeting in Jeddah in August, there was a large turnout of the royal family.

As we had agreed on the flight, Cheney began by saying that we thought the Kingdom might be in danger. Iraqi forces might continue south from Kuwait and seize the Saudi oil fields too. There was nothing to stop them. He then turned it over to Schwarzkopf, who erected a stand and placed satellite photography and maps on it. During our rehearsal on the aircraft I had been afraid that the briefing was not persuasive. I thought that again when I heard it now; we had no evidence that Iraq was intending to keep going, even though I believed it possible either now or in the future.

Cheney concluded the presentation, promising that U.S. forces would come only to defend the Kingdom. President Bush wanted the King to know that he had the President's word that the U.S. forces would leave as soon as the threat was over, or whenever ordered to do so by the King.

The King turned to his brothers and solicited their views. Despite our presence, a debate erupted over the very idea of having U.S. troops in the Kingdom. "They will never leave," one prince said in Arabic. Our interpreter whispered a translation. "It violates Koranic principles," said another. The argument seemed to be going against us. What we then learned was that the King had just received a report that a Saudi National Guard unit had stumbled upon an Iraqi army force near or slightly over the poorly marked Saudi border. Maybe they were going to keep going. Cheney's staff began asking if we should be staying the night there.

Sitting next to the King translating our English for him was his ambassador to the U.S. and nephew, Prince Bandar. Bandar had flown out hours ahead of us in his own aircraft. A favorite of the King and a darling of the Washington social set, Bandar agreed with the need to deploy U.S. forces and had tried to persuade the King before the meeting. The tension in the room, both among the Americans on one side of the hall and the Saudi princes forty feet across the room, was almost electric. Neither group knew what the King would say next, but we all knew that what he decided would have huge implications for years to come.

Physically turning to his right, the King literally turned his back on his brothers and looked directly at Cheney. "I trust President Bush. Tell him to have his Army come, come with all they have, come quickly. I have his word that they will leave when this is over." He then launched into a lengthy monologue about what he and his family had built in the desert Kingdom, turning a backward collection of nomadic tribes into a modern nation. He was not about to let Saddam Hussein steal it.

As we prepared to leave the palace, Cheney called a huddle. The Americans formed a tight circle in the foyer. "Poker faces leaving here. All the cameras out there are going to be looking at your faces to see the King's decision. Don't let Saddam know. If he thinks we're coming in, he may jump off and seize the oil fields before we can get there." When the doors to the palace opened, however, the humidity was so intense that our glasses instantly fogged. Rather than having poker faces, the American team stumbled toward its cars, rubbing its glasses, looking confused.

The Saudi princes left by another door. Some of them had thought of an alternative to the Americans. Unknown to the Americans at the time, the intelligence chief, Prince Turki, had been approached by the Saudi who had recruited Arabs to fight in the Afghan War against the Soviets, Usama bin Laden.

With the Afghan War over, bin Laden had returned triumphantly to Saudi Arabia in 1989. Prince Turki had reportedly asked him to organize a fundamentalist religion–based resistance to the Communist-styled regime in South Yemen. (The contacts that bin Laden made then in Yemen proved valuable to al Qaeda later.) Bin Laden had also kept some of the Afghan Arab fighters organized. When Kuwait was invaded, he offered to make them available to the King to defend Saudi Arabia, to drive Saddam out of Kuwait. After we left the palace, perhaps bin Laden was told of the King's decision.

His help would not be required. He could not believe it; letting nonbelievers into the Kingdom of the Two Holy Mosques was against the beliefs of the Wahhabist branch of Islam. Large numbers of American military in the Kingdom would violate Islam, the construction magnate's son thought. They would never leave. He feared the King had made a fatal mistake, but he did not break with the regime. He continued his work transforming his front organization, the Afghanistan Services Bureau, into a network that linked returning Afghan war veterans in Algeria, Chechnya, Bosnia, Egypt, and the Philippines.

Returning to the guest palace, Cheney sought to debrief the President. His staff had trouble installing a secure telephone, then found out that it was incompatible with the unit in the Oval Office. When the call did go through, Cheney's Military Assistant was told by someone that the President was in a meeting. Incredulous at the delays, Cheney's implacable facade cracked and he finally erupted, "Well, pull him out of the meeting. We may be going to war."

Schwarzkopf was having better luck with his phone. Talking to Tampa, he ordered, "Stand by to lift the 82nd Airborne in and the tactical fighters." Apparently asked how many fighters, he answered, "What's ever in the plan." The plan, which coincidentally CENTCOM had just exercised in a tabletop war game, called for hundreds of aircraft. It was imprecise as to where they would be based, how they would all fit.

The Saudis were eager for us to involve other Arab nations. Cheney flew on to Cairo to persuade Egyptian leader Hosni Mubarak to send troops to the Kingdom. Wolfowitz and I flew on to Bahrain, Abu Dhabi, and Salalah to gain approvals for American aircraft to land at air bases in the smaller Gulf countries. In the United Arab Emirates, we were greeted by the unusual sight of all of the emirs of the seven federal states sitting together led by President Zayed. They had expected us to ask to land forty-eight fighter aircraft. When we asked to base two hundred, there was an audible gasp. Zayed, however, had been trying to warn America for weeks that Saddam would invade Kuwait. A week earlier he had asked for U.S. tanker aircraft to help his aircraft defend UAE oil fields from Iraq. He now knew that the Americans were serious this time and ordered construction of more fighter aircraft support areas immediately.

In Bahrain, the emir was equally stunned by the size of our proposed aircraft deployment. "Of course you may come, but there is not enough room at the airport and my fighter base is still being built." We offered to finish it.

We found the sultan of Oman in a fifteenth-century fortress by the sea in Salalah, glued to CNN. When he turned to us, it was clear that he knew from our previous stops that we would be asking for permission to land a major air force. "Of course they may all come," he said with a smile. A graduate of the British military academy, he was a strategic thinker. He also loved aircraft. "Will you bring the Stealth? May I ride in it?"

As we received approvals for U.S. aircraft to bed down in the Gulf countries, we quickly relayed that information to Schwarzkopf's command. The aircraft had already left the U.S. Now, as we flew over Dhahran, on the way out of the Gulf, we could see U.S. heavy-lift transports landing with the lead units of the Airborne. They were equipped with rifles and had only the bullets they carried on them. Schwarzkopf called them "speed bumps" if Iraq kept going.

Listening on the headsets, we heard the U.S. AWACS aircraft circling over Saudi Arabia being called by incoming squadrons of fighters, "Sentinel, this is Tango Foxtrot 841 with twelve birds, exactly where are we supposed to land, in what country?"

All along our return route, across the Mediterranean and then the Atlantic, we heard the chatter of hundreds of U.S. military aircraft that formed a bridge reaching out from their American bases to the Kingdom of Saudi Arabia and the states of the Gulf. The access agreements and pre-positioning that we had achieved to stop the Soviet Union were now being utilized for the first time—but to stop Iraq.

In the months that followed, President Bush and Secretary Baker engaged in a diplomatic tour de force. They created a consensus coalition of over one hundred nations, many of which agreed to send forces to defend Saudi Arabia and the Gulf states. My job was to coordinate the solicitations for military units and to find space for the immense Tower of Babel military force that was heading to the Gulf: French, Syrians, Egyptians, units from South and Central America, Africa and Asia. At one point when I told Cheney that the Australians had made a decision to send F-111 aircraft, he threw up his hands in frustration, "Dick, we do not have room for any more allies. Stop asking them." Cheney's attitude then foreshadowed his attitude twelve years later: we can deal with Iraq militarily by ourselves and everybody else is just more trouble than they are worth.

By contrast, Bush and Baker knew that the thought of an American army going to war with an Arab nation could be enormously damaging to America's image in the Muslim world. They believed that the only way to inoculate against that damage was by extraordinary, unprecedented diplomatic effort and coalition building. Both spent long hours on the telephone for months, building and holding together the eclectic coalition. They knew that for that alliance to stay united, they had to demonstrate that they had taken the time and given Iraq every opportunity to avoid war. It could not just look that way, it had to be a really exhaustive effort to achieve a peaceful outcome. Only then could American forces go on the attack, along with the militaries of seven Arab nations. Their historic efforts are in marked contrast to the go-it-alone, hell-bent-for-war policy pursued by George W. Bush and Dick Cheney twelve years later.

When Bush's and Baker's diplomatic efforts failed to persuade Saddam Hussein to abandon Kuwait, the U.S. plan changed from defending Saudi Arabia to invading Kuwait. The Saudis supported the offensive plan, fearing the effects in their own country if hundreds of thousands of U.S. troops had to stay for years defending the Kingdom against a possible Iraqi invasion.

The Iraqis expected a frontal assault on Kuwait, supplemented by amphibious landings by U.S. Marines. So did I, until late November 1990 when Schwarzkopf asked me to fly around the Gulf to visit American units and give speeches to the troops about the coming war and why we had to fight. I was with the 101st Airborne in a forward desert camp one night when I learned that we had a trick planned. After my speech, the fifth of a very long day, the general who was the division commander, and I stood in the chow line with the troops and then grabbed an outdoor table alone. "Aren't those fine troops?" the general asked as we ate baked beans.

"They are, but I'm sick at the thought that many of the guys I talked to today will be killed in a few weeks," I admitted. The general looked surprised. "Hell, Dick, the Hail Mary will catch Saddam off guard. We'll envelop him before he knows what hit him. He'll still be looking for the Marines landing, which ain't ever gonna happen."

I asked the general to show me in the sand. He drew a dramatic left hook from Saudi Arabia into Iraq, which would attack the Iraqis in Kuwait from the rear. Barry McCaffrey's 24th Division was to lead the sweep around. (Twelve years later, renamed the 3rd Infantry, the same division would race to Baghdad in three weeks.) I smiled. "Well, General Shelton, if we can pull that off we ought to be able to eliminate Saddam's army once and for all."

Hugh Shelton smiled back. "That's the idea." Shelton had no fear of boots on the ground in Iraq then. When it came to boots on the ground in Afghanistan in 1999, he would be Chairman of the Joint Chiefs and would think otherwise.

At Schwarzkopf's request, I had placed some of my staff in his bunker in Riyadh. He asked them, although civilians, to dress in camouflage uniforms. He requested one of my staff, John Tritak, who had a newly minted degree in war studies from London's Kings College, to conduct a series of seminars for his senior commanders on how wars end. Tritak explained the "unconditional surrender" logic that Churchill had insisted on in World War II. My staff in Riyadh also provided Schwarzkopf with informal reports on the latest bureaucratic maneuvering in Washington. What Schwarzkopf also knew was that my guys kept me well informed about his plans.

As soon as the air phase of the U.S. attack began, Iraqi missiles landed on Israel. Initial reports reaching me in the State Department Operations Center spoke of chemical clouds coming from the missiles. If that were true, I knew the Israelis could not be held back from responding. Seymour Hersh reported in his book *The Samson Option* that Israel actually prepared missiles for launch against Iraq during this period and they did so in a way that the United States detected. The Patriot missiles in Israel fired at the incoming Iraqi warheads, but still the warheads landed. My Israeli counterpart, David Ivry, told me of their plans to send Airborne forces into western Iraq to clean out the Iraqi missile launchers. If that happened, if it became the U.S. and Israel attacking Iraq, the U.S.-Arab coalition might rupture before the ground war had even begun.

My staff in Riyadh were reporting that Schwarzkopf was refusing to pull U.S. aircraft off scheduled bombing missions to search for Iraqi missiles in the west. I used my unauthorized back channel to

Schwarzkopf and called him. "Norm, you said to call you directly anytime I needed to. Well, I need to. I'm hearing that we don't have a lot of assets hunting for the Scuds. The Israelis are about to go nuts."

"To hell with them, not one Israeli has died from the Scuds," Schwarzkopf fumed. "Those things are just big firecrackers. The bombing missions I am running are eliminating Iraqi units that will kill American troops if those Iraqis are still alive when the ground war starts." He was right, not one Israeli had died at that point and we did need to bomb the front-line Iraqi troops. He was also wrong. If we did not do something about the Scuds, Israeli parachutists would be the first troops into Iraq.

Schwarzkopf was ordered by Cheney and Powell to divert bombing missions to do Scud hunting. A diplomatic mission to Israel by Deputy Secretary Larry Eagleburger, and promises that U.S. forces would take out the Scud missile launchers, persuaded Israel to stand down. (The Scud-hunting bombing missions failed to destroy a single Iraqi missile.)

Once the ground war started, Schwarzkopf's plan worked perfectly. Iraqi units began to flee Kuwait. Meanwhile, McCaffrey drove his division farther and faster than any American unit had ever gone in combat, moving into position to cut the withdrawing Iraqis from behind. But then the pro-war tenor of U.S. news reporting began to change. American television carried stories of American aircraft slaughtering retreating Iraqi troops. Returning pilots were interviewed plane-side talking about "turkey shoots."

Schwarzkopf's view was that these withdrawing Iraqis were combat units with their equipment intact, repositioning. Individual Iraqis who had abandoned their weapons were not being attacked by U.S. aircraft. The repositioning units were, however, a threat. They were elite Republican Guard divisions with the best equipment the Iraqi army had. They could resume combat at any time. He wanted McCaffrey and the air strikes to eliminate them. Washington thought otherwise. The war was coming up on its hundredth hour, Iraq was abandoning Kuwait, and there was no sense risking adverse U.S. media coverage. Schwarzkopf was ordered to stop. Although he writes in his memoir that he agreed with the order, it seemed otherwise to some in his headquarters who were sitting behind him on the secure phone to me.

In the field, McCaffrey was stunned. A few more hours and he could have eliminated any future Iraqi military threat to anyone by destroying the Republican Guard divisions. Without them, the chances of Saddam Hussein being overthrown increased. Many in Washington, however, had come to take it as a given that the Iraqi military would in any event oust the adventurous Saddam once the war ended.

Schwarzkopf was sent to negotiate a surrender with Iraqi generals at Safwan, near Kuwait. A joint U.S.-U.K. working group I led had discussed proposed surrender terms, including the destruction of the heavy armor of the Guard divisions. In the talks at Safwan, however, the Iraqi units were allowed to withdraw intact. At the request of the Iraqis, the no-flying rule was amended to permit the Iraqi army to fly its helicopters. The U.S. forces inside Iraq would withdraw, although Iraqi units could not be stationed near the Kuwaiti border.

There had never been a U.S. plan to march on Baghdad, nor an advocate in Washington for doing so. The Arab nations with large numbers of troops fighting in the coalition (Saudi Arabia, Egypt, Syria) were not eager to see American troops occupy an Arab country, nor did they want to see the Shi'a Muslim majority take over Iraq and set up a pro-Iranian regime. Thus, the Saudis and Egyptians had backed U.N. Security Council resolutions authorizing only the liberation of Kuwait.

The Bush administration also shied away from the enormous task of occupying Iraq. How much would that cost? What Iraqi would we put in charge? What would we do with the Shi'a majority in Iraq? Left to their own devices, they thought, the Iraqi army would no doubt pick some Sunni general, but one who would be less dangerous than Saddam. After all, this defeat in Kuwait followed hard on the heels of the defeat in the long war with Iran, which was also started by Saddam's desire to expand his territory into another nation's oil fields. The Iraqis had now suffered hundreds of thousands of dead because of his lunacy. The Bush White House was convinced, wrongly, Saddam would not last.

In the postwar period, of course, Saddam was not overthrown. Quite the contrary, he used his surviving Republican Guard units to massacre those who did rise up against him, notably the Shi'a, the "marsh Arabs" in the south, and the Kurds in the north. Iraqi helicopters mowed down the rebels. U.S. forces stood by. Years later, the Shi'a would remember how Washington had called on them to rise up, but then did nothing as they were slaughtered.

It can and has been well argued as to whether the United States should have continued the war for a day or a week to destroy the Republican Guard, as had been originally intended. To me it was obvious then and now that another seventy-two hours of combat was needed. After all we had been through, we needed to insure that the Iraqi military was not strong enough to pose a future threat, otherwise we would have to keep our military in Saudi Arabia for the indefinite future.

Some even believe, wrongly, that we should have gone on to Baghdad. I can see how people can make that argument, although continuing into Baghdad would have shattered the coalition and left the U.S. holding the very messy bag of an occupied Iraq. What I cannot understand is how anyone can defend the Bush administration's decision to stand by and let the Republican Guard mass-murder the Shi'a and the Kurds. We had it within our power to resume the bombing of the Republican Guard and regime targets. Our Arab coalition partners and the world in general would have had to respect an American decision to renew hostilities for the limited purpose of stopping the slaughter. If we had bombed the Republican Guard and defended the Shi'a and Kurds, the Bush calculus that Saddam Hussein would fall without our occupying Baghdad might have proved true. Since we did not, a moral outrage was committed and Saddam Hussein stayed in power, and the U.S. had to keep forces in Saudi Arabia to defend against a renewed strike on Kuwait by a reconstituted Republican Guard.

WEAPONS OF MASS DESTRUCTION had figured little in the justification for the war. Nonetheless, before the end of the war, my U.K.-

U.S. working group on the postwar period had focused on Iraq's weapons of mass destruction. We proposed a Special Commission, run by the U.N. that would require Iraq to destroy its chemical, biological, nuclear, and missile programs. The U.N. would call it the United Nations Special Commission, UNSCOM.

Now, after the war, I developed plans for UNSCOM to have a forward base in Bahrain, equipment from various allies, and expert staff drawn heavily from the U.S. and U.K. I asked Bob Gallucci, who had been teaching at the War College, to be the top American and the Deputy Director of the Commission.

Although UNSCOM was shown tons of chemical weapons and some missiles, U.S. and British intelligence indicated that Iraq was hiding other programs, notably its nuclear weapons effort. U.N. teams found an enormous nuclear weapons research and development campus, which had been unknown to CIA prior to and during the war. Thus, it had never been bombed. The program was much further along than CIA had known.

Prior to the war, Israeli intelligence had urgently reported that Iraq was close to developing a nuclear weapon. When pressed by doubting CIA analysts, however, Israel had refused to provide corroboration or reveal sources. Now it began to appear that Israel may have been right.

We then received a report that the records of the Iraqi nuclear program had been removed and hidden in the Agricultural Ministry. Working through the Special Commission, we and the British overtly planned an inspection on another nearby site, but at the last minute it would turn into a surprise raid on the ministry. U.S. and British Special Forces would be among the inspectors and would smash locks and break into files quickly before the Iraqis could react. The problem with the plan, we knew, was how the inspectors would get out once they discovered the nuclear bomb records. Gallucci and I agreed on a standoff, the U.N. inspectors would not leave the site or give up the documents. Meanwhile, the U.S. would prepare a renewed bombing campaign. I gave Gallucci a satellite phone and promised him that we would use it to instruct him to leave the records and depart the area before the bombing started.

The raid worked. Nuclear records were found before the Iraqis figured out what was going on. Iraqi security units arrived quickly, however, and surrounded the ministry. They demanded the documents be returned to them. Gallucci refused and the standoff we anticipated ensued. When Gallucci called in on the satellite phone, I gave him the telephone numbers of U.S. television news organizations, which interviewed him live during the standoff. National Security Advisor Brent Scowcroft approved a plan to renew bombing and sent it to the President. Scowcroft seemed pleased at the prospect of renewed bombing, perhaps thinking that it might create another chance for the Iraqi military to topple Saddam. The targets were Special Republican Guard units and other units that propped up Saddam.

Gallucci, from the parking lot in Baghdad, called me again in the State Ops Center. I told him how proud we all were: "Bob, this is working. You were great on CNN. Remember, 'The whole world is watching!' " Gallucci and I had both been anti–Vietnam War protesters in the 1960s.

"Yeah, I remember that well," Bob whispered over the satellite telephone, "but Dick, we've found the smoking gun here. These guys almost had the bomb. But the Iraqis are never going to let me out of here with this document."

Arabic translators on the inspection team had found the annual report of the nuclear weapon program and rendered it into English. It revealed that the design was complete and that enriched material would soon be available in sufficient quantity to conduct the first nuclear explosion. Prior to the outbreak of the war, Iraqi scientists estimated that they were less than a year from that detonation.

"Well, can you hook up a fax machine to the sat phone? We have to get the proof out to the world, to the U.N." I could taste success, but there were still risks. The standoff in the fenced-in parking lot could get out of hand. The Iraqis surrounding it were well armed.

"No. The fax doesn't work with the satellite phone." Gallucci and his team had already looked at the options. "We have what they call a digital camera, no film, but we can't get that to work well enough either." Digital cameras were something very new to us.

"Okay, Bob, you know Beverly Roundtree pretty well, you worked together in PM?" My assistant, Bev, had previously worked for Gallucci when he directed an office in the Pol-Mil Bureau. "She can take dictation for hours. I'm going to put her on the sat phone."

It did take hours. With the world's television cameras and the Iraqis' guns pointed at the UNSCOM team, a relay of inspectors read Beverly Roundtree the smoking-gun document, which was on the desk of the President and the U.N. Secretary General when they came to work in the morning. As they did, Beverly left the State Department Operations Center and went home to sleep.

Faced with the prospect of renewed U.S. bombing, however, Secretary Baker returned to Washington and convinced President Bush to accept a negotiated settlement of the standoff. Baker held a strong influence over Bush. He had a dedicated telephone on his State Department desk that ran directly to the Oval Office. By my own observation, Baker did not hesitate to initiate calls on that line. In private, Baker did not treat Bush with all the deference a Secretary of State usually accords a President. Baker thought that he had made Bush the President, through Baker's political maneuvering.

Baker also sometimes doubted Bush's skills. At a NATO summit in London early in the administration, Baker had stunned me by coming to sit next to me in an auditorium, as I listened to President Bush's press conference. As Bush batted the reporter's questions, the Secretary of State provided me with a personal color commentary whispering in my ear: "Damn he flubbed that answer . . . I told him how to handle that one . . . Oh, no, he'll never know how to deal with that . . ." I was one of Baker's Assistant Secretaries, but I could not understand why he would go out of his way to disdain the President to an audience of one, me. Over time I came to understand that Baker often doubted the President's judgment. Baker would never have gone to war in the Gulf and made that clear at several points in the months after the Iraqi invasion of Kuwait. The two friends and rivals did, together, demonstrate how an international coalition should be built and how America can get done what it needs without creating self-inflicted wounds. They did, however, fail to manage the postwar challenges, as their successors would also fail to do twelve years on.

After the Gulf War, with Saddam still in power and his army reconstituting, it would be necessary for large-scale U.S. forces to remain in the region, especially in Saudi Arabia where most of the residual forces were based. I was given a Gulfstream jet and told by Baker to fly around the Gulf locking down new agreements with the six Gulf states so we could keep some of our military forces in their countries.

Shuttling up and down the Gulf, we obtained basing agreements with Kuwait, Qatar, Bahrain, and Oman. No longer would we have only secret access arrangements with limited and hidden prepositioned equipment. A temporary arrangement was also struck with the United Arab Emirates, pending agreement on how to handle U.S. personnel who might break local laws, but U.S. aircraft carrier battle groups could regularly dock near Dubai.

Saudi Arabia, however, would not negotiate a basing agreement. Neither, however, did the King order all U.S. forces to leave as Cheney had said he could. The continued presence of Saddam and his army had changed the King's prewar calculus that the Americans could and would leave when the war in Kuwait was done. The enormous American military presence rapidly dwindled after the war, but it gradually became clear to the Saudi public that some would remain. Fighter squadrons and support aircraft would stay at several air bases. The U.S. military headquarters would also stay active, although at smaller levels. The Saudis also went on a shopping spree for new U.S. arms. With each arms deal came more American civilians to make the weapons work.

Saudi dissidents who had protested the original U.S. presence now complained again that the American forces in the Kingdom were a sacrilege. CIA did not know much about these dissidents, who they were, what they said. The Saudis kept us well away from their internal debates. Among the dissidents was bin Laden, who grew more critical of the King. The Saudi government moved against the dissidents, threatening them with legal and economic punishments. Despite his past work for Prince Turki in Afghanistan and Yemen, bin Laden was no exception to the government's crackdown. In bin Laden's case the government also threatened his extended family and its vast economic holdings. Invited to Khartoum by Hasan al-Turabi, the fundamentalist fanatic who had taken charge in Sudan, a bitter bin Laden decamped across the Red Sea. Soon thereafter, he summoned his Afghan Arabs to join him.

Saddam was still in power. U.N. inspections were being more restricted. U.S. forces were settling in throughout the Gulf. Usama bin Laden had broken with the Saudi regime and moved in with a radical state sponsor of terrorism. It was 1991. As the year ended, the Soviet Union ceased to exist as a legal entity. During the Cold War every military action by one superpower had drawn a reaction by the other. Thus, large-scale shifts of military assets such as the movement of a half million American troops to the Persian Gulf would have risked some dramatic Soviet countermove. Moreover, nations that significantly increased their military relationship with one superpower knew they risked subversion from the other. Thus, the kind of cooperation the United States enjoyed in the First Gulf War would have been impossible during the Cold War.

The Cold War had also served to suppress some traditional ethnic and religious rivalries beneath the heavy glacier of the Communist totalitarian state, particularly in the Balkans and Central Asia where there were many Muslims. To the extent that religion was a political force during the Cold War, it was a weak one promoted by the United States as a counterpoint to the anti-religious ideology of the Soviet Union.

When the Cold War ended, the United States could move massively into the Persian Gulf during a crisis there, ethnic and religious tensions could erupt in the Balkans and Central Asia, and religious fervor could no longer be directed at the Communists. Those feeling disadvantaged by the global system and wishing to blame their lot on foreign forces had only one world-dominant nation to blame for their troubles, one major target to motivate their followers: America.

Chapter 4

Terror Returns (1993–1996)

In 1993 the Clinton administration came to office with an agenda to deal with the post–Cold War era, and terrorism was not on it. Terrorism had not been a major issue in the preceding Bush administration either. George H. W. Bush had issued no formal policy on counterterrorism and had chosen to deal with the single major anti-U.S. act of terrorism during his tenure (the bombing of Pan Am 103) through diplomacy, not the use of force. America seemed to be enjoying a period largely free of anti-American terrorism after the tumultuous years of the Reagan administration and its bombings of Lebanon and Libya.

In January 1993 the new National Security Advisor, Tony Lake, had taken the unusual step of asking me to stay on in the White House when the Bush team left. Lake, on Madeleine Albright's advice, asked me to work on post–Cold War issues such as peacekeeping and failed states. While terrorism was in my portfolio of "Global Issues," it was far down on the new team's priority list. All that was about to change, quickly.

The large, white telephone console blurted. I had never heard it ring before and wasn't initially sure what the noise was. In the little window on the console a name popped up: "Scowcroft." Brent Scowcroft, the National Security Advisor to the first President

Bush, had left the White House the month before, along with almost all of his staff except me and a few other holdovers. How was he calling me now on this highly secure phone? I reached for the handset.

"Did the Serbs do it?" It was Tony. I had no idea what he was talking about. "Did the Serbs bomb it? Was it a bomb?"

"I don't know yet, Tony." I faked it. "We're checking. Let me get back to you as soon as we have something, soon."

My next call was to the Situation Room. "Did something just get bombed?"

"Well, something just exploded, we don't know if it was a bomb, sir. The World Trade Center," a young Navy officer replied. "I know you handle terrorism, sir, and we're supposed to tell you when something happens that might be terrorism, but do you want to know when things happen in the United States too? Do you guys handle domestic crises too?"

The notion that terrorism might occur in the United States was completely new to us then. The National Security Council staff, which I had joined in 1992, had only ever concerned itself with foreign policy, defense, and intelligence issues. "Yes, yes we do," I vamped, making up my view as I answered. "Anything that happens in the U.S. that could involve foreign agents is our job. Just like the shooting at CIA." A month earlier, only four days into the Clinton administration, a young Pakistani named Mir Amal Kansi had walked down Virginia Route 123 and shot motorists stopped at a traffic light, waiting to drive into CIA headquarters. Three people had died. Kansi had successfully flown out of the country after the shooting. Neither CIA nor FBI had found out anything interesting about who Kansi was or to what group he belonged. "So what do we know about this explosion in New York?" I asked.

"Well, sir, we're hearing that it was a transformer that erupted, but we will keep you posted. And, sir, we will let you know right away in the future when things blow up, anywhere."

I turned to Richard Canas, a DEA agent on my staff. "You know anyone in NYPD?"

I HAD JOINED THE NATIONAL SECURITY COUNCIL STAFF in 1992 under President Bush and his National Security Advisor, Brent Scowcroft, whom I had come to know during the Gulf War and its aftermath. Scowcroft had been brought back from retirement to do a second tour as National Security Advisor (he had held the position under President Gerald Ford) to clean up the mess that Ollie North and others had made of the NSC Staff. North had been a junior staffer assigned to worry about terrorism. Terrorism had shot to the top of the agenda after the Beirut bombings of our embassy and the Marine barracks, the kidnapping of Americans in Lebanon, the hijackings of American aircraft in the Middle East, and Libya's bombing of a U.S. Army hangout in Berlin.

North had responded vigorously to the problem—a little too vigorously. He and National Security Advisor John Poindexter had crossed the line into secret policies and procedures that were shortsighted and, in some cases, probably illegal, when they arranged to sell arms to Iran in hopes of the release of American hostages held there, and then diverted some of the proceeds to the anti-Communist Contra rebels in Nicaragua. Congress had outlawed aid to the Contras, and trading arms for hostages violated Reagan's oft-stated insistence that we never negotiate with terrorists. President Reagan and Vice President Bush had escaped, barely, without being shown to be personally culpable. When Bush became President in 1989, he had asked Scowcroft to run a less-activist NSC Staff and to play down the U.S. response to terrorism. Luckily for Scowcroft, with the exception of the attack on Pan Am 103, there had been little anti-American terrorism on his watch. Bush's and Scowcroft's response to Pan Am 103 had been muted, at best. Despite the death of 259 passengers at the hands of Libyan intelligence agents, the United States had not retaliated with force. Instead, it had sought U.N. sanctions on Libya.

When I went to the NSC Staff, it had been to head up a new office to worry about proliferation of missiles and chemical, biological, and nuclear weapons. Secretary Baker didn't like the idea of that increasingly important issue being run out of the NSC Staff, however, and told Scowcroft so. My assignment was changed to "International Programs," issues that did not fit into any of the regional offices of the

NSC. Among those issues was terrorism, and it was still there and still a low priority, when Tony called about the explosion at the World Trade Center.

Meanwhile, Richard Canas had used his law enforcement skills and White House clout to call through to the police commander on the scene at the World Trade Center. "Dick, I've got a Deputy Commissioner on the line. NYPD has had its bomb guys get down into the hole. They say it's definitely a bomb." I convened the Counterterrorism Security Group in the Situation Room. Six people were dead in New York, hundreds wounded.

Within days of the World Trade Center bombing, FBI made an arrest. The FBI's magicians, the forensics specialists, had gone through the wreckage in the basement of the tower and determined which vehicle had held the bomb. They had earlier amazed us all by rebuilding Pan Am 103 from pieces scattered over hundreds of square miles, and then determining which suitcase had held the bomb. Now they were able to identify the specific Ryder rental truck and trace it back to a franchise in nearby northern New Jersey. Incredibly, the rental agency said that the person who had rented the truck was scheduled to return the next day to collect the deposit on what he said was a stolen truck.

With the arrest of Muhammad Salameh, the case broke open. A suspicious rental storage facility operator called the FBI to suggest that the terrorists might have used one of his lockers to prepare the bomb. Pulling on those strings of information, the FBI developed a list of the cell that had performed the bombing: Egyptians, a Jordanian, an Iraqi, a Pakistani—it was not the Serbs. The CSG met again.

"Okay," I started, "so you know the names of the guys who did it. What is the group? Or to quote from a great movie, who *are* these guys?" I was asking Bob Blitzer, who represented the FBI in the meeting.

"Nobody we know," Blitzer answered, obviously chagrined. "New York thinks there may be some links to the guy who shot a rabbi up there last fall. They all seem to be related to a Muslim preacher from Egypt, a guy in Brooklyn or Jersey City."

CIA's representative, Winston Wiley, had compared all the names with those in a database. "They are not known members of Hezbollah or Abu Nidal or Palestinian Islamic Jihad, or any other terrorist group. The bureau gave us some overseas telephone numbers these guys called and we're trying to run them down, but we didn't recognize any of the numbers."

"So, what are you telling me," I asked. "That these guys met at a pickup basketball game at the Y in Brooklyn or Jersey City and decided to blow up the World Trade Center 'cuz they were bored? You expect me to believe that?"

"Could be." Wiley shrugged.

"How did they get in?" I wondered. "What does their visa application say, terrorist?"

Blitzer explained: "Well, two of them just showed up at JFK last year without any documents or even false docs. One of the two was detained because he had 'How to Make a Bomb' manuals on him." The other man was Ramzi Yousef.

"So, let me get this straight, we let a guy go who was with a bomb builder, we let him get into a cab at JFK even though he shows up here without a passport?" I could not believe it. Immigration had given Yousef a citation to appear before an immigration magistrate at a later date and let him walk into the country. Ramzi Yousef was now the one FBI was fingering as the cell's leader. He had disappeared overseas after the attack.

"Don't worry, Dick, we'll pick them all up," Blitzer assured me. "We'll track them down. We'll find out who they worked for."

The New York City FBI Office is so big that the head of it is an Assistant Director of the FBI, not a Special Agent in Charge, as is the title in most cities. In fact, the head of the New York Office actually has three special agents in charge, or SACs, reporting to him. One of the SACs was responsible for national security cases. Although that had once meant keeping track of Soviet spies, it also involved the supervision of a Terrorism Task Force. As in every city, the FBI in New York works closely with the local federal prosecutor, the U.S. Attorney, and the Assistant U.S. Attorneys on the staff. Following the World Trade Center attack, the New York FBI Office and the U.S. Attorney's Office set to finding out exactly what we were facing.

Within two weeks of the bombing, FBI had taken four of the cell into custody. Ahmed Ajaj had been held since he arrived at JFK Airport the previous year. Muhammad Salahme was arrested while seeking his deposit at the Ryder office on March 4. Nidal Ayyad, a U.S. citizen, was arrested on March 10. Abdul Yasim, interrogated on March 4, was released because he convinced the FBI he was not involved and would cooperate. He flew immediately to Iraq, where, we believe, he was incarcerated by Saddam Hussein's regime. Eyad Ismoil fled to Jordan and stayed out of sight until he was arrested two years later. The cell leader, Ramzi Yousef, disappeared and became the CSG's most wanted terrorist, only later showing up in the Philippines.

The New York investigation soon revealed a network that had supported the plotters. Spread across Brooklyn, Queens, and north Jersey, the network seemed to center on Omar Abdel Rahman, a blind Egyptian, who served as a spiritual leader to Egyptian radicals. Rahman had been sentenced in absentia for terrorism in Egypt. He was on the State Department visa lookout list, but somehow he had managed to get a visa at the U.S. embassy in Sudan and had moved to New York. Egyptian government requests that he be extradited had apparently been made and rejected.

By keeping a close eye on Rahman, within months the FBI uncovered another cell planning bombings in New York. This time it would be the Lincoln and Holland Tunnels, the United Nations headquarters, and other landmarks. By the end of June 1993, the plotters and Rahman were in the federal government's Manhattan Metropolitan Detention Center. It seemed like the counterterrorism machinery was working well.

It wasn't. The FBI and CIA should have been able to answer my question, "Who *are* these guys?" but they still could not.

The real answer was a group that the FBI and CIA had not yet heard of: al Qaeda. The first member of al Qaeda arrested in the United States—as we later discovered—was El Sayyid Nosair, who assassinated Rabbi Meir Kahane, the fiery leader of the radical Jewish Defense League, in New York in 1992. The FBI's investigation into the World Trade Center suspects connected them to Nosair. Nosair's legal bills were ultimately paid by bin Laden. His apartment had materials connecting him to something called the Afghan Services Bureau; yet many of the Arabic-language materials would go untranslated by the FBI for years after his arrest. The four initially arrested for the World Trade Center bombing in 1993 were quickly linked to the Al Kifah Center in Brooklyn. That center was funded by and openly affiliated with the Afghan Services Bureau (Mahktab al Kiddimah), run by bin Laden. The blind sheik had spent time in Afghanistan with bin Laden. The blind sheik was a member of the Egyptian Islamic Jihad, which was already tied to bin Laden. Ahmed Ajaj had been detained at JFK Airport for carrying bomb-related materials, including a manual on the cover of which was the phrase "al Qaeda." Ramzi Yousef had even called bin Laden from New York.

Usama bin Laden had formed al Qaeda three years earlier. Not only had no one in the CIA or FBI ever heard of it, apparently they had never heard of bin Laden either. His name never came up in our meetings in 1993 as a suspect in the World Trade Center attack. We did hear about someone who appeared to be Ramzi Yousef's uncle. He went by various names, and he appeared to be behind Yousef's mysterious money. One name he used was Khalid Sheik Muhammad. It was not clear exactly what his role was, but he was connected, and therefore the FBI wanted him, wherever he was.

As it happened, I was the one in Washington who first saw evidence of a true act of terrorism by Saddam against us, and the irony is that President Clinton's response to it successfully deterred Saddam from ever again using terror against us.

I had the daily habit of reading hundreds of intelligence reports, embassy messages, and translations of foreign media that the Situation Room dutifully forwarded to my office computer. During the week, I skimmed many of them. On weekends, however, I had more time. One Sunday in April, I saw a subject line that grabbed my eye. An Arab-language newspaper in London was reporting that the Kuwaiti police had prevented an assassination attempt on former President Bush.

There had been no such report from the Secret Service, FBI, CIA, or the embassy. Nonetheless, something suggested to me that I should not dismiss the report. Instead, I called our ambassador in Kuwait, Ryan Crocker, a career officer and expert on the Arab world.

"Ryan, have you seen this report in a London paper about an attempted assassination on former President Bush?"

He had not seen it, but did tell me what a great time Bush had in Kuwait. Then he paused, "Dick, knowing you, you could not possibly be instructing me to ask the Kuwaitis about the report . . . because you know, of course, that we are told never to accept instructions directly from the White House staff." One of the continuing legacies of Ollie North's excesses was a ban on NSC Staff directly ordering ambassadors to do things.

"No, no, of course not, Ryan. Thought never crossed my mind," I chuckled back across the secure line.

"As it happens, now that I know about the story, I might just ask someone I happen to be seeing tonight . . ."

The next morning there was a sealed envelope on my desk, a message so sensitive that it could not be sent to me electronically from the Situation Room. It was a report from our Ambassador in Kuwait which stated that the Kuwaitis were covering up a plot that they had foiled. The plot was aimed at killing former President Bush and had almost succeeded. Several people were being held and they had implicated the Iraqi intelligence service.

I called Lake: "Saddam tried to kill Bush."

After I explained, the National Security Advisor gave me instructions: "Tell State to make it clear to the Kuwaitis. They have to come clean with us."

That allowed me to draft an instruction cable to Crocker and ask if the State Department would send it to him on its behalf. Crocker then confronted the Kuwaiti government with our knowledge of the plot and formally asked for access to the prisoners. There were sixteen.

Two were Iraqi nationals, who admitted that they had been recruited in Basra by the Iraqi intelligence service and given a Toyota Land Cruiser, in which a sophisticated bomb had been installed. They were to park it near the university in Kuwait City and then detonate it by radio when President Bush and the Emir drove by. It would have killed everything up to four hundred yards away. The Iraqi assassination plot failed only because a Kuwaiti policeman discovered the bomb-laden SUV after it was involved in a traffic accident and the Kuwaitis started to make arrests.

On instructions from Tony Lake, I asked Secret Service, FBI, and CIA to send teams to Kuwait. Attorney General Janet Reno and CIA Director Woolsey agreed to conduct two separate but parallel investigations, one in law enforcement and one in intelligence channels. It took over a month, but in early June the two reports were in draft. Both agencies had corroborated the prisoners' story. The bomb materials were also definitely from Iraqi intelligence.

On June 23, Lake had his usual Wednesday lunch with Secretary of Defense Les Aspin and Secretary of State Warren Christopher in Lake's West Wing office. During the lunch, he called and asked me to join them. "We'd like you to plan a retaliation mission against Iraq. Only you, and one person each from Defense and State. When can we have the plan, the checklist?"

Someone from CIA was added to the circle, and in a day we had a target list developed by the Joint Chiefs of Staff and the CIA. Secretary Christopher argued strongly on legal grounds that the list be limited to one facility, the Iraqi intelligence headquarters. He also wanted it hit on Saturday night, to minimize casualties. Christopher won.

We developed the plan. The ships would move into firing position. An "execute order" from the Joint Chiefs to CENTCOM (the U.S. military regional command for the Middle East and the successor to the Rapid Deployment Joint Task Force) had been prepared. Personal messages would go out in staggered fashion from the President to the Emir of Kuwait, the King of Saudi Arabia, the British Prime Minister. To avoid leaks, they would be sent from the White House rather than through the State Department. Instructions would be sent to the U.S.

mission at the United Nations to ask for an emergency session of the Security Council. Justice and CIA would have detailed white papers to release to the press and foreign embassies, outlining the evidence. congressional leaders would be called individually by the President. Former President Bush would be told. American embassies and troops in the region would be placed on heightened alert against Iraqi countermoves. CIA stations and FBI offices would place Iraqi agents under surveillance. The President would make a short announcement from the Oval Office. A stark warning would be passed to the Iraqis, threatening dire consequences for any further terrorism against the United States.

I put the checklist, a timeline, and the implementing documents in a book and gave it to Lake on Friday. He looked at it and said, "That's good. Take it down and show the President. I'll tell him you're coming. Then, do it."

NSC Staff, even Special Assistants to the President like me, had not popped in on the President in my experience. Brent Scowcroft had talked to the President for us. Sometimes Brent had allowed a staff member to sit in for a while. Now, I was being asked to go see the President about the first use of force in his administration. There had been a secretive Principals meeting with the President on the subject earlier and Clinton had seemed resolute. But there were doubts among the right wing that Clinton would ever use force.

Presented with the detailed plan, Clinton was pragmatic. "Well, this may teach him a lesson, but if it doesn't, we will have to do more." Saturday morning, White House Press Secretary Dee Dee Myers, who did not know what was about to happen, told the White House press corps that "the lid" was on, that nothing would happen the rest of the day. A group of White House reporters then left for a baseball game in Baltimore. As they did, I began sending the messages out from the Situation Room.

Shortly after 6:00 p.m. a small group of senior administration officials began assembling in Lake's office. I went to the Oval Office to help the President with his last few calls notifying congressional leaders. The cruise missiles had just been launched.

"So when will we get the pictures from the missiles?" the President asked me.

"Well, we don't get pictures from the missiles, sir, but we will have bomb damage images from satellites available to show you first thing in the morning," I explained.

"Tomorrow morning? I'm going on TV in an hour to say we blew up this building—I want to know first that we did. Why don't the missiles have cameras in them?" the President insisted.

"Well, if the missiles communicated, someone might see them coming or interfere with them. But we know how many we fired and when, so we can calculate how many will hit and when—"

"We can't communicate with the missiles? What if I wanted to turn them back?" the President asked.

"You don't want to sir, do you? . . . because you can't . . . there is no mechanism to . . ." I stammered.

"No I don't, but I do want to know for certain that we blew this place up before I go telling the world that I did."

I went back to Lake's office with the news. Admiral Bill Studeman, the number two man at CIA, began making calls. Satellites were redirected. "We got nothin'," he reported. "The missiles should have hit several minutes ago, but nothing we have can tell us that . . . not for a while."

A glum mood settled over the office as we wondered how we would get the President to go on national television. Then, as we talked, he did it. On all networks, the Saturday evening news anchors were told something and announced a surprise address by the President. "We don't know why," one said.

Clinton read the short statement and then, almost immediately, showed up in Lake's office with Vice President Al Gore. "We thought you were not going to go on," Lake confessed. "We thought you needed proof that the missiles hit."

Gore urged the President to tell us something that the two highest leaders in the land clearly found funny. "Okay, okay," Clinton agreed. "I needed relative certainty that the missiles had hit and none of you guys could give me that . . . so I called CNN . . . they didn't have anybody in Baghdad tonight, but their cameraman in their Jordan bureau had a cousin or some relative who lived near the intelligence headquarters, so they called him." Most of the room looked horrified. "The cousin said, yeah, the whole place blew up. He was certain . . . so I figured we had relative certainty."

Clinton using force was not going to be a problem. The next day, however, he was clearly upset with reports that some of the missiles had fallen short and killed the leading female artist of the Arab world, who happened to have a house across the street from the Muhabarat—Iraqi intelligence.

I was initially disappointed that the retaliation had been so small, that targets had been taken off the list, and that the raid was scheduled in the middle of the night when few Iraqi intelligence officers would be present. My friends from the Bush administration told me vaguely that they heard that the Bush family were also upset that the response was so limited.

My disappointment faded with time because it seemed that Saddam had gotten the message. Subsequent to that June 1993 retaliation, the U.S. intelligence and law enforcement communities never developed any evidence of further Iraqi support for terrorism directed against Americans. Until we invaded Iraq in 2003.

THE FIRST YEAR OF THE CLINTON ADMINISTRATION also tested the new President's willingness to use force a second time, in Somalia. In retrospect, it is possible that the October Battle of Mogadishu may have been a second case of an al Qaeda role in an attack on Americans. President Bush had sent troops to Somalia to help end an enormous famine that had placed approximately 700,000 people on death's door. Their fellow Somalis with guns were stealing and selling relief supplies. International relief organizations could not obtain security for their operations. Following his defeat in a bid for reelection, President Bush had sent the troops into Somalia to insure the delivery of the relief supplies. Brent Scowcroft had asked me to be the White

House coordinator for the operation, and in January 1993 he had asked me to brief his successor, Tony Lake, on the subject.

I found Lake in the Presidential Transition Office, a floor of a private office building on Vermont Avenue. I had never seen him before. He and the "National Security" area on the floor were the only indication of calm in a flurry of young staffers and a sea of résumés. "Well, thank you for coming, but I gather that we won't have to worry too much about Somalia because the U.S. will be largely out by Inauguration Day," Lake said.

"Ah, no, actually, the U.S. troop movement into Somalia will not be complete until the end of January," I replied, pulling out a Pentagon chart that showed the staged deployment of U.S. units.

Lake looked suspiciously at the chart. "We were told that the U.N. would take over. That the U.S. troops would be out." He did not say precisely who told him, but I gathered it was my bosses at the White House.

"The U.N. is dragging its feet, Mr. Lake. Boutros-Ghali thinks it would strain the U.N. to take over." Lake's reaction made him look like a man who had just been told he had cancer. In a way, he had.

U.N. Secretary General Boutros Boutros-Ghali grudgingly accepted a U.N. role, but the arrival of a U.N. peacekeeping force was slow in coming. He urged the United States to provide an American to be the head of the U.N. operation, to insure close coordination between the U.N. and the U.S. Lake persuaded Scowcroft's deputy, Admiral Jonathan Howe, to take the job. Shortly after Clinton came to office, coordination of the Somali operation shifted from the White House to the State Department and its Bureau of African Affairs. Howe was soon tested by the Somali warlords, particularly by Farah Aideed. In June, Aideed's men slaughtered two dozen Pakistani troops who were operating under the new U.N. command.

Howe's response was firm. If the Somalis thought they could get away with killing the Pakistanis, it would be all over for the international relief effort. Aideed needed to be arrested and his militia smashed. Howe had only recently retired as a four-star admiral. He knew U.S. military capability well. He drafted a detailed list of additional forces immediately, including Delta Force commandos to arrest Aideed and AC-130 aerial gunships to blow up the militia's infrastructure. He got the gunships, but only for a few strikes. Despite pressure from the NSC, the Pentagon refused to send the commandos or most of what Howe needed and the Pentagon stopped the AC-130 strikes before Aideed's militia infrastructure was destroyed.

Aideed was moving about Mogadishu openly with little or no security in June. A Delta team could have arrested him with little difficulty. Following the AC-130 attack on his arms warehouses, however, he went underground and ordered more attacks on the coalition, including American troops. In September, three American troops were killed by Aideed's forces.

Only then did the Pentagon agree to send in the commandos. The Joint Special Operations Command (JSOC), which included what the public called Delta, had mastered the art and science of surprise nighttime operations and low-profile, covert operations. In Mogadishu, however, they acted in broad daylight with dozens of helicopters clattering into the city. The operations were repetitive and the Somalis learned by watching them. On October 3, 1993, in the famous *Black Hawk Down* incident, the Aideed militia responded and engaged JSOC, shooting down two helicopters with rocket-propelled grenades. Eighteen Americans and probably 1,200 Somalis were killed.

When the National Security Council cabinet members met with the President in the Cabinet Room, Clinton was irate. Somalia was not his idea of how to spend his first year in office. He had inherited it and the military had let him down. He had followed the Pentagon's advice, not Howe's, in June and they had been wrong. When Aideed could have been captured in June, they had let him go. When the military had finally agreed to send in JSOC to Mogadishu, they had acted as though there were no hostile forces operating against them, ignoring their usual tactics, and creating a disaster. Clinton sat silently, red-faced, in the Cabinet Room listening to Warren Christopher, Les Aspin, and Colin Powell. I realized that he was letting them have their time, but he had already decided something. He was done listening to them on Somalia.

When they had talked themselves out, Clinton stopped doodling and looked up. "Okay, here's what we're gonna do. We are not running away with our tail between our legs. I've already heard from Congress and that's what they all want to do, get out tomorrow. We're staying. We are also not gonna flatten Mogadishu to prove we are the big badass superpower. Everybody in the world knows we could do that. We don't have to prove that to anybody.

"We are going to send in more troops, with tanks and aircraft and anything else they need. We are going to show force. And we are going to keep delivering the food. If anybody fucks with us, we will respond, massively. And we are going to get the U.N. to finally show up and take over. Tell Boutros he has six months to do that, not one day more. Then . . . then we will leave."

As the meeting broke up, Clinton indicated for Lake and me to follow him through the side door into the outer area of the Oval Office. "I want us running this, not the State Department or the Pentagon." He looked at me. "No more U.S. troops get killed, none. Do what you have to do, whatever you have to do."

In the days that followed, American snipers were placed on the roofs and walls of the U.S. compounds. When they saw any Somalis in the area with guns, they took them out. There was little or no publicity about these deaths. When the U.S. forces went back on the streets, they went with tanks. Six months later, the United States finally handed over the operation to the United Nations peacekeeping force. There had been no more American casualties.

During those six months I repeatedly pressed CIA to track down rumors in the foreign press about terrorists who might have trained Aideed's militia. They discounted them. I asked my friends Mike Sheehan and Roger Cressey, who had worked in Mogadishu in 1993, what they thought. "How the shit would CIA know," Mike replied. "They had nobody in the country when the Marines landed. Then they sent in a few guys who had never been there before. They swapped people out every few weeks and they stayed holed up in the U.S. compound on the beach, in comfy trailer homes that they had flown in by the Air Force."

Apparently Sheehan and Cressey were right. Although CIA did not know it in 1993 and 1994, evidence later emerged and was included in the U.S. indictment of bin Laden that al Qaeda had been sending advisors to Aideed and had helped to engineer the shoot-down of the U.S. helicopters. Indeed, al Qaeda had bombed a hotel in Yemen in December 1992, thinking that U.S. Air Force personnel supporting the Somalia operation were living there. (The Americans had been evacuated because Yemeni security had heard rumors of the plot.) CIA had not been able then to figure out who had bombed the hotel.

Thus, when the Clinton administration looked back on the terrorism of 1993, they did not include the events of Somalia in that category. Nor did they think about bin Laden or al Qaeda, because they had not yet been told that that terrorist or his organization existed.

Al Qaeda and bin Laden, however, thought about the United States. Even though the U.S. had not "cut and run" under congressional pressure, they perceived that it had. The additional six months stay and the orderly handoff to the U.N. had not impressed them. The failure to flatten Mogadishu had registered. Once again, they told one another, the United States had been humiliated by a Third World country. Just like Vietnam. Just like Lebanon. Just like the Soviets in Afghanistan.

What al Qaeda did not seem to understand is that the United States had never intended to stay in Somalia. It had gone there for a limited time until the creaky U.N. peacekeeping bureaucracy could field a force. By its own limited definition of an objective, the U.S. had done what it set out to do. Was Clinton right not to respond with some large-scale retaliation to the murder of the eighteen U.S. commandos? I was not sure then and I am not sure now. We had killed over a thousand Somalis in a day. Should we have done more? We could have kept up the hunt for Aideed, but that would have placed the prestige of the United States against the resourcefulness of one man hiding in his own country. Did our self-restraint reduce our deterrence? I feared then that it would, but I had no good idea about how to do anything about it. After the murder of 278 Marines in Beirut, Reagan had invaded Grenada in part to show that we were still able to exercise force. I had no doubt that Clinton would use force again soon, in Bosnia and maybe in Haiti, not just to demonstrate resolve but because those situations demanded it. In retrospect, I doubt that there was anything that could have been done then to deter al Qaeda. Killing more innocent Somalis would not have helped.

JUST BEFORE 1993 CAME TO A CLOSE, I received one last, memorable lesson in terrorism. Tony Lake and his Staff Director, Nancy Soderberg, had urged me and my staff to deal directly with the families of the victims of terrorism, especially the families of the Pan Am 103 attack. Pan Am 103 had been destroyed by Libyan terrorists in 1988. The families were upset with their handling by the Bush administration. In particular, they could not understand why their request for a memorial in Arlington National Cemetery had been turned down, especially when many of the victims were military personnel.

We met with the families. We heard their stories and we put pictures of their fallen children on our desks. The aircraft had exploded above and around Lockerbie, Scotland, killing some of the town's residents as well. The town had opened its hearts to the families of all of the victims. Lockerbie had donated stones for a cairn, a Scottish memorial rock pile, one rock for every victim. Joined by my colleague Randy Beers, we drove to the cemetery and selected a site for the cairn.

On the fifth anniversary of the attack, the President drove to the site to say a few words and turn the dirt to begin the construction of the cairn. It was just before Christmas, cold and wet and windy. The President asked a little boy who had lost his father on the plane to join him with the shovel. He kneeled by the boy and whispered to him. A lone piper from Lockerbie played "Amazing Grace."

As people moved to their cars and out of the rain, I asked the boy's mother what the President had said. "He said, 'My father died before I was born too. Be good to your Mom.' "

That night the network news showed tape of the President heading out from the Oval Office for the cairn event, as the White House reporter talked over the tape about allegations of impropriety made by former Arkansas state troopers. They did not mention Pan Am 103.

ALTHOUGH NEITHER CIA NOR FBI had yet heard of al Qaeda, because of the many known terrorism events of 1993, the Clinton team, from the President down, was seized with the issue by 1994. Clinton, Lake, and I believed our response to terrorism should be high on the list of measures to shape the post–Cold War world.

Part of that response was developing a new policy on counterterrorism to replace what Reagan had signed seven years earlier. There had not been a formal counterterrorism policy in the first Bush administration. As I would discover, turf battles could derail even the best efforts at counterterrorism, and (as Tom Ridge would much later demonstrate) it is easier to waste time on bureaucratic reorganization than it is to accomplish anything concrete. Three policy issues emerged as I drafted and circulated a new policy for approval by all of the relevant departments and agencies. First, was terrorism a law enforcement issue or an intelligence issue? While the question was posed that way, what it meant was, would CIA be in charge? or did we just plan to arrest and prosecute terrorists as if they were organized criminals?

The answer that Clinton approved, correctly I believe, was that we would use all the resources of any department or agency that could contribute. If the FBI could contribute by, for example, reassembling the wreckage of Pan Am 103 and determining who put the bomb on board, that was a capability we wanted utilized. CIA did not have significant forensics capabilities and was not good at interviewing hundreds of witnesses to stitch together a post-attack investigation. If we can chase down individual terrorists and arrest them, drag them back to the United States for trial and punishment, we should—even if the FBI has to do it. We had to use every agency that had something to bring to the effort. There were those who said such arrests and trials did not deter terrorists. I did not think that was knowable. I did know that there would be times when the criminal justice process would be feckless in dealing with terrorism and we needed intelligence, military, and diplomatic responses as a result.

If the FBI liked the response to the first policy question, they were less than thrilled with the reply to the second. The second question had to do with the role of the White House and its National Security

Council in domestic events. It was the question posed to me by the Situation Room watch officer, "Do you guys do domestic incidents?" In the wake of the World Trade Center bombing and the plots by the blind sheik, I thought the question answered itself. If there are foreign agents involved, we are involved. Until we know there are no foreign agents involved, we assume there are. The immediate problem that policy ran up against was the secrecy of the FBI. Institutionally, the fifty-six FBI offices talked only to the U.S. Attorneys around the country. There was also some communication between the field and FBI headquarters and somewhat less between FBI headquarters and the Justice Department.

To deal with that obstacle Lake, accompanied by his deputy, Sandy Berger, and me, drove over to the Attorney General's cavernous office. In a room that could have accommodated a few of the Saudi King's throne rooms, the three of us met with Janet Reno and the FBI. I explained the problem. If the NSC was going to coordinate counterterrorism policy and keep the President informed about what needed to be done, we needed to know what the FBI knew. The FBI officials present explained that information developed in a criminal investigation could not be shared with "civilians."

Reno, whom I did not really know at the time, sat silently taking notes on her legal pad. I wondered to what extent she had already been captured by the Bureau, or to what extent she would have the courage to stand up to them. She had shown incredible public courage in taking the blame for the disastrous siege of the religious cultists at Waco, Texas. In doing so she had taken the blame for an incident that was started by federal police in another department (Treasury's ATF agents had raided the compound initially) and ended with dead children when the FBI had given her bad advice. Now, she turned to the FBI and the White House guys present and issued her ruling: "If it's terrorism that involves foreign powers or groups, or if it could be, the Bureau will tell a few senior NSC officials what it knows." Lake and Reno agreed to sign a Memorandum of Understanding enshrining that principle. They never did. FBI and Justice Department lawyers slow-rolled the document for years. Nonetheless, it was the principle that we operated under and when I knew about people or events I was able to use the "Lake-Reno Agreement" to pry out information. Sometimes, a few senior FBI personnel even volunteered information to us. Usually, however, the FBI acted like Lake-Reno was a resort in Nevada.

The third policy issue was one that uniquely reflected the personality of the Clinton administration. It was: what should be the role of the federal government in dealing with the victims of terrorism? For Clinton, Lake, and Reno this issue loomed large. They now knew personally the families of the Pan Am 103 victims, who had told them how they were informed about the deaths of their loved ones, not by the government but by the airline. Often the news had been delivered badly and there was no one to work with to make arrangements for dealing with the deaths. From now on there would be a federal government role, to help in the grieving process and to provide information about the ongoing investigations.

I had a fourth issue that I wanted to add: weapons of mass destruction and terrorism. There were no signs of a terrorist group attempting to acquire weapons of mass destruction, but there was a disturbing correlation between the list of countries we labeled as state sponsors of terrorism and the list of countries that had chemical weapons. My previous work on nonproliferation had told me that the counterterrorism and nonproliferation "communities" in the government hardly knew each other. That had to change. No one in the departments objected to my including a policy on counterterrorism and weapons of mass destruction, they just thought it was odd.

With these issues agreed upon, President Clinton signed Presidential Decision Directive 39 (PDD-39), "U.S. Policy on Counterterrorism." It reiterated the "no concessions" policy, which the Reagan administration had violated by trading arms to Iran for the release of American hostages. It called for both offensive and defensive actions in order to "reduce terrorist capabilities" and in order to "reduce vulnerabilities at home and abroad." Law enforcement, intelligence, military, and diplomatic tools would be used and coordinated. Finally, there would be "no greater priority than preventing the acquisition of weapons of mass destruction" by terrorists, or if that failed there would be no greater priority than "removing that capability."

THE NEW POLICY SOUNDED GOOD, but it depended on intelligence that remained spotty. The search for the two remaining World Trade Center bombers continued in 1994, with Ramzi Yousef getting the most intensity. He was busy, but his activity did not gain the notice of U.S. intelligence. Unknown to us at the time, he engaged in unsuccessful plots to kill the Pope and later President Clinton, both in the Philippines. Then in January 1995, Manila police responded to a fire in an apartment building.

The message from Manila popped up on my computer screen on a Saturday morning. I printed it and ran from my office in the Executive Office Building across the parking lot known as West Exec to the West Wing. I interrupted a meeting Tony Lake was having on Bosnia and announced: "They found Ramzi Yousef."

"That's great news," Lake replied.

"No it's not. He got away," I exhaled. "And he was planning to blow up U.S. airliners in the Pacific with bombs smuggled on board, bombs we won't notice, using liquid explosives. They're assembled on board in the bathroom and then left there. The terrorist then gets off at the first stop and the plane continues on and blows up. The Filipinos found some of the bombs, but not all. He had the flights all picked out, United, Northwest . . . eleven of them, 747s."

Lake got the image. The man who blew up the World Trade Center, who had eluded capture for almost two years, was on the loose with bombs designed to create more Pan Am 103s, several simultaneously over the Pacific.

"Have you grounded the aircraft?" Lake asked. I had already called FAA and told them to call the airlines and stop flights originating in the Pacific. FAA said it would, but they also told me that only the Secretary of Transportation could ground flights. I told Lake all this.

"Get me the Secretary of Transportation," Lake said, picking up the phone to his assistant. Then he looked back at me, "Who the hell is the Secretary of Transportation?" Lake asked White House Chief of Staff Leon Panetta to join us, as various people tried to locate Secretary

Federico Peña. "Well," Panetta decided, "if the secretary has the authority, the President does too. Tell the airlines to ground them by order of the President."

U.S.-owned airlines originating flights in the Pacific were told to ground them. Flights in the air were turned around. Cabin crews were instructed to search above the ceiling tiles in the bathrooms, and anywhere else a bomb made of batteries, a watch, and a contact lens cleaning fluid bottle could be hidden. Nothing was found. Beginning the next day, when flights resumed, no passenger could carry any liquid on board. Hand searches disposed of perfumes and colognes. Ramzi Yousef had again eluded capture.

The CSG had already decided to issue a reward for Yousef and had authorized the distribution of matchbooks throughout the Middle East and South Asia, noting our $2 million bounty. There was a flood of people claiming to know where he was and seeking the reward. Virtually all of them were worthless leads. In early February, however, one of the callers actually did know. When questioned by State Department security officers from our embassy in Islamabad, Pakistan, the source gave details that made him credible. What happened next was a model apprehension. It happened quickly. The Ambassador sought and obtained Pakistani support for an arrest and extradition from that country. While an FBI arrest team flew in from New York, the embassy cobbled together its own team of State Department security officers, DEA agents, and a regional FBI officer from Thailand. In the early morning hours of the day on which Ramzi Yousef planned to take a bus to Afghanistan, he was rudely awakened by Pakistani and American officers. A few days later, he was back in New York.

Ramzi Yousef had many aliases. He was born Abdul Basit in Pakistan and grew up in Kuwait, where his father worked. After his arrest, he became a man of as much mystery and attention as when he was at large. With almost every terrorist incident or similar event, an urban legend develops that challenges the official story. After the events of 9/11, one widespread legend had it that Israel had attacked the World Trade Center and had warned Jews not to go to work that day. After TWA 800 crashed, the legend was that the U.S. Navy had shot down the civilian 747. With Ramzi Yousef, the legend was that there were actually two people: one was the man arrested by the FBI in Pakistan and the other was a mastermind of Iraqi intelligence, the Muhabarat. This legend was part of the theories of Laurie Mylroie.

For those in the U.S. government who knew Iraqi intelligence, the phrase "Iraqi intelligence mastermind" was an oxymoron. The Muhabarat had a well-deserved reputation as the Keystone Kops of the Middle East. Moreover, Ramzi Yousef, or Abdul Basit, was implicated in the World Trade Center attack by a large number of eyewitnesses, fingerprints, and other evidence. That did not stop author Laurie Mylroie from asserting that the real Ramzi Yousef was not in the federal Metropolitan Detention Center in Manhattan, but lounging at the right hand of Saddam Hussein in Baghdad. Mylroie's thesis was that there was an elaborate plot by Saddam to attack the United States and that Yousef/Basit was his instrument, beginning with the first World Trade Center bombing. Her writing gathered a small cult following, including the recently relieved CIA Director Jim Woolsey and Wolfowitz.

As reported by Jason Vest in the *Village Voice* (November 27, 2001): "According to intelligence and diplomatic sources, Powell—as well as George Tenet—was infuriated by a private intelligence endeavor arranged by Wolfowitz in September. Apparently obsessed with proving a convoluted theory put forth by American Enterprise Institute adjunct fellow Laurie Mylroie that tied Usama bin Laden and Saddam Hussein to the 1993 World Trade Center bombing, Wolfowitz, according to a veteran intelligence officer, dispatched former Director of Central Intelligence and cabalist James Woolsey to the United Kingdom, tasking him with gathering additional 'evidence' to make the case. Woolsey was also asked to make contact with Iraqi exiles and others who might be able to beef up the case that hijacker Mohammed Atta was working with Iraqi intelligence to plan the September 11 attacks, as well as the subsequent anthrax mailings." It turned out there was only one Ramzi Yousef, he was not an Iraqi agent, and he had been in a U.S. jail for years.

More than anyone in the Clinton administration, I wanted an excuse to eliminate the Saddam Hussein regime. Having been involved in the Gulf War's planning and execution, I had been furious when the war had stopped without eliminating the Republican Guard, and when Saddam had been permitted to mow down the Kurdish and Shi'a opposition while the U.S. stood idly by. I had hoped the UNSCOM parking lot incident that I had helped to contrive would have blossomed into a renewed round of major bombing that would have weakened the regime. For the same reason, I had pressed for a major round of bombing of Iraq in 1993 after the Bush assassination attempt was uncovered. More than anyone, I *wanted* the World Trade Center attack to be an Iraqi operation so we could justify reopening the war with Iraq—but there was no good evidence leading to Baghdad's culpability. By 1994, there was a lot of evidence beginning to point to another organization, whose name and outline was still unknown, but which involved a man that the CIA kept referring to as "terrorist financer Usama bin Laden."

The Saudis, fed up with bin Laden's continued anti-regime propaganda, had revoked his citizenship in 1994. Rumors suggested that a gunfight at bin Laden's house in Khartoum had been an attempt by Saudi intelligence to kill him using Yemeni mercenaries. His name popped up in intelligence in connection with terrorist activity in places as widely dispersed as the Philippines and in Bosnia. Beginning in 1993 Lake and Nancy Soderberg joined me in pestering CIA for more information about the man and his organization. CIA doubted initially that there was an organization.

Although bin Laden's name surfaced with increasing frequency in raw intelligence in 1993 and 1994, CIA analyses continued to refer to him as a radicalized rich kid, who was playing at terrorism by sending checks to terrorist groups. CIA knew of the existence of the Afghan Services Bureau, but did not see it as the public face of a covert terrorist network. Senior CIA officers explained to the Counterterrorism Security Group that the bureau was what it purported to be, a sort of Veterans of Foreign Wars for Arabs who had fought in Afghanistan. They allowed as how there may be some terrorists who were using some of its officers or services, but they did not say that it was now run by Usama bin Laden and was recruiting, paying, and arranging transportation for terrorists in a dozen or more countries. But it was.

Two months after Ramzi Yousef's arrest on a Sunday afternoon in March, I got the news that there had been a terrible explosion in downtown Oklahoma City. It had terrorism written all over it. But in Oklahoma? I called the White House from Haiti and reached my deputy, Steve Simon, in the Situation Room. He had stepped out of a CSG meeting to take the call. I felt guilty interrupting the meeting. "Who's chairing the meeting while you're talking to me?" I asked.

"Oh, don't worry, it's in good hands," Simon answered dryly. "Bill Clinton's chairing the CSG."

My only advice was to not assume the bombing in Oklahoma City was by an Arab or Islamic group. It didn't smell right. Simon had already figured that out and the White House was publicly cautioning that no one should leap to conclusions regarding who did it, and that no one should engage in reprisals against any ethnic or religious group. Hours later it became clear that the bombing was done by Americans.

The President's repeated appearances and speeches after the Oklahoma City bombing did much to comfort a shaken nation, but also to focus it on the problem of terrorism. Clinton talked incessantly about what it would be like if terrorists used a weapon of mass destruction to attack in a U.S. city. Not content to work with what we had, Clinton decided to seek more legal authority and more money to increase our ability to go on the offensive against terrorism. I was asked to inventory what we needed.

It was the first of several terrorism funding reviews that I led between 1995 and 2000. At a time of a decreasing federal budget, we took the federal counterterrorism budget from $5.7 billion in 1995 to $11.1 billion in 2000. The counterterrorism budget of the FBI was increased over 280 percent over that period. We also sought additional authorities for the FBI, including extending organized crime wiretap rules to terrorists, making funding of terrorist groups a felony, easing access to terrorists' travel records, and accelerating deportation of those associated with terrorist front groups. While most of the funds I sought in 1995 were approved by the White House and its Office of Management and Budget, some were not passed by the Congress. There was not one fund for counterterrorism, but several department budgets. We sought to fund programs in the Department of Energy, the Health and Human

Services Department, the Defense Department, the Justice Department, the Federal Emergency Management Agency, and other departments whose congressional appropriators did not see "their" agencies as being counterterrorist departments.

I sought the new legal ban on fund-raising for terrorist groups because several people in the administration had thwarted the CSG's attempts to go after terrorist money. In January 1995 we had persuaded the President to issue an Executive Order making it a felony (under the International Emergency Economic Powers Act) to raise funds for or transfer funds to designated terrorist groups or their front organizations. Rick Newcomb, the head of an obscure but powerful office in the Treasury (the Office of Foreign Assets Control), was eager to use the new authority. Newcomb was a dedicated, bright career bureaucrat who knew the rules and procedures in this area better than anyone.

Newcomb and I reviewed the case of the Holy Land Foundation of Richland, Texas. We were convinced that it was in violation of the Executive Order. Newcomb used the Customs police to enforce his edicts and, after CSG review, he had them set to raid the HLF, break the locks, seize the records and assets, and plaster posters on the doors and windows proclaiming that the place had been raided. Then FBI Director Louis Freeh and Treasury Secretary Bob Rubin objected. Freeh was concerned with alienating Arabs in America and claimed that use of the International Emergency Economic Powers Act might be challenged in court. Rubin claimed that he feared the law might not hold up under a challenge. He had also been reluctant to support any moves against money laundering for fear that it would cause capital flight from the U.S. and raise objections from other nations concerned with the sanctity of "bank secrecy." (In a case of strange bedfellows, Republicans like Congressman Dick Armey also opposed infringement on "bank secrecy.")

The raid did not occur. The Holy Land Foundation continued its activities, and I could only seek a new law that would be unassailable, a clear expression of congressional intent against terrorist fund-raising.

Incredibly, the legal authorities we sought were not approved by the Congress in 1995. I had thought these issues were bipartisan, but the distrust and animosity between the Democratic White House and Republicans in the Congress was strong and boiled over into counterterrorism policy. The World Trade Center attack had happened, the New York landmarks and Pacific 747 attacks had almost happened, sarin had been sprayed in the Tokyo subway, buses were blown up on Israeli streets, a federal building in downtown Oklahoma City had been smashed to bits, but many in the Congress opposed the counterterrorism bill. Republicans in the Senate, such as Orrin Hatch, opposed expanding organized crime wiretap provisions to terrorists. Tom DeLay and other Republicans in the House agreed with the National Rifle Association that the proposed restrictions on bomb making infringed on the right to bear arms. We would have to try again in 1996 to strengthen our ability to fight terrorism.

Chapter 5

THE ALMOST WAR, 1996

IF THE CLINTON NATIONAL SECURITY TEAM had come to office in 1993 without a thought to terrorism, by the beginning of 1996 they were preoccupied with it and feared a major terrorist attack would happen in the year ahead. But it wasn't al Qaeda that they expected to attack. CIA had not begun to use that phrase in its reports.

The radical theocracy that had replaced the Shah of Iran in 1979 had not cooled in its zealotry. Although the American hostages in Tehran were released at the beginning of 1980, the regime continued on a path of action against America. Iran had played a major role in the three truck bomb attacks on U.S. facilities in Lebanon, in which Hezbollah terrorists had killed Americans in the 1980s. It had been the behind-the-scenes mastermind of the prolonged hostage takings of Americans in Lebanon, including journalists, a Marine colonel, and a CIA station chief, both of whom were tortured and killed.

Throughout the 1980s, Iran was engaged in an eight-year war, defending itself from the invasion by Saddam Hussein. That war had spilled over into the Gulf, involving Iranian (and Iraqi) attacks on oil tankers. Defending oil tankers, the U.S. Navy had engaged in firefights with Iranian ships and aircraft. Then, in 1989, in the middle of such a firefight with Iranian small boats, the USS *Vincennes* had mistaken an Iran Air passenger plane for an attacking Iranian fighter plane, and shot it down, killing 290 civilians.

When I received the word of the shoot-down, I thought it would be the end of our "neutrality" in the war between Iran and Iraq. We had been supporting Iraq with intelligence, escorting its oil in Kuwaiti tankers, and cracking down on military supplies flowing to Iran.

Nonetheless, we said we were neutral. Now that we had killed hundreds of Iranian civilians, I assumed that Tehran would attack us directly in retaliation, thus drawing us into the war overtly on Saddam's side.

Instead, our mistaken shoot-down of the Iran Air flight ended the war. Bled dry by an eight-year war, the leaders of the Iranian Revolution were looking for an excuse to end the war and this would be it. Publicly they claimed that the United States was starting to fight them overtly and that they could not stand up to both Iraq and America at the same time. They said that further fighting could result in circumstances in which the Revolution would be undone, presumably by a U.S. invasion. Iran declared a cease-fire. Saddam Hussein, whose people and resources were also drained by his misadventure against Iran, eagerly accepted the cease-fire. The Iran-Iraq War was over. Three hundred and fifty thousand people lay dead.

The covert export of the Iranian Revolution continued, however, through the Iranian Revolutionary Guard Corps (IRGC), its special branch called the Qods Force (Jerusalem Force), the Ministry of Intelligence and Security (MOIS), and their own foreign legion of nationals from other countries, Hezbollah. The Arabic word for "Party of God," Hezbollah was initially Iran's instrument among the Lebanese and Palestinians in Lebanon. Tehran then extended it, establishing Hezbollah chapters in countries as near as Saudi Arabia and as distant as Brazil and Uruguay. The Iranian government pumped out extreme anti-American propaganda and welcomed terrorists from throughout the Islamic world for conferences on the struggle against Israel and the United States.

In response, the United States continued the economic sanctions that it had instituted in 1980 and kept Iranian assets in the U.S. frozen in escrow accounts. Despite those sanctions, Iran had continued to export oil to the United States, as much as $1.6 billion worth in 1987. During the "Tanker War," the U.S. added sanctions to further weaken Iran in its war with Saddam Hussein, ending the import of Iranian oil and banning the export to Iran of militarily useful civilian products.

Evidence mounted of Iran's procurement of modern weapons and materials to make chemical, biological, and nuclear arms. Tehran sought to acquire missiles and aircraft from Moscow and Beijing, and signed a deal with Russia to build a civilian nuclear power plant. No longer drained by fighting Iraq, its aid to Hezbollah increased, as did Hezbollah's attacks on Israel. Congress and the Administration competed with each other in originating further sanctions against Iran, while Hezbollah activity only mounted. In 1992 Senator John McCain sponsored the Iran-Iraq Nonproliferation Act, extending sanctions on third-country entities that exported "advanced conventional" weapons or components to either of those two countries.

In 1992, the Israeli embassy in Buenos Aires was bombed. In 1994, a Jewish cultural center in Buenos Aires was bombed, killing eighty-five. Intelligence indicated that Hezbollah and Iran were behind the attacks, but the Argentine government seemed reluctant to accuse them.

In 1995 Senator Alfonse D'Amato introduced legislation to ban all trade with Iran (except humanitarian items) and prohibit U.S. subsidiaries in third countries from trading in Iranian oil. In response, the Clinton administration instituted its own similar ban, using Executive Order authority. That action ended a billion-dollar deal that Conoco had in the works with Iran. As the head of Halliburton, Dick Cheney opposed the U.S. sanctions. Clinton also ordered Vice President Gore to coordinate efforts to build oil and gas pipelines that would tap the resources of Central Asia (chiefly in Kazakhstan) and pump them out using routes that did not cross Iranian territory, thus denying Iran the economic benefit it had hoped to gain from new pipeline deals. The White House and the State Department launched a concerted effort to persuade allies to cut economic ties with Iran, although to little avail.

Not content with administrative action, as 1995 ended Congress passed additional statutory sanctions against Iran and a secret appropriation to fund covert action by the CIA aimed at the Iranian regime. That secret leaked in the *Washington Post* a month later, in January 1996. The *Post* report alleged that a small amount, $18 million, had been added at the insistence of Speaker of the House Newt Gingrich. It said that Gingrich had wanted the funds to "overthrow" the Iranian regime, but had settled with the Administration on language that would permit the funds to be used to "change the behavior" of the government in Tehran.

Although the U.S. had promised not to seek the overthrow of the revolutionary regime as part of the agreement releasing the U.S. Embassy hostages in 1981, the Iranian government still believed and feared that Washington wanted to restore the Shah. The story that Gingrich had now persuaded Clinton to fund subversion set off alarms throughout the Iranian hierarchy. In a mirror image of the U.S. action, the Iranian Majlis, or parliament, publicly passed funding for covert action against the United States. The Majlis action was largely a propaganda move; the IRGC and MOIS were already actively engaged in anti-U.S. efforts around the world.

In March 1996 four suicide bombings took place in Israel in nine days, killing sixty-two people. Israeli intelligence believed that Hezbollah and Iran had a role in the attacks. Although suicide bombings in Israel would later become almost commonplace, in 1996 the world was shocked. President Clinton quickly orchestrated a summit of twenty-nine Arab and European leaders, which Egypt hosted at Sharm el-Sheikh. The International Summit on Terrorism produced proof that Arab governments rejected terrorism. Iran did not attend.

Fearing Iranian-sponsored terrorism against the U.S., the Counterterrorism Security Group formed a team to examine what Iran might do and how we could move to deter and prevent its attacks. One possible target we considered was the International Olympics planned for August 1996 in Atlanta. The FBI said it was the lead federal agency for the security of the Olympics and had been planning for the event for over a year, so I asked it to brief the CSG in April.

John O'Neill was the FBI man on the CSG and he arranged for FBI personnel from Headquarters and the Atlanta Field Office to come to the White House Situation Room with a briefing on all they had done. John proudly introduced the team and we all sat back to listen and to view their PowerPoint slides. The briefing was short and uninformative. The team could not answer most of the questions thrown at them by the interagency members of the CSG. I could see O'Neill was embarrassed and so I quickly brought the meeting to an end. As the group filed out of the Situation Room, I pulled O'Neill into the empty White House Mess next door.

"That wasn't encouraging, John."

"Know what I'm thinkin'?" O'Neill smiled. "Road trip. The whole CSG. Let's go down there and see how fucked up this thing really is."

Two weeks later, two dozen Washington counterterrorism experts from eight agencies landed and boarded a bus for an unusual tour of Atlanta to look for security vulnerabilities. After the ride, the Washington team met with the local authorities and the Atlanta representatives of the federal agencies that had been working on Olympics security for two years. We had a few questions.

Lisa Gordon-Hagerty of the Energy Department went first. "I noticed when we were touring the Olympic Village that it's really the Georgia Tech campus." Everyone nodded. "And that there is a nuclear reactor in the middle of the campus." A few nodded. "And I didn't see any real security on the reactor building, but I assume that it probably has spent fuel on site." Nobody nodded. People left the meeting to plaçe calls.

Steve Simon of the NSC Staff followed. He was a student of military history, as well as being a real expert on the Middle East. "Atlanta is a big railroad hub, all the north-south and east-west trains in the South pass through downtown Atlanta. That's why it was such an important hub for the Confederacy and such a key target for the Union." Again nods, but more carefully. I was thinking that perhaps we should not have mentioned the war in which a Washington department had ordered Atlanta burned to the ground and Scarlett O'Hara had become homeless. "But when you drive around downtown, you don't see any train tracks," Steve continued. Someone from Atlanta talked about the many underground tunnels. "Problem is those tunnels go right under the Olympic Stadium," Simon went on, "and those trains carry highly explosive and hazardous materials, even without a terrorist placing anything on them. You have a plan for searching the train cars or diverting the traffic?" They did not.

"Well, the nuclear reactor and the chemical train cars raise the whole question of the plan and the assets to respond to a chem, bio, or radiation incident," R. P. Eddy from the NSC Staff put in. "Can we get a briefing on the plan for that?" There was none.

The Washington representative of the Secret Service asked about access control on the Olympic venues, especially the Olympic Stadium where the President would be sitting. "Who is going to mag and search everyone as they come into the stadium?" After he explained that the verb "to mag" meant to search for metal such as guns using handheld or stationary walk-through magnetometers, the Atlanta Olympic Committee representative revealed its plan to have citizen volunteers at each gate to the stadium. They would not be using mags.

Mindful of Ramzi Yousef's plot to blow up 747s and the images of Pan Am 103, I asked about aircraft. "What if somebody blows up a 747 over the Olympic Stadium, or even flies one into the stadium?"

The Special Agent in Charge of the Atlanta FBI Office was steaming under the cross-examination from the Washington know-it-alls. "Sounds like Tom Clancy to me," he sneered. I glared at him. "But if it happens well, that's an FAA problem," he answered.

"Okay. Admiral Flynn?" I turned to Cathal Flynn, the retired Navy SEAL who ran FAA security. Born in Ireland and having spent twenty-five years in the U.S. Navy with the first name Cathal, Flynn liked to be called "Irish."

"Well, Dick, we could ban aircraft from over the Stadium during the events by posting a Notice to Airmen," Irish responded.

"But what if a terrorist hijacks an aircraft and violates that ban?" I asked.

"Then we would call the Air Force if we saw the aircraft violate the ban on radar. But by then it would be too late," Flynn intoned in his deep baritone. "But, of course, we would not even see them on radar if they shut down the transponder on the aircraft. You see, our radars are not air defense radars. Our air traffic control radars rely on the aircraft sending out a radio signal to us to tell us its altitude."

The Defense Department representative then explained to us about the *posse comitatus* law and how it prohibited the military from using force in the U.S. Jim Reynolds from the Justice Department helpfully pointed out that *posse comitatus* could be waived and had been waived to allow Army Special Forces to assist in suppressing a prison riot "right here in Atlanta" a few years earlier. "Yeah, but there is also an international law, to which we are a party, that bans shooting down a civilian aircraft. We learned all about that after we shot down the Iranian Airbus," came the DOD reply.

"Okay, okay. So whose job is it to stop a hijacked aircraft from flying into the Olympic Stadium?" I asked in frustration.

"Don't let them hijack an aircraft in the first place," the Atlanta FBI man offered.

We returned to Washington. On the flight back, I wondered aloud with John O'Neill how we would ever get the departments back in Washington to do the right thing about Atlanta Olympics security, spending the money, moving the teams. There was not much time left. Nominally, Vice President Gore chaired a committee on the Olympics, but it was one of dozens of jobs that President Clinton had piled on him. Leon Feurth was Gore's national security advisor. Feurth understood security and terrorism issues as well as anyone I knew. We went to Feurth.

A week later, the Vice President of the United States was in a short motorcade up Pennsylvania Avenue to the Headquarters of the FBI. O'Neill had arranged for the large Flag Room on the first floor to be set up for a CSG meeting in which every department would, again, present a briefing on plans for their role in Atlanta Olympics security. I sent the word to the departments that I would not be chairing the CSG that day; Gore would be. The level of attendance rose.

In the car on the way to the J. Edgar Hoover Building, I painted the picture for Gore one more time. "Here are some questions you might like to ask, innocently," I said, passing a list of what we had asked in Atlanta. "Then, after a while, you ought to look really mad."

"I do mad well." Gore smiled. He did have an impressive temper when he thought bureaucracy was unresponsive.

After the introductions and a few of the briefings, Gore slipped the questions out of his suit jacket. Some of the CSG regulars saw it coming. "Well, I know you all have briefings, but let me just ask a few questions that have been troubling me . . ."

The answers had not gotten any better. "Look, guys," the Vice

President said, "I know General Shelton over there could probably personally scare away most terrorists, but we can't put Hugh on every corner. We need a better plan than this." Shelton was then the head of Special Operations Command and, in his jump boots, had towered over Gore during the handshaking at the start of the meeting. Turning to me on his right, Gore handed me all the authority I needed. "Dick, I am going to ask you to pull that together, use whatever resources these agencies have that are needed. Anybody got any problems with that?" We were off to the races.

I had been helpful to the U.S. Customs Service in its efforts to persuade Congress to convert old Navy P-3 anti-submarine aircraft into flying radar platforms to find small planes smuggling drugs from South America. I called Customs and asked if they would move their P-3s to Atlanta during the Games. I also asked if they would move in some of their Blackhawk helicopters and place Secret Service snipers with .50 caliber rifles on board to warn off, or take out, aircraft threatening the Olympics. The Defense Department agreed to set up a joint air coordination post with the FAA and to place an Army radar on a hill outside Atlanta. They also agreed to have National Guard fighter aircraft on strip alert. After weeks of persuading the General Counsel of the Treasury (Customs and Secret Service were then both Treasury bureaus), we began to have an air defense plan.

Lisa Gordon-Hagerty and Frank Young went to work creating a response team to deal with chemical, biological, or nuclear incidents. Special medical stocks were moved in, as were decontamination units, and thousands of protective suits and hundreds of detection and diagnostic packages. Personnel from the Energy Department's nuclear labs, the Health and Human Services Department, the Army's chemical weapons command, and DOD's Joint Special Operations Command commandos would work together in a task force at an air base outside the city, where an interagency command post would be created.

Secret Service began to survey every Olympics venue for vulnerabilities and developed a plan to search everyone entering them. Hundreds of Secret Service personnel would be moved to Atlanta. O'Neill insured that hundreds of FBI agents would also be added, patrolling the streets undercover and sitting in key locations with rapid-response SWAT teams. The Transportation Department persuaded the railroads to reroute hazardous material cargos and to move additional railroad police in to surveil the trains. Flights going into Atlanta would get special passanger screening. The Energy Department ordered the nuclear reactor shut down temporarily and the nuclear waste moved.

By May we had a plan to move several thousand federal personnel and their equipment into facilities in and around Atlanta at a cost that ran into scores of millions of dollars. It dawned on us that the package of preventive and responsive measures we had assembled, along with the restrictions we had imposed, would be needed again elsewhere. For a while after the Olympics, when talking about using this security blanket approach to an event, we referred to them as "Atlanta Rules."

Yet, much to our chagrin, the Atlanta Rules failed to stop a lone bomber from striking at the Olympics. The fact that it was a small bomb did not matter, nor the fact that it had gone off in a public square and not at an event. What we needed quickly were two things: a reassuring show of force, without making the Olympic Games look like a military exercise; and we needed to know who had set off the bomb that killed one person and injured 111.

The reassuring and not threatening show of force turned out to be the easier of the two requirements. We asked the Treasury and Justice Departments to quickly provide hundreds of uniformed federal agents, even if the uniforms were raid jackets and baseball caps. Border Patrol agents were flown in from Texas and California on Air Force jets. Customs, INS, Park Rangers, and Bureau of Prisons guards were dispatched and walked the streets of Atlanta. The Games continued.

Finding out who had placed the bomb, however, was more difficult. I heard a rumor that the FBI had someone in custody and called a friend at the Bureau's Command Center. "They got a guy all right. Louis Freeh is on the phone now telling Atlanta what questions to ask him. Freeh thinks it's him." His tone suggested there was more to it.

I asked, "So what do you think?"

"Atlanta doesn't like this guy for the bomb. He's a rent-a-cop who was at the scene. But don't say we don't know who did it, 'cuz Louis has decided."

The rent-a-cop was named Richard Jewell. He had discovered the bomb and cleared the area of many potential victims. Freeh's theory was that he had staged the incident to get a full-time job with the police. After his life was ruined by the negative publicity of the detention and media leaks by the FBI, Jewell was released. The real bomber turned out to be Eric Rudolph, who went on to commit several other acts of terrorism. When the FBI finally set its sights on Rudolph in 1998, Freeh went to North Carolina to lead the search, using FBI helicopters and hundreds of agents, without success. Rudolph was later arrested by local police in 2003.

After the Olympics in 1996, in order to institutionalize what we had learned in Atlanta, I suggested that we create an official designation of "National Security Special Events." The CSG could formally designate upcoming public ceremonies as such, and the agencies involved could request Congress for funds in advance, unlike in Atlanta where I had to promise the departments that I would find the money to pay them back. FBI agreed, with the condition that they be put in charge of all NSSEs. After their performance in Atlanta, I would not agree. Despite FBI objections, I insisted that the Secret Service share the lead. Secret Service had shown in Atlanta that they were better equipped and trained to think about preventing a terrorist attack by eliminating vulnerabilities.

In the following years, the CSG designated several National Security Special Events, including the celebration of the United Nations Fiftieth Anniversary in New York, NATO's Fiftieth Anniversary in Washington, the Republican National Convention in Philadelphia, the Democratic National Convention in New York, and the 1997 and 2001 Presidential Inaugurations. Heightened security was obvious at all of those events. Less obvious were the thousands of special response units with menacing-looking vehicles hidden in buildings nearby, or the hundreds of undercover federal agents on the streets, the Coast Guard cutters in the rivers, or the aircraft above. Invisible were the intelligence activities performed at the events and around the world by FBI, CIA, Secret Service, NSA, Customs, Immigration, Diplomatic Security, Coast Guard, and Defense Department to detect and prevent terrorism. Unfortunately, the teamwork and integration forced on the departments for special events did not always continue when the events were over.

IN MAY 1996, shortly before the Atlanta Olympics, word reached Washington of a remarkable discovery made by the Belgian authorities. They had intercepted a shipment en route to Germany. Inside what was labeled as "pickles" was a custom-designed weapon best described as the largest mortar ever seen. The weapon was designed to lob a large explosive charge a short distance, such as over the walls of an Israeli or U.S. embassy compound. The shipment was traced to Iran.

The Defense Department agreed to our request to station an additional aircraft carrier battle group in the waters off Iran temporarily, as a deterrent signal to Tehran. The Navy was growing increasingly concerned with anti-ship missiles that Iran was placing on islands in the Persian Gulf and on its coastline, particularly at the narrow point in the Gulf leading to the Indian Ocean, the Straits of Hormuz. In early May, DOD announced that Iran had acquired long-range missiles from North Korea and was engaged in a program to protect its missiles in hardened bunkers.

The Navy relied on two ports in the Persian Gulf. Only one, in the United Arab Emirates, could handle an aircraft carrier. That port, near Dubai, saw more U.S. Navy ships anchored and more U.S. sailors ashore than any harbor outside the United States during the 1990s. It remained, however, a commercial facility with no permanent U.S. Navy facility. The U.S. Navy base was a few hundred kilometers up the Gulf in the island nation of Bahrain. There, thousands of U.S. sailors lived and worked. After the Tanker War and then the first Gulf War, the little Navy base at Bahrain had mushroomed into a large and active facility. In 1996, DOD announced that the base would now be headquarters to a new entity, the Fifth Fleet. With the Soviet navy rusting at Siberian ports and the Iraqi Navy sitting on the bottom of the Persian Gulf and Shatt al-Arab, the Fifth Fleet had only one possible enemy: Iran.

Bahrain was ruled by the Khalifas, a Sunni Muslim family. The Shah of Iran had laid claim to their country, based on a relationship lost in antiquity. A United Nations commission decided against the Iranian claim in 1970 and the island remained an independent nation. It had few oil or gas deposits, so the Khalifas had turned the small island nation into a Western-style destination, with shopping, banking, and entertainment for Saudis and others who were inhibited in their own countries. More than half of Bahrain's citizens were, however, Shi'a Muslims who felt disenfranchised by the Khalifas. They provided fertile ground for Iran.

In early June, the Bahraini ambassador to Washington called me and asked, on behalf of his foreign minister, for an urgent meeting at the White House. He presented me with pictures of bombs and other weapons that had been found in Bahrain the day before. He handed over a document outlining a plot by the Iranian Revolutionary Guard Corps to stage an armed attack on the Khalifas and install a pro-Iranian government in Bahrain. Tehran's instrument was something called Hezbollah-Bahrain, a group of Bahraini Shi'a created in Qum, Iran in 1993. It had been training terrorists in Iran and Lebanon for over two years. Twenty-nine Hezbollah had been arrested in Bahrain; others had fled to Iran. The ambassador offered details from the interrogations of the Hezbollah prisoners.

Although little noticed by the Western press, the attempted coup in Bahrain was further evidence of Iran's support for terrorism and its attempt to drive the U.S. military out of the region. In two weeks, we had still more.

The American military had come to Saudi Arabia in August 1990 and was still there in 1996, although in smaller numbers. They were spread out over a half dozen facilities. In the Eastern Province, where most of the minority Shi'a lived, the U.S. Air Force had been given a high-rise housing complex near the village of Khobar. On June 25, 1996, it was attacked by terrorists using a devastating truck bomb. Nineteen Americans died.

In fact, Khobar was the second attack on a U.S. military facility in Saudi Arabia. In November 1995, the Riyadh headquarters of the U.S. military training mission to the Saudi National Guard had been bombed, killing five Americans. Within days, the Saudi authorities had arrested four men, obtained their confessions, and executed them. Despite U.S. appeals to hold up the executions so that an American investigation could be completed, the Saudis decapitated the four. The Saudis provided scant details about who they were or why they had acted.

To avoid a repeat of the previous incident, I asked Clinton to write to the King seeking full cooperation in a joint investigation of the Khobar attack and announcing that he was sending an FBI team. I also suggested that Clinton appoint retired four-star general Wayne Downing to head an independent U.S. inquiry into the security of U.S. facilities in the region and, in particular, what had gone wrong at Khobar. I had known Wayne since he was a major and had no doubt that he would tell us the truth. Clinton agreed. The Pentagon, civilian and military, was outraged that the President would launch an investigation of military laxness.

After a CSG meeting to coordinate relief efforts, I met with the NSC staff counterterrorism team. We went over every CIA, NSA, Defense, and State Department report on threats in Saudi Arabia for the past two years. A few dozen reports, culled from thousands on file, told a clear story. The Iranian Revolutionary Guard Corp's Qods Force had created Hezbollah groups in Bahrain, Kuwait, and Saudi Arabia. They had secretly recruited terrorists and sent them off for training in Iran and then in Lebanon. Saudi Arabia had learned of this activity and protested to Iran. Iran had denied the allegation. One night, the Saudi border guards were using a bomb-sniffing dog suggested by the United States that noticed something in a car at a customs post. The car was found to have a load of sophisticated plastic explosives. The ensuing Saudi interrogation and investigation led to arrests of Hezbollah operatives in the Kingdom and established that the car was operated by Saudi Hezbollah and originated at a camp in Lebanon's Beqaa Valley. The camp was nominally run by a Saudi named Mugassal, but he worked for the Qods Force, the Iranian Special Forces. The bomb was intended for an attack on a U.S. military facility in Saudi Arabia.

The Saudis had told us none of this. They had quietly asked the Syrians to close the Hezbollah camp in Lebanon's Beqaa Valley, which was under Syrian control, and to hand over the Saudi Hezbollah terrorists. Syria had professed ignorance.

The day after the Khobar attack, we presented Tony Lake with a detailed NSC Staff report placing the blame on Iran's Qods Force and their front, Saudi Hezbollah. Lake believed us and wondered why CIA had not reached the same conclusion. He sent the report to CIA Director John Deutch, who replied only that ours was one of many theories.

At the FBI, Director Louis Freeh responded eagerly to the White House request for an FBI investigation. It was one of the few times Freeh did anything eagerly that the White House had asked him to do. Freeh had told senior FBI officers that the White House staff were all "politicals" who could not be trusted. Many of his senior officers, however, had been working with me and other career national security officials in the White House for years on sensitive counterterrorism, counterintelligence, and anti-narcotics activities. They continued to do so, while admitting that they were no longer telling Freeh about all their meetings at the White House complex.

For Freeh, who had worked on narcotics and organized crime cases in New York, international affairs was a new arena. Soon after the Khobar attack, Freeh was sought out by Saudi Ambassador Prince Bandar. Bandar charmed Freeh at frequent meetings at the Saudi's Virginia estates. Bandar facilitated meetings in Saudi Arabia for Freeh, who went there to coordinate the investigation personally. John O'Neill accompanied Freeh to the Kingdom. O'Neill told me he was struck by the contrast between the fawning protocol the Saudis showed to Freeh and their mendacity whenever the conversation got around to the investigation. Freeh, according to O'Neill, did not seem to detect the duplicity.

Behind the glad hand, the Saudis had no intention of cooperating with the FBI. The attack had revealed an internal vulnerability in the Kingdom, the armed opposition of Shi'a Muslims from the Eastern Province. The Saudis did not want that embarrassment publicly revealed. Saudi Interior Minister Nayef denied the FBI access to evidence and witnesses. When the Saudis traced the attack back to Mugassal and Iran, they arrested some of the Saudi Hezbollah group still in the country, but denied the FBI access to the prisoners and refused to admit to the FBI that the attack was orchestrated by Iran. Nayef and others in the royal family worried about what the U.S. would do with that information.

Almost a year after the attack, the Saudis did convey one interesting fact. They claimed that they had traced a member of the terrorist cell to Canada. They asked that the United States intervene with the Canadians to return the suspect to Saudi Arabia. I thought otherwise, suggesting to the CSG that we put the suspect, Hani el-Sayegh, under surveillance to see whom he met with, whom he talked to. Unfortunately our agreements with Canada prohibited us from unilateral operations there. FBI, therefore, requested Canadian surveillance. After a short time, the Canadians complained that they did not have the staff or the funds to continue constant surveillance.

Louis Freeh had a solution.

He proposed confronting Sayegh and soliciting his cooperation in exchange for a light sentence. That was the way Freeh had handled organized crime cases, rolling up the gang by "flipping" lower-level members, getting them to implicate their bosses in exchange for leniency. Freeh asked if the White House and State Department would go along with Sayegh testifying before a grand jury even if the result might be indictments of Iranian officials. The NSC Principals Committee met and agreed that we should indict whoever we had evidence against, including Iranian government officials.

I didn't think Freeh's plan would work with Sayegh and asked the director, "Why should he agree to go to jail when we have no evidence against him? If we bring him here, you will have to release him and he can walk out onto the streets in the U.S. a free man."

I could not convince Freeh, who proceeded with the confrontation of Sayegh. When detained, the Saudi talked freely to the Canadian authorities and FBI in Canada. He admitted that the Khobar attack was directed by the Saudi Hezbollah leader, Mugassal, and the Iranian Qods Force. Surprisingly, Sayegh agreed to come to the United States and testify before a grand jury. He was told that he would be sentenced to prison for his role in anti-U.S. terrorism, but he would be given a light sentence. Sayegh agreed to the bargain and was trundled off.

Yet once in the United States, Sayegh refused to cooperate and sought political asylum, noting that he would be tortured and then decapitated if he were returned to Saudi Arabia. Of course, he would have been decapitated for killing Americans, but nonetheless his asylum request was placed into the State Department and Justice Department systems for review. When asked about the attack on Khobar and the role of Iran, he clammed up. His government-appointed lawyer moved for his release, pending the asylum review. The FBI had no evidence against him. Sayegh was about to walk out the door of a federal building onto the streets of the United States. Then Freeh came up with an idea that showed real creativity. He ordered Sayegh detained on the grounds that he was in the United States illegally, even though it was the FBI that had brought him in.

Two years later, in 1999, Sayegh was placed into Saudi custody, without ever having testified before a grand jury or having given one bit of evidence from the time he stepped foot in the United States. FBI agents accompanied him to Saudi Arabia, reminding him throughout the flight that it was not too late to turn the plane around if he would testify. Sayegh ignored them.

During the two years of Sayegh's detention in the United States, Freeh sought to understand from Prince Bandar why the FBI was not getting better cooperation from the Saudi government. I learned that Bandar had explained to Freeh that the White House did not want the Saudis to cooperate with Freeh. Clinton, Bandar claimed, did not want the evidence that Iran had bombed an American Air Force base; Clinton did not want to go to war with Iran. Freeh believed it. It fit with his own dim view of the President, the man to whom he owed his rapid elevation from a low-level federal job in New York. In the White House, we heard that Freeh began to repeat Bandar's explanation for the failed Khobar investigation, telling Congressmen and reporters of the supposed Clinton cover-up.

Freeh should have been spending his time fixing the mess that the FBI had become, an organization of fifty-six princedoms (the fifty-six very independent field offices) without any modern information technology to support them. He might have spent some time hunting for terrorists in the United States, where al Qaeda and its affiliates had put down roots, where many terrorist organizations were illegally raising money. Instead, he reportedly chose to be chief investigator in high-profiles cases like Khobar, the Atlanta Olympics bombing, and the possible Chinese espionage at our nuclear labs. In all of those cases, his personal involvement appeared to contribute to the cases going down dark alleys, empty wells. His back channels to Republicans in the Congress and to supporters in the media made it impossible for the President to dismiss him without running the risk of making him a martyr of the Republican Right and his firing a cause célèbre.

In actuality, Clinton had been pursuing the opposite path to what Freeh imagined. In discussions with Saudi officials, the U.S. made very clear at presidential direction that there must be full cooperation, not the rapid decapitation of suspects as had been done in the Riyadh case. Having been advised that the Saudis were reluctant to see the United States start another war in the Persian Gulf by retaliating against Iran, we assured the Saudi leadership that there would be no surprises, that the U.S. would consult fully with the Saudis before responding to whatever it learned about those behind the attack. Clinton was promised that Saudi Arabia would tell us all it knew and cooperate fully with the FBI. They proceeded to do the exact opposite.

Some in the Saudi royal family, like Bandar's father, Minister of Defense Sultan, reportedly welcomed the possibility of a U.S. war with Iran, if America could remove the Tehran regime. Bandar, in private talks with senior American officials in 1996 and 1997, suggested that all that was stopping the Saudis from implicating Iran was the fear that the American retaliation would be halfhearted. If the U.S. could promise a full-scale fight to the finish, then the Kingdom would probably tell all that it knew about the Iranian role in the Khobar attack. Sandy Berger told Bandar that the United States could not promise what it would do on the basis of evidence it had not seen.

Others in the Saudi royal family thought any war with Iran would end up with a Pyrrhic victory. The U.S.-led war with Iraq had almost bankrupted the oil-rich Saudis. They had spent so much money subsidizing U.S. and coalition forces and then buying more arms from America that they had few funds left for anything else and were falling behind in payments owed to foreign suppliers. The presence of American troops in Saudi Arabia had been destabilizing. Another war would bring the Americans back in large numbers. The Crown Prince was reportedly of this school of thought. With the King largely incapacitated, Crown Prince Abdullah was making the decisions. Without telling the United States, he entered into talks with Iran.

After many months, what was agreed between the Saudi and Iranian leadership was essentially this: Iran would not sponsor or support terrorism in Saudi Arabia; Saudi Arabia would not permit the United States to launch attacks on Iran from the Kingdom.

The White House pressure on the Saudis to cooperate in the investigation continued over three years, with letters from the President and demarches by National Security Advisors Lake and Berger. Vice President Gore demonstrated his famous temper in one such meeting, pounding on the table and asking a Saudi prince what sort of country hid the identity of people who had killed American military personnel stationed in that country defending it and its royal family.

When enough time had passed to convince the Saudis that America had cooled down and was not about to bomb Iran, the FBI was finally granted access to the suspects. Five years after the bombing, indictments were handed down by a U.S. grand jury.

While Freeh had been pursuing the Saudis, the White House had been preparing for war. We had convinced Tony Lake that Iran launched the Khobar attack, and CIA soon agreed and suggested that further Iranian-sponsored terrorism against the U.S. was likely. Clinton told us that if it came to using force against Iran, "I don't want any pissant half-measures." Lake convened what he called the Small Group, CIA Director Deutch, Defense Secretary William Perry, Secretary of State Christopher, and the Vice President's National Security Advisor, Leon Feurth, to examine options.

Separately, Lake sent his deputy, Sandy Berger, and me to see Chairman of the Joint Chiefs John Shalikashvili. The Joint Chiefs had made a practice of never showing their war plans to civilians, despite being hectored to do so over the years by various Pentagon civilians. I knew the number of the war plan for Iran and asked Lake to call Shali and ask him to brief us on that plan.

John Shalikashvili was an unlikely person to be the senior American military officer. Born in Poland to a family from Soviet Georgia, he still had an accent. Out of uniform, he looked like a kindly pediatrician. I had first heard his name when, in 1991, as Assistant Secretary of State for Politico-Military Affairs, I was asked to set up a meeting between a U.S. commander and an Iraqi commander, in order to tell the Iraqis to clear out of northern Iraq. U.S. forces were about to intervene to save the starving Kurds, who were fleeing into snow-covered mountains in Turkey. Looking at a large, detailed map of northern Iraq, I found a town near the Turkish border named Zakho.

"Tell the U.S. mission at the U.N. to get the Iraqi ambassador. Tell him to have a flag rank officer meet a U.S. general in, let's see, how about Zakho at noon the day after tomorrow," I instructed my executive officer, Martin Wellington. "Then tell the Pentagon to send a U.S. general to Zakho."

Wellington returned in a few hours, saying "The Iraqis want to know where in Zakho they are supposed to meet Shalikashvili?"

"Meet who? Are the Russians trying to get involved?" I asked Wellington, who assured me that was the name of an American general. Shali went on to perform heroically in rescuing the Kurds and moving them safely back from Turkey to their homes in Iraq. When it came time to replace Colin Powell as Chairman of the Joint Chiefs in 1993, many of us urged the selection of Shali. Unlike Powell, who had bristled at the use of the U.S. military in minor engagements, Shali had thought there was a role for the military in creating stability in situations short of all-out war.

In our meeting in the Pentagon in July 1996, Shali was talking about all-out war. The military had a plan for almost any contingency. The plan on the shelf for war with Iran looked like it had been drawn up by Eisenhower. Several groups of Army and Marine divisions would sweep across the country over the course of several months. "What if we wanted to do something a little bit less first?" Berger asked.

"Well," Shali said, reaching for another map, "CENTCOM also has a plan to bomb their military facilities along the coast: navy ports, air force bases, missile installations."

"Let's suppose for the sake of argument that we did that, bombed their coastal stuff," I asked. "What happens next?"

"If you're asking what I personally think happens next, Dick, is that they attack us again, with hidden missiles, with little boats, with terrorist cells going against us and the Saudis and the Bahrainis," Shali mused.

"Not good," Berger said, shaking his head, "tit for tat. Then we have to hit them again." Clinton had told Lake, Berger, and me that he did not want to get into a round of gradually escalating mutual attacks. If we were going to do this, he wanted a massive attack that would frighten the Iranians into inaction. In 1989, the Iranians had stopped the war with Iraq because they said they were convinced that the United States and Iraq together would take actions that threatened the continuance of the Iranian Revolution. Could we get them to think that way again?

"What about the old nuclear strategy concept of escalation dominance," I asked, "where you hit the guy the first time so hard, where he loses some things he really values, and then you tell him if he responds, he will lose everything else he values?"

"We could do that," Shali suggested. "Let me talk to the boys down in Tampa." It was clear that he was going to do that even without my input. Shali had not liked the choices CENTCOM gave him any more than we did.

The Small Group examined what we were now dubbing the Eisenhower Option and others too. One option was attacking Iranian-sponsored terrorism camps in Lebanon. Another was a Presidential Envoy to Europe and Japan to try again to convince our allies to engage in an economic boycott, but this time promising a U.S. military response on Iran if they did not join us in economic action. There was also an intelligence operation option. When the Small Group was presented with the intelligence option, Leon Feurth said, "Well, we ought to do that anyway just for the hell of it."

The intelligence operation had intrinsic merit, as Feurth had noted, but if combined with a stark private-channel threat to the Iranians, it would give that message greater credibility: We have just demonstrated what we can do to hurt you. If your agents continue to engage in terrorism against us, we will hurt you in ways that will severely undermine your regime. Such a one-two punch would be escalation dominance. If it failed to deter Iran, then we could turn to CENTCOM's new plans. Unfortunately, it would take months to put CIA assets in place and to choreograph a more or less simultaneous series of intelligence actions around the world.

SOMETHING HAPPENED DURING OUR DEBATES about how to respond to Khobar that almost made that debate a foregone decision for all-out war with Iran. On a hot summer night just three weeks after the bombing of Khobar Towers, the Coast Guard and the Air Force were conducting a joint nighttime search-and-rescue exercise off Long Island, using cutters and aircraft. At 8:31 many in the exercise saw a huge fireball in the sky east of the island, at about fifteen thousand feet. It was TWA 800, a 747 from Kennedy Airport on its way to Paris. There were 230 people on board.

Shortly after 9:00 p.m., the CSG met via secure video conference connecting the Situation Room with operations centers at FAA, FBI, Coast Guard, State, CIA, and the Pentagon. Racing in from Virginia, I dreaded what I thought was about to happen. The Eisenhower Option, invading Iran.

The description provided by the Coast Guard was graphic. If there had been anyone alive, the fact that there was a rescue operation under way even before the explosion took place would have meant that the victims might have been saved. But no one was alive. Scores of naked bodies that had been floating on the water were now piling up on the cutters and the dock at the little Coast Guard boat station at nearby Moriches. Their clothes had been blown off by the force of the explosion and their rapid flight through the air. Debris was also everywhere.

The FAA was at a total loss for an explanation. The flight path and the cockpit communications were normal, the aircraft had climbed to 17,000 feet, then there was no aircraft. "A lot like Pan Am 103," Irish Flynn suggested, "but too early to tell."

FBI had mobilized in a big way. John O'Neill reported that hundreds of FBI agents from New York City were en route to Kennedy Airport and to Long Island to establish a crime scene and begin interviewing witnesses. Jim Kallstrom, the head of FBI New York, had ordered a mobile command post to roll out to the Moriches Coast Guard station so that FBI could take charge of the operation.

"John, I admire that response," Irish Flynn began, "but somebody has to point out that the National Transportation Safety Board is in charge of an airline incident."

"Not if it's a criminal act, they aren't," O'Neill shot back. "Besides, what assets does the NTSB have anyway?"

We agreed it would be a parallel investigation, until we knew what happened. We all thought we knew what had happened and it would end up being an FBI problem.

Yet in the days that followed, no intelligence surfaced that helped advance the investigation. Many witnesses described things that sounded like a surface-to-air missile just before the explosion. TWA, having learned from Pan Am's mistakes in the Lockerbie crash, had a plan for dealing with the victims' families. They flew them to Kennedy Airport and put them up in an airport hotel where they could be briefed. Initially, there was nothing to brief them on. Then, during dinner, a Long Island coroner showed up with pictures of bodies for them to identify. The outraged and distraught families were featured prominently on the evening news. Bill Clinton was watching.

He called us into the Oval Office. "I want to go up there tomorrow, to see those families."

That did not seem like the best idea I had ever heard. The families were looking to lynch someone. If the president of TWA was unavailable, they might settle for the President of the United States.

I suggested there might be a problem with meeting the families in their current mood. "In addition, you are going to Atlanta tomorrow to the Olympics." That thought frightened me too.

"Get a French interpreter too. Many of the families are from France," the President continued as though I had never objected. "I'll go on to Atlanta from Kennedy." As we were leaving the Oval Office, he had one more thought. "And I want to announce new airline security measures while I'm at Kennedy. So develop some."

We had been working with Evelyn Lieberman, the Deputy Chief of Staff of the White House, and Kitty Higgins, the Cabinet Secretary, on the idea of a Commission on Aviation Safety and Security. A low-cost airline, ValuJet, had crashed into the Everglades earlier in the year because of hazardous cargo that should not have been on board and had exploded. Almost two hundred people had died. The airline industry needed something to restore confidence in air travel, as industry leaders had been telling Lieberman. From my perspective, a commission would highlight all the shortcomings in airport security that Irish Flynn and I had been discussing. Now, however, the President wanted some new security measures announced immediately. I called Flynn, "Tell your lawyers they're not going home tonight."

In the morning, I flew with the President and First Lady to Kennedy International and briefed them aboard Air Force One on the announcements he would make. From now on, no one would be allowed on board an aircraft without a government-issued photo ID that matched the name on the ticket. Random passenger and cargo searches would be increased. Cars would temporarily not be permitted to park near terminal buildings. Curbside check-in would be temporarily discontinued. Vice President Gore would head a new Commission on Aviation Safety and Security, which would include family members of victims from flights that had crashed. The commission would recommend permanent changes to enhance security and safety.

Upon arriving at the airport hotel, we went into a ballroom where the families were waiting. There were a lot of them. The President spoke from a small podium, pausing for consecutive translation into French. When he had finished, Mrs. Clinton left to meet with Red Cross and other rescue workers who were gathered nearby. The President, to my chagrin and to the horror of the Secret Service, stepped into the crowd. He began to gather them in small family groups, praying with them, hugging them, taking pictures with them, looking at the pictures of their now dead loved ones, and listening intently. I thought he was about to cry. I knew I was, so I slipped out of the ballroom. I opened a door into the next room, which had been set up as a chapel. Alone in the room, on her knees, Mrs. Clinton was praying. I stepped outside. There a cluster of television cameras and reporters waited to interview the irate families. They emerged slowly in small groups, after having had their time with the President. "Did you tell the President how angry you are about the way you've been treated?" one reporter yelled. "The President was so good to come to us," a woman who might have been a grieving mother replied. "He's so kind."

It went on for a long time. When it was over, the President stood at a podium in front of Air Force One and made the new security announcements. He then left for the Olympics. His statement also made clear that we did not yet know if the crash had been a terrorist act. I knew he thought it was a terrorist act and he was bracing himself for what he would have to do in response. After the blue and white 747 took off for Georgia I was left alone on the tarmac. An FBI agent drove me to LaGuardia to catch the shuttle back to Washington. A long line snaked out of the Marine Air Terminal. The guy in front of me explained, "New security stuff. You have to have a photo ID."

A few weeks later I returned to LaGuardia with John O'Neill. He had an FBI helicopter waiting next to the shuttle's jetway. O'Neill was lobbying me to get the FBI some money to pay for the enormous operation they were undertaking to recover the wreckage and to reconstruct it. In a giant hanger in Bethpage, Long Island, where NASA had originally built part of the Apollo moon mission, the 747 was being rebuilt. Rebuilding a 747 that was in thousands of pieces looked like it might be as hard as the moon mission. On the hop out to Bethpage, O'Neill told me that the eyewitness interviews were pointing to a missile attack, a Stinger.

I tried to dissuade him from the Stinger theory. "It was at 15,000 feet. No Stinger or any other missile like it can go that high. The distance and angle are too far from the beach, and even from a boat right under the flight path, you can't get that high." John wanted proof from the Pentagon. I agreed to get it.

At Bethpage, O'Neill urged me to wander around, talk with the technicians and visit the lab that the Bureau had created on site. It was a strange, quiet place. Airline seats were being placed around the floor. A window was propped up nearby. One room was filled with luggage. There was a giant tail section.

I stopped to ask one technician what he was doing. "Looking to see the pitting and the tear," he explained. "See, a bomb causes a certain type of pitting on the metal nearby, little bumps. And a bomb causes sharp tear lines where the metal separates."

"So this is from near where the bomb exploded?" I asked. "Where on the plane was it?"

"The explosion was just forward of the middle, below the floor of the passenger compartment, below row 23. But it wasn't a bomb," he added. "See the pitting pattern and the tear. It was a slow, gaseous eruption, from inside."

"What's below row 23?" I asked, slowly sensing that this was not what I had thought it was.

"The center line fuel tank. It was only half full, might have heated up on the runway and caused a gas cloud inside. Then if a spark, a short circuit . . ." He indicated an explosion with his hands.

"Yeah, but wait a minute," I said. "How do you get a spark inside a fuel tank?"

"These old 747s have an electrical pump inside the center line fuel tank . . . fuel eats away the insulation. If a spark . . ." His hands did an explosion again.

There was no pitting or tear, no indication of an inbound explosion from a Stinger-like missile and no indication that a bomb had been on board. (The engines, once raised from the ocean, would show nothing to suggest that they were hit by a missile either. A simulation of the crash would later indicate that what witnesses saw as a streak of a missile going up toward the aircraft was actually a column of jet fuel from the initial explosion and rupture, falling and then catching fire, sending flame ascending prior to a second, larger fuel explosion. The FBI concluded in November 1997 that there was no evidence of a criminal act. In May 1998, the NTSB ordered inspection and possible replacement of fuel tank wiring insulation on 747s.)

That summer day in 1996 I returned to the White House from

Bethpage and asked to meet with Tony Lake and Leon Panetta. By now they had been conditioned to equate my asking for a meeting with the probability that something was about to explode. I sketched the 747 design and explained about the fuel tank. "Does NTSB agree with you, or does FBI?" Lake asked.

"Not yet," I admitted. Nonetheless, we were all cautiously encouraged.

Unfortunately, the public debate over the incident was clouded by conspiracy theory. Conspiracy theories are a constant in counterterrorism. Conspiracy theorists simultaneously hold two contrary beliefs: a) that the U.S. government is so incompetent that it can miss explanations that the theorists can uncover, and b) that the U.S. government can keep a big and juicy secret. The first belief has some validity. The second idea is pure fantasy. Dismissing conspiracy theories out of hand, however, is dangerous. I learned early on in my government career not to believe that the government experts knew it all. The list of major intelligence failures and law enforcement errors is far too long to dismiss alternative views. Because I was personally skeptical about what agencies told me and always intrigued by the possibility of the unlikely explanation, I encouraged my analysts to have open minds and perform due diligence on every claim. For that reason we had always looked for Iraqi involvement in the World Trade Center attack of 1993, to no avail.

For that reason too, in 1996 I asked the Senior Director for Counterterrorism at the NSC Staff, Steve Simon, to drive over to the Georgetown townhouse of Pierre Salinger. The former White House Press Secretary had publicly claimed to have evidence that TWA 800 was shot down. Simon was gone a long time. When he returned, he looked like someone who had been on a far more difficult and frustrating mission than a two-mile drive to a fashionable Washington neighborhood.

"What the hell happened to you?" I asked after Simon stormed into my office and stood silently steaming, his arms folded across his chest, and a look of intense disgust on his face.

Finally he blurted out, "Plucky Pierre is whacked; he's lost it. The real world is a planet he left long ago." With that Simon spun around and went back to the office that had once belonged to Ollie North. When he calmed down, I got a real debriefing. Salinger thought a U.S. Navy F-14 had shot down TWA 800 and he had a set of accompanying fantasies. Defense Department, FAA, and FBI evidence all convincingly proved that theory wrong.

ANOTHER CONSPIRACY THEORY intrigued me because I could never disprove it. The theory seemed unlikely on its face: Ramzi Yousef or Khalid Sheik Muhammad had taught Terry Nichols how to blow up the Oklahoma Federal Building. The problem was that, upon investigation, we established that both Ramzi Yousef and Nichols had been in the city of Cebu on the same days. I had been to Cebu years earlier; it is on an island in the central Philippines. It was a town in which word could have spread that a local girl was bringing her American boy friend home and that the American hated the U.S. government.

Yousef and Khalid Sheik Muhammad had gone there to help create an al Qaeda spinoff, a Philippine affiliate chapter, named after a hero of the Afghan war against the Soviets, Abu Sayaff. Could the al Qaeda explosives expert have been introduced to the angry American who proclaimed his hatred for the U.S. Government? We do not know, despite some FBI investigation. We do know that Nichols's bombs did not work before his Philippine stay and were deadly when he returned. We also know that Nichols continued to call Cebu long after his wife returned to the United States. The final coincidence is that several al Qaeda operatives had attended a radical Islamic conference a few years earlier in, of all places, Oklahoma City.

FROM WHERE I SAT, Khobar, TWA 800, and the Atlanta Olympics bomb had given the impression of a renewed wave of terrorism against the United States, and even in the United States, even if some of that impression was mistaken. It was a good time to play the Washington game of seeking increased funding. I prepared an Emergency Supplemental request and took it to White House Chief of Staff Leon Panetta.

Emergency Supplementals, budget requests sent up to Congress after the President's Budget, were anathema to another part of the White House, the Office of Management and Budget. The normal budget preparation process took months and OMB controlled the outcome. Getting money for counterterrorism was not easy in the normal process because the departments often did not ask for the funds. That meant that the NSC Staff then had to argue that we knew better than the Cabinet members what should be in their budgets. I had done well in pumping up the counterterrorism funds in the last two budgets, but had not gotten everything we needed. When OMB heard I was putting an Emergency request together, they were more than a little unhappy. They knew that if the Administration asked for counterterrorism money in a Presidential election year (which 1996 was), Congress would vote for every penny and more. The new level would then become a baseline for the next budget. OMB's chief concern was balancing the budget and driving down the deficit. They had been doing a good job of it.

The OMB staff, however, took solace in the fact that Leon Panetta had come to the Chief of Staff's job from having been Director of OMB. He would see things their way.

We met around Panetta's long conference table: the Chief of Staff, me, and six OMB officials. Panetta, doodling on a legal pad and half looking up at the group, asked, "What do you need, Dick?" The OMB staff shuffled papers; that was not the way they wanted to begin the meeting.

"Little over a billion." There were both gasps and groans from OMB. I continued, "Four-thirty for airline security upgrades, four-thirty for force protection for DOD bases like Khobar, some more for FBI, some more for CIA."

Panetta had sat through the meetings that summer thinking about war with Iran. OMB had not. Paying to prevent terrorism was a lot more attractive decision than those he had thought we might be faced with. "Okay, sounds good. Let's get it up to the Hill this week. Anything else, anyone?" Panetta rose from the table. Meeting over.

We had the money. We also did the intelligence operation against the Iranians.

Professor Crane Britton's study of revolutions claimed that there were predictable phases in the life of any revolution. When the movement became the government, its ardor ultimately cooled, a stage that Britton called Thermidor. We have been waiting since 1979 for Tehran's Thermidor. It has been like waiting for Godot.

Following the intelligence operation, and perhaps because of it and the serious U.S. threats, among other reasons, Iran ceased terrorism against the U.S. War with Iran was averted, giving Thermidor more time to arrive, giving the Iranian people more time to take complete control of their government. Despite the election of "moderate" President Khatami in 1997, the Iranian security services continued to support escalating terrorism against Israel and allowed al Qaeda safe passage and other support.

Clinton had ended 1995, after the Oklahoma City attack, with a speech to the United Nations fiftieth General Assembly focusing on terrorism, the need to end sanctuaries, to go after their money, to deny them access to weapons of mass destruction. In November, he had gone back to Arlington Cemetery to unveil the finished Pan Am 103 cairn and speak again about the continuing threat of terrorism. In April 1996, after Khobar, he gave another address on terrorism at George Washington University, declaring a war on terror before the term became fashionable:

"This will be a long, hard struggle. There will be setbacks along the way. But just as no enemy could drive us from the fight to meet our challenges and protect our values in World War II and the Cold War, we will not be driven from the tough fight against terrorism today. Terrorism is the enemy of our generation, and we must prevail. . . . But I want to make it clear to the American people that while we can defeat terrorists, it will be a long time before we defeat terrorism. America will remain a target because we are uniquely present in the world, because we act to advance peace and democracy, because we have taken a tougher stand against terrorism, and because we are the most open society on earth. But to change any of that, to pull our troops back from the world's trouble spots, to turn our backs on those taking risks for peace, to weaken our opposition against terrorism, to curtail the freedom that is our birthright would be to give terrorism the victory it must not and will not have."

Shortly thereafter, on September 9, 1996, Clinton formally requested $1.097 billion for counterterrorism-related activities. One month to the day after he filed the request, the funds were approved by Congress: money for more CIA and FBI counterterrorism agents, for Immigration to look for possible terrorists entering the country, for Rick Newcomb at Treasury to hire staff to go after terrorist financing, for the State Department and Department of Defense to harden overseas facilities, for improving security on federal buildings, for training and exercising counterterrorism disaster response units in major cities, and for weapons of mass destruction terrorism–related programs at the Centers for Disease Control and the Department of Energy.

The Commission on Aviation Safety and Security (the Gore Commission) requested and got funding for programs involving baggage screening, carry-on luggage checks, passenger profiling, screener training, research on aircraft hardening, and to hire more FAA security agents. The Gore Commission did not, however, agree to recommend that the federal government assume the role of airport passenger and luggage screening. It would continue to be the job of the airlines, which in turn would continue contracting out the mission to firms using low-wage staff.

It was clear even at the time that the Gore Commission had not been sufficiently ambitious about the job of airport security and passenger screening. Having the federal government assume the mission of passenger screening would, however, have meant hiring fifty thousand new federal employees and spending billions more, at a time when both the Administration and the Congress were taking pride in cutting the number of federal employees and the federal budget. Instead, the Gore Commission agreed that there would be more testing and inspection of the rent-a-cops involved, new machines to screen bags, and a passenger-profiling system. The events of 1996 (the ValuJet crash from an exploding oxygen tank and the TWA crash from a worn wire in a fuel tank) had not provided the political circumstances needed for the massive change in how the federal government performed aviation security. No one in the Administration or Congress would have backed a new 50,000-person Transportation Security Administration.

One proposal that would actually have made things worse was narrowly averted. The FBI proposed eliminating the FAA's small Federal Air Marshal program. The Bureau was concerned that if an aircraft were hijacked, any Marshal on board would just get in the way of the FBI's Hostage Rescue Team, which was trained to seize a hijacked aircraft. The FBI was unable to say how the Marshals posed any greater risk to the Hostage Rescue Team than the hundreds of FBI, Secret Service, Drug Enforcement, State Police, and other law enforcement officers who flew armed every day. Nor did the FBI address the problem that for the Hostage Rescue Team to deal with a hijacked aircraft, the plane had to land first.

The Secret Service and Customs had teamed up in Atlanta to provide some rudimentary air defense against an aircraft flying into the Olympic Stadium. They did so again during the subsequent National Security Special Events and they agreed to create a permanent air defense unit to protect Washington. Unfortunately, those two federal law enforcement agencies were housed in the Treasury Department and its leadership did not want to pay for such a mission or run the liability risks of shooting down the wrong aircraft. Treasury nixed the air defense unit, and my attempts within the White House to overrule them came to naught. The idea of aircraft attacking in Washington seemed remote to many people and the risks of shooting down aircraft in a city were thought to be far too high. Moreover, the opponents of our plan argued, the Air Force could always scramble fighter aircraft to protect Washington if there were a problem. On occasions when aircraft were hijacked (and in one case when we erroneously believed a Northwest flight had been seized), the Air Force did intercept the airliners with fighter jets. We succeeded only in getting Secret Service the permission to continue to examine air defense options, including the possibility of placing missile units near the White House. Most people who heard about our efforts to create some air defense system in case terrorists tried to fly aircraft into the Capitol, the White House, or the Pentagon simply thought we were nuts.

Chapter 6

Al Qaeda Revealed

THE FIRST YEARS OF THE CLINTON ADMINISTRATION had seen a staccato drum roll of terrorism. Eleven "terrorist" events rose to high-level attention in the United States, from the first World Trade Center attack, to the shootings outside CIA headquarters, to the Atlanta Olympics bomb, and others. Not one of them had been blamed on anything called al Qaeda by CIA or by FBI. The story of when, and how, the U.S. first began to focus on Al Qaeda has been garbled in various recent accounts. It is time to set the record straight.

A man named Usama bin Laden, a so-called financier, had been remotely and tentatively related to one or two events but not blamed for them. Maybe, CIA said, he was connected to a failed attack on Americans in Yemen in 1992 and perhaps there was some connection between him and Ramzi Yousef, who had attacked the World Trade Center in 1993 and then plotted in the Philippines. The supposedly known perpetrators of terrorist attacks discussed by the media were an unrelated hodgepodge of apparently containable threats: Iraqi intelligence for the attempt on former President Bush, Iranian intelligence for the attack on the U.S. Air Force at Khobar Towers in Saudi Arabia, a lone wolf from Baluchistan for the attack on the CIA gatehouse, two odd ducks from the American right wing for the Oklahoma City bombing, an Egyptian cleric for the plot to blow up the New York City tunnels, a wannabe cop turned security guard for the Atlanta Olympics bomb, a crafty Palestinian-Kuwaiti for the World Trade Center attack, a group of now beheaded Saudis for the bombing of the U.S. military training mission in Riyadh, and a mystery man in a boat off Long Island or perhaps even a U.S. Navy pilot for the downing of

TWA 800. By 1997, the two hostile intelligence services had been checkmated by our bombing of Iraq's service headquarters, and by the intelligence operation against Iran. Most of the other actors were in jail or dead, and the rent-a-cop and U.S. Navy had been exonerated of the Atlanta bomb and the TWA crash. If there was a pattern in all of this, U.S. intelligence and federal law enforcement did not see it.

Nonetheless, this regular diet of destruction and death was enough for us to generate a White House response. The Clinton administration had begun a steady escalation in counterterrorism funding. For the first time in forty years, an Administration had designed and funded a major program for homeland defense. Clinton had focused on terrorism in a string of major speeches: at the Air Force Academy, Oklahoma City, George Washington University, Annapolis, twice at the United Nations, twice at the Pan Am 103 cairn, at the White House, at Lyon, France, and Sharm el-Sheikh, Egypt. Most of the media ignored the pattern of the administration's response and warnings. While some federal employees were alarmed at the rise of terrorism and worked diligently against it, others in the FBI, CIA, and the Defense Department did not see the urgency.

We now know that the World Trade Center attack in 1993 was an al Qaeda operation, as were the failed plots to attack New York landmarks and U.S. airliners over the Pacific. At the time, however, these events were attributed by FBI and CIA to Ramzi Yousef and the blind sheik, both of whom were behind bars by 1995. Rumors circulated of Arab involvement in the events against American troops in Somalia, but neither the Defense Department nor the CIA could verify them.

The details of the attack on the U.S. military training mission in Riyadh were not well established due to the lack of Saudi cooperation. The larger attack in Saudi Arabia at Khobar was conducted by Saudi Hezbollah under the close supervision of Iran's Revolutionary Guard Corps and its Qods Force. Iran had also staged terrorist attacks in Israel, Bahrain, and Argentina.

Outside of New York the attacks in the U.S. were conducted by deranged loners. We had not been able to connect Mir Amal Kansi, the CIA gatehouse shooter, to any known group. The Oklahoma City and Atlanta attacks had been conducted by right-wing Americans, with tenuous ties to homegrown militias and religious extremists. Another, potentially devastating attack had involved Americans in a right-wing militia planning to explode a gas storage facility in Fresno. FBI surveillance of the militias had averted that calamity.

DESPITE THE LACK OF EVIDENCE of a bin Laden hand in the series of terrorist events, Lake, Berger, Soderberg, and I had persisted in 1993 and 1994 in asking CIA to learn more about the man whose name kept appearing buried in CIA's raw reporting as "terrorist financier Usama bin Laden." It just seemed unlikely to us that this man who had his hand in so many seemingly unconnected organizations was just a donor, a philanthropist of terror. There seemed to be some organizing force and maybe it was he. He was the one thing that we knew the various terrorist groups had in common. And we kept coming back to the incredible notion offered by CIA and FBI that the gang that bombed the World Trade Center had just come together as individual agents who happened upon one another and decided to go to America to blow things up.

In 1991 the Saudi government had given up trying to persuade Usama bin Laden to stop his criticism of the royal family, its military alliance with the United States, and the continuing presence of U.S. forces. Despite threats to the large, wealthy, and well-connected bin Laden family and construction company empire, Usama kept crossing the line. A frustrated Saudi government told him to leave the country.

He chose to go to Sudan, which at the time was the quintessential safe haven for terrorists of all stripes. The government of Sudan was dominated by the National Islamic Front, whose leader was Hasan al-Turabi. Although allegedly a religious scholar, Turabi preached a particularly violent flavor of hatred. Bin Laden and Turabi had known each other through the growing international network of radical Islamists. When bin Laden came under pressure from the Saudi government, Turabi invited him to set up shop in Sudan. Bin Laden came with his money and his men, the Arab veterans of the Afghan War.

Most of these veterans faced jail cells if they returned home to Egypt, Kuwait, Algiers, or Morocco.

As is well known by now, Turabi and bin Laden set up several joint projects: a new construction company, a new investment firm, control of the Sudanese commodities markets, a new airport, a road between the two largest cities, new terrorist training camps, a leather factory, Arab Afghan War veterans housing, arms shipments to Bosnia, support to Egyptian terrorists plotting to overthrow President Mubarak, and development of an indigenous weapons industry (including chemical weapons). The two radical fundamentalists were soul mates, sharing a vision of a worldwide struggle to establish a pure Caliphate. The two also socialized together, taking meals at each other's homes. In bin Laden's spare time he went horseback riding with Turabi's son.

Before going to Sudan, bin Laden had returned to Afghanistan, the site of his now widely acclaimed role in the war against the Soviets. He had found the post-Soviet Afghanistan factionalized by tribal groups unwilling to take his counsel or direction. Although fighting continued there, it was not jihad against non-Muslims. Jihad was available to a limited extent in the Philippines, where Muslims in the south had been fighting the Christian government for centuries. Bin Laden sent key lieutenants there, including his brother-in-law Muhammad Jamal Khalifa, Ramzi Yousef, and Yousef's uncle and mentor, Khalid Sheik Muhammad. Jihad was also available in Russia, where oppressed Muslims took advantage of the fall of the Soviet Union to seek independence for the province of Chechnya. Bin Laden sent Afghan Arab veterans, money, and arms to fellow Saudi ibn Khatab in Chechnya, which seemed like a perfect theater for jihad.

The ingredients al Qaeda dreamed of for propagating its movement were a Christian government attacking a weaker Muslim region, allowing the new terrorist group to rally jihadists from many countries to come to the aid of the religious brethren. After the success of the jihad, the Muslim region would become a radical Islamic state, a breeding ground for more terrorists, a part of the eventual network of Islamic states that would make up the great new Caliphate, or Muslim empire. Bosnia also seemed to fit the bill. The fall of Communism in Yugoslavia had sent the ethnic republics of that artificial union spinning off into their own orbits. The predominately Muslim province Bosnia had long been discriminated against by the Christian center, and Bosnia's attempt at independence in 1991 was brutally countered by the Serb-dominated Belgrade government. Despite an international outcry, the George H. W. Bush administration had done little to stop the slaughter. General Scowcroft and his close friend Deputy Secretary of State Lawrence Eagleburger judged the dissolution of Yugoslavia to be a hopeless quagmire best left to the European community to fix. (Eagleburger, a former U.S. ambassador to Yugoslavia, had almost unerring instincts in foreign policy, but his years in Belgrade made him reluctant to involve the U.S. too deeply in Balkan affairs. He became Secretary of State briefly in 1992 when President Bush virtually ordered a reluctant Jim Baker to manage the Bush reelection campaign.)

Unlike the jihad in Chechnya, which Russia tried to keep away from the scrutiny of the world, Bosnia was a center of attention during its struggle with Serbia. It was also a center for scrutiny by West European and American intelligence. What we saw unfold in Bosnia was a guidebook to the bin Laden network, though we didn't recognize it as such at the time. Beginning in 1992, Arabs who had been former Afghan mujahedeen began to arrive. With them came the arrangers, the money men, logisticians, and "charities." They arranged front companies and banking networks. As they had done in Afghanistan, the Arabs created their own brigade, allegedly part of the Bosnian army but operating on its own. The muj, as they came to be known, were fierce fighters against the better-armed Serbs. They also engaged in ghastly torture, murder, and mutilation that seemed excessive even by Balkan standards.

The hard-pressed Bosnians clearly wished they could do without these uncontrollable savages, but Bosnian President Alija Izetbegovic decided to take aid where he could. America talked a good game, but was doing little to stop the Serbian military. Iran sent guns. Better yet, al Qaeda sent men, trained, tough fighters. European and U.S. intelligence services began to trace the funding and support of the muj to bin Laden in Sudan, and to facilities that had already been established by the muj in Western Europe itself.

The ties led to the Finsbury Park Mosque in London, to the Islamic Cultural Center in Milan, to the Third World Relief Agency in Vienna. They also led to the Benevolence International Foundation in Chicago and to the International Islamic Relief Organization in Saudi Arabia. These charities were providing funds, jobs, identification papers, visas, offices, and other support to the international brigade of Arab combatants in and around Bosnia. Western governments, including our own, did not find adequate legal grounds prior to September 11 for closing these organizations.

Many of the names that we first encountered in Bosnia showed up later in other roles, working for al Qaeda. Among the top jihadists in the Bosnia fighting were: Abu Sulaiman al-Makki, who would later show up standing next to bin Laden in December 2001 as al Qaeda's leader extolled the September 11 attacks; Abu Zubair al-Haili, who would be arrested in Morocco in 2002 plotting to attack U.S. ships in the Straits of Gibraltar; Ali Ayed al-Shamrani, who was arrested in 1995 by Saudi police and quickly beheaded for involvement in attacking the U.S. military aid mission in Saudi Arabia; Khalil Deek, who would be arrested in December 1999 for his role in planning attacks on American facilities in Jordan at the Millennium; and Fateh Kamel, who would be fingered as part of the Millennium Plot cell in Canada. Although Western intelligence agencies never labeled the muj activity in Bosnia an al Qaeda jihad, it is now clear that is exactly what it was.

Although not seeing it entirely for what it was, the United States did begin to act against the jihadist presence in Bosnia. U.S. officials made clear to Izetbegovic that the jihadists would have to leave, that he was riding a tiger that would swallow him at some point. The Clinton administration also made stopping the war in the Balkans its highest foreign policy priority, introducing U.S. forces and hammering out the Dayton Accord. (That peace agreement took the dedicated and diligent labor of Clinton, Lake, Berger, Albright, Ambassador Dick Holbrook, and General Wes Clark. In its pursuit, Holbrook's team faced personal tragedy. An armored vehicle in their convoy careered off a ridgeline and burst into flames. Clark dragged out some of those inside before the vehicle exploded. Three died, including my NSC Staff colleague Nelson Drew.) A part of that Dayton Accord called for the eviction of the muj from Bosnia following the end of the fighting. We didn't know they were al Qaeda, but we knew they were international terrorists.

Diplomacy and peacekeeping were not the only tools we employed. In 1995 Abu Talal al-Qasimy, the leader of the Egyptian muj in Bosnia, disappeared. He had earlier run an office of the International Islamic Relief Organization in Peshawar on the Pakistan-Afghan border. He had worked with Ayman Zawahiri, leader of Egyptian Islamic Jihad (later bin Laden's deputy) in exile in Denmark. His disappearance was responded to with a car bomb directed at Croatian police. The bomber was a Canadian working for the Vienna-based Third World Relief.

As it became clear that diplomacy had not entirely worked, in 1998 French troops raided one of the remaining muj facilities still operating in Bosnia in violation of the Dayton Accord. They arrested eleven, including two Iranian diplomats and nine muj. The facility was filled with explosives, arms, and plans for terrorist attacks on U.S. and other Western troops. Also in 1998 a shipment of C-4 plastic explosives was intercepted en route to an Egyptian Islamic Jihad terrorist cell in Germany. Indications were that the explosives were intended for a round of attacks on U.S. military installations in Germany. The same year, an Egyptian Islamic Jihad cell in nearby Albania disappeared. The group, led by Abu Hajir (Mahmoud Salim), was plotting to blow up the U.S. embassy in Tirana.

The United States threatened Bosnian President Izetbegovic with a termination of military aid, then a cessation of all assistance, if he did not fully and faithfully implement Dayton by evicting the muj. The Bosnians claimed that they had evicted them, except for sixty men who had married Bosnian women and become Bosnian citizens. Not until 2000 in his last week in office, did Izetbegovic expel the remaining muj leader, Abu al-Ma'ali. (The Netherlands welcomed him.) And Izetbegovic never did expel everyone. Al Qaeda cells in Bosnia were identified by the United States and raided by Bosnian police as late as 2002.

Despite Izetbegovic's lapses, Bosnia was largely a failure for al Qaeda. They invested men and money, but were unable to establish a major, permanent base, unsuccessful at turning another country into part of the Caliphate. They did, however, gain further experience and burrow deeper into Western Europe. For the United States, Bosnia was largely a success. Although late to address the issue, the U.S. was the major reason that the Islamic government in Bosnia survived. The U.S. also blocked Iranian and al Qaeda influence in the country. Moreover, CIA was able to cripple parts of the al Qaeda network and uncover others. Much of what was uncovered was in Europe, where al Qaeda had taken advantage of refugee policies and other forms of international openness to lay down roots. Although West European governments knew what was present in their countries, many continued to turn a blind eye to al Qaeda's presence. The Finsbury Park Mosque in London, the Islamic Cultural Center in Milan, and similar gathering places for terrorists continued to operate without interference.

THROUGHOUT BIN LADEN'S YEARS in Sudan, that country served as a base for arms and fighters going not just to Bosnia, but also to terrorists in Egypt, Ethiopia, Uganda, and even Qadhafi's Libya. Sudan's intelligence service and military supported the terrorists. Then in June 1995, Egyptian President Hosni Mubarak flew to Ethiopia for a meeting in Addis Ababa of the Organization of African Unity. Aware that Sudanese-based Egyptian terrorists were plotting to kill Mubarak as they had assassinated his predecessor, Anwar Sadat, Mubarak's intelligence advisor insisted on an armored limousine and rooftop snipers along the routes from the airport. Without them, Mubarak would have been dead. Islamic Jihad terrorists attempted to block the road, fire on the limousine, and bomb the motorcade. They narrowly failed. Evidence tied the attack to terrorists in Sudan, and all of that evidence indicated support from the Sudanese government.

Following that event, Egypt and we (joined by other countries in the region) sought and obtained the United Nations Security Council's sanction on Sudan. Only Libya had previously been subject to U.N. sanctions because of terrorist sponsorship. In the Counterterrorism Security Group we considered the sanctions a rare diplomatic success. The CSG also considered direct action, examining options for attacks on bin Laden's and/or Turabi's facilities in and around Khartoum. The White House requested the Pentagon to develop plans for a U.S. Special Forces operation against al Qaeda–related facilities in Sudan. Weeks later a Pentagon team briefed National Security Advisor Tony Lake and other Principals in Lake's West Wing office. There were options to raid a terrorist facility that the Pentagon briefing labeled "Veterans' Housing for Afghan War Fighters," a plan to blow up a bank in downtown Khartoum that was thought to house bin Laden's money, and a few other options. While the Joint Staff dutifully briefed on the plan, they recommended strongly against it. "I can see why," Lake replied after seeing the details. "This isn't stealth. There is nothing quiet or covert about this. It's going to war with Sudan."

The military briefing leader nodded: "That's what we do, sir. If you want covert, there's the CIA." The CIA, however, had no capability to stage significant operations against al Qaeda in Sudan, covert or otherwise.

The Saudis or perhaps the Egyptians may have been thinking along similar lines about the need for some covert operation against bin Laden in Sudan. Reports reached us from Sudan of two incidents in which someone had attempted to kill bin Laden in Khartoum. We also knew that Mubarak was sending the word to Khartoum to rein in the terrorists, or else. Egypt had moved troops and aircraft to the Sudan border once before and had even used its air force to bomb an anti-Egyptian radio station in Khartoum in the early 1980s. Now, Mubarak was threatening another military buildup. The weak Sudanese military could beat up Christian tribes in the south, but it was no match for the Egyptian military. It was getting a little too hot there for the al Qaeda leader.

Afghanistan was looking better to bin Laden in 1996. The puppet government the Soviets had left behind in Kabul had fallen and, after ten years of factional fighting, Pakistan had intervened to stabilize the situation. Hoping to see the return of millions of Afghan refugees in Pakistan, the Pakistan military intelligence service (ISID) had armed and trained the Taliban religious movement to gain control of much of Afghanistan. The leader of the Taliban was much like Sudan's Turabi, a religious zealot seeking to create theocracy at the point of gun. Like Turabi, Mullah Omar was known to bin Laden and was eager to have his men and money back.

Turabi and bin Laden departed as friends, and pledged to continue the struggle and to use Khartoum as a safe haven.

In recent years Sudanese intelligence officials and Americans friendly to the Sudan regime have invented a fable about bin Laden's final days in Khartoum. In the fable the Sudanese government offers to arrest bin Laden and hand him over in chains to FBI agents, but Washington rejects the offer because the Clinton administration does not see bin Laden as important or does and cannot find anywhere to put him on trial.

The only slivers of truth in this fable are that a) the Sudanese government was denying its support for terrorism in the wake of the U.N. sanctions, and b) the CSG had initiated informal inquiries with several nations about incarcerating bin Laden, or putting him on trial. There were no takers. Nonetheless, had we been able to put our hands on him then we would have gladly done so. U.S. Attorney Mary Jo White in Manhattan could, as the saying goes, "indict a ham sandwich." She certainly could have obtained an indictment for bin Laden in 1996 had we needed it. In the spring of 1998, she did so. The facts about the supposed Sudanese offer to give us bin Laden are that Turabi was not about to turn over his partner in terror to us and no real attempt to do so ever occurred.

Had they wanted to, the National Islamic Front government could have arrested bin Laden just as they had arrested the legendary terrorist Ilyich Sánchez ("Carlos the Jackal") when he was uncovered in Khartoum by CIA and then by French intelligence in 1994. Carlos, however, was a lone wolf doing nothing for the NIF. Usama bin Laden was an ideological blood brother, family friend, and benefactor of the NIF leaders. He also had many well-armed followers.

Turabi and bin Laden decided to relocate al Qaeda's leadership to Afghanistan to reduce international pressure on the NIF and to help the Taliban finish putting another nation into the Caliphate. Sudan, they thought, was already well on the path. (Turabi was later jailed by the Sudanese military in 2002 and the NIF largely thrown out of government positions.)

The CSG did not, however, stop considering U.S. military or CIA raids into Khartoum. Following bin Laden's departure in 1996, a series of intelligence reports established that a bin Laden associate named Abu Hafs al-Muratani was in Khartoum engaged in supporting terrorist cells elsewhere. The reports became so specific that we knew his hotel and the room in the hotel he was using. I referred the reports to National Security Advisor Sandy Berger with a recommendation that we snatch the terrorist. My CSG colleagues from every agency concurred.

Snatches, or more properly "extraordinary renditions," were operations to apprehend terrorists abroad, usually without the knowledge of and almost always without public acknowledgment of the host government. One terrorist snatch had been conducted in the Reagan administration. Fawaz Yunis, who had participated in a hijacking of a Jordanian aircraft in 1985 in which three Americans were killed, was lured to a boat off the Lebanese shore and then grabbed by FBI agents and Navy SEALs. By the mid-1990s these snatches were becoming routine CSG activity. Sometimes FBI arrest teams, sometimes CIA personnel, had been regularly dragging terrorists back to stand trial in the United States or flying them to incarceration in other countries. All but one of the World Trade Center attackers from 1993 had been found and brought to New York. Nonetheless, the proposed snatch in Khartoum went nowhere. Several meetings were held in the White House West Wing with Berger demanding the snatch. The Joint Staff had an answer that they used whenever asked to do something that they did not want to do:

- it would take a very large force;
- the operation was risky and might fail, with U.S. forces caught and killed, embarrassing the President;
- their "professional military opinion" was not to do it;
- but, of course, they would do it if they received orders to do so in writing from the President of the United States;

- and, by the way, military lawyers said it would be a violation of international law.

Fletcher School professor Richard Shultz came to similar conclusions about how the U.S. military would refuse to fight terrorism prior to September 11. His study is summarized in the article "Show Stoppers" in the January 21, 2004 *Weekly Standard.*

The first time I had proposed a snatch, in 1993, the White House Counsel, Lloyd Cutler, demanded a meeting with the President to explain how it violated international law. Clinton had seemed to be siding with Cutler until Al Gore belatedly joined the meeting, having just flown overnight from South Africa. Clinton recapped the arguments on both sides for Gore: Lloyd says this. Dick says that. Gore laughed and said, "That's a no-brainer. Of course it's a violation of international law, that's why it's a covert action. The guy is a terrorist. Go grab his ass." We tried, but failed. We learned that often things change by the time you can get a snatch team in place. Sometimes intelligence is wrong. Some governments cooperate with the terrorists. It was worth trying, however, because often enough we succeeded.

But in the 1996 discussion of Sudan, Berger turned to George Tenet, asking if CIA could snatch the man in the Khartoum hotel room. Tenet responded that they had no capability to do that in that hostile environment, nor could they find a friendly intelligence service that could (or would) do it.

Mike Sheehan, the Army Special Forces colonel who had worked with me on terrorism, Somalia, and Haiti, offered to go to Khartoum and do the snatch himself. He was only half joking. "This guy doesn't even have bodyguards. Hit him over the head and throw him in a Chevy Suburban." To the complete frustration of Berger, Albright, and me, the CIA finally admitted it could do nothing to effect a snatch in Khartoum. DOD was only able to generate options, once again, that looked like going to war with Sudan. Two years later Sheehan was visiting the headquarters of the Joint Special Operations Command (which includes Delta Force) at Fort Bragg. He struck up a conversation with two fellow Green Berets. They told each other stories about operations they had done and about "the ones that got away," missions planned but not carried out. The two told Sheehan about the plan they had to snatch an al Qaeda leader in a Khartoum hotel. "Woulda been so sweet. Six guys. Two cars. In and out. Easy egress across the border and fly out, low-risk."

"Really?" Sheehan asked, pretending not to know about the proposed snatch. "What happened? Why didn't you get to do it?"

"Fuckin' White House," the Green Beret said in disgust. "Clinton said no."

"How do you know that?" Mike innocently inquired.

"Pentagon told us all about it."

Whether it was catching war criminals in Yugoslavia or terrorists in Africa and the Middle East, it was the same story. The White House wanted action. The senior military did not and made it almost impossible for the President to overcome their objections. When in 1993 the White House had leaned on the military to snatch Aideed in Somalia, they had bobbled the operation and blamed the White House in off-the-record conversations with reporters and Congressmen. What White House advisor would want a repeat of that? Often though, we learned, senior military officers let the word spread down the ranks that the politicians in the White House were the ones reluctant to act. The fact is, President Clinton approved every snatch that he was asked to review. Every snatch CIA, Justice, or Defense proposed during my tenure as CSG chairman, from 1992 to 2001, was approved.

Skipping ahead in the chronology, I should mention that CIA was able to operate near Khartoum in 1998. Reports had been reaching us for several years that Sudan sought to make chemical weapons. The reports from several sources, including UNSCOM, indicated that Sudan was making chemical bombs and artillery shells. There were few places in Sudan where the needed chemicals could be created. One was a chemical plant at Shifa. The intelligence reports indicated that the plant had benefited from investment by the Sudan Military Industry Commission, which in turn had received investments by bin Laden. Bin Laden had created an investment company, Taba Investments, upon moving to Khartoum. Separately, there were numerous sources reporting that bin Laden was seeking chemical weapons, even nuclear weapons. Prior to the reports of the chemical plant in Sudan, it was not clear from where he would obtain the weapons.

Satellite photography of Shifa revealed a plant like many others in the world, capable of compounding a variety of chemicals both innocent and military. In 1991 and 1992, I had worked with Arms Control Director Ron Lehman to write an international chemical ban with an inspection procedure that could verify compliance. In the process of that negotiation I had literally crawled through chemical plants and learned a lot from chemical engineers. In the international negotiation that followed in 1992, the nations participating had agreed that many chemical plants were capable of making nerve agent one day and paint, fertilizer, or medicine the next. The Chemical Weapons Convention Treaty, therefore, provided for international inspection of "innocent" chemical plants to insure they had not recently been used to make weapons material. The Treaty provided that the international inspectors could take soil samples from inside and outside the plants in order to do trace analysis. Sudan had refused to sign the Treaty.

There were also two other facilities near Shifa. One was a high-walled, heavily secured set of buildings that human sources said was a weapons-related facility. The other was an artillery shell storage site. It was very plausible that chemical weapons precursor compounds were created at Shifa occasionally, and moved to the nearby development site for mixing into lethal agents and insertion into artillery shells, which were then moved to the storage dump down the road.

CIA sought to determine whether the Shifa plant might be spending some of its time making lethal gas for weapons. To do so, CIA sent an agent to Khartoum to collect trace material that would have floated away from the plants in the air or in liquid runoff. It was a risky mission to drive up to the plant and scoop up soil samples, but it was successfully conducted. The samples were then taken to an independent, nongovernmental analysis laboratory with a well-established reputation for reliability. Their tests revealed a chemical substance known as EMPTA.

EMPTA is a compound that had been used as a prime ingredient in

Iraqi nerve gas. It had no other known use, nor had any other nation employed EMPTA to our knowledge for any purpose. What was an Iraqi chemical weapons agent doing in Sudan? UNSCOM and other U.S. government sources had claimed that the Iraqis were working on something at a facility near Shifa. Could Sudan, using bin Laden's money, have hired some Iraqis to make chemical weapons? It seemed chillingly possible. The Khartoum regime was, after all, engaged in a campaign that seemed intended to eradicate the blacks who lived in southern Sudan. Numerous international relief organizations had provided evidence of such outrages as bombing feeding stations. Chemical weapons would allow Khartoum to accelerate the killing and to chase the survivors out of the country. It was also likely that bin Laden's friends in the Khartoum regime might provide the terrorists with some of the chemical weapons production.

In 2001 during questioning conducted by Assistant U.S. Attorney Pat Fitzgerald, al Qaeda operative Jamal al-Fadl matter-of-factly described his role in traveling to Sudan for his terrorist organization. He said that his assignment was to follow the work al Qaeda had under way in Khartoum to develop chemical weapons.

DURING HIS FIRST FOUR YEARS IN SUDAN, bin Laden had kept in the shadows, not overtly confronting the U.S. There were signs in 1995 of his money and support in Bosnia, Chechnya, the Philippines, Egypt, Morocco, and in Europe. Rumors connected him to attacks in New York, Somalia, Saudi Arabia, and Yemen. But they were only rumors. He might know Khalid Sheik Muhammad, who might be the uncle of Ramzi Yousef, who attacked the World Trade Center in 1993 and had tried to attack 747s over the Pacific. Perhaps one of bin Laden's brothers-in-law, Muhammad Jamal Khalifa, moved money to terrorist groups like the bag carrier in the 1950s television show *The Millionaire.* (In January 1995, Khalifa was detained by U.S. Customs at San Francisco International. Jim Reynolds at the Justice Department tried hard, at my request, to find grounds to indict Khalifa in connection with the World Trade Center attack or any other crime. Unfortunately, the Justice Department could not generate an indictment and Khalifa was extradited to Jordan, where he was subsequently released for lack of evidence there too.)

In the summer of 1995, bin Laden had written a public letter to Saudi King Fahd, denouncing the U.S. troop presence. CIA, under White House pressure and with the support of staff in its Counterterrorism Center, began to develop plans for a station dedicated to investigating what they now agreed was a "bin Laden network." Not wanting to risk putting the station in Khartoum, where bin Laden was, they began to develop a proposal for an innovation, a "virtual station." The virtual station would be structured like an overseas office. Physically, it would not even be in CIA headquarters.

Then in the spring of 1996, two chess pieces moved. Bin Laden flew to Afghanistan, closing some of his Khartoum companies and houses. After he left, Jamal al-Fadl, who had been privy to much of the "bin Laden network" based in Sudan, sought U.S. protection. He had been siphoning off funds and feared al Qaeda would kill him. Fadl's interrogation helped the new virtual station discover the size and shape of the network. What they found was widespread and active, with a presence through affiliate groups or sleeper cells in over fifty countries. Ramzi Yousef and the blind sheik had been part of it. Bin Laden was not just its financier, he was its mastermind.

The network also had a name, we learned: the foundation or base, as in the foundation of a building. Usama bin Laden, son of a building contractor, had called his terrorist network by an Arabic word, al Qaeda. It was the first piece, the necessary base for the edifice that would be a global theocracy, the great Caliphate.

The Taliban welcomed bin Laden enthusiastically back to Afghanistan. He had been funding terrorist training camps there while in Sudan. Fighters caught in Chechnya and Bosnia had been taught at these facilities. Now the camps expanded with new recruits from across the Islamic world. Those who did well graduated either to the 55th Brigade, a unit bin Laden created to help the Taliban fight its Afghan opponents, or were dispatched to sleeper cells around the world.

By 1996 and 1997 the CSG was developing plans to snatch bin

Laden from Afghanistan. One plan called for an Afghan snatch team to drive a bound-and-gagged bin Laden to a dirt strip on which a CIA-owned aircraft would briefly land and then head back out of Afghanistan, flying low to evade radar. Although normally reluctant to operate inside Afghanistan, CIA made an exception long enough to inspect the dirt strip to see if it could support the aircraft's landing, turn-around, and takeoff. The unmarked aircraft was flown into position in a nearby country.

The flaw that developed in the snatch was our inability to know when it would occur. If the grab would take place when the opportunity arrived and not at a time of our choosing, the snatch team would have to hold him for almost a day until the aircraft arrived. During that day, bin Laden's men and the Taliban would be hunting for him. The chances of them detecting the aircraft, and perhaps capturing CIA staff, were large.

A variation on the plan was developed. The Afghan snatch team would not just wait for bin Laden to drive by, they would go pick him up at his "farm" at the same time the CIA aircraft was flying into the country. It sounded good. I asked to see photographs and maps.

Tarnak farm looked more like Gunga Din's fort than Dorothy's farm in *The Wizard of Oz*. It certainly wasn't in Kansas. The farm complex was several dozen houses surrounded by a twelve-foot wall. At each corner of the wall there was a machine gun nest. Parked outside were two T-55 tanks. A frontal assault by the Afghan team would probably have resulted in the deaths of the few assets the CIA had in that country. The CSG unanimously decided against an assault. (One of the many urban legends about al Qaeda that emerged after September 11 was that Attorney General Janet Reno had vetoed the operation. Not true. George Tenet and I did, to avoid getting all of our Afghan assets killed for nothing.) Instead, the CIA's Afghans would look for another way to get the leader of al Qaeda.

ALTHOUGH WE FAILED TO SNATCH BIN LADEN, the CIA did succeed in another revenge snatch in 1997. Ever since Mir Amal Kansi had shot Agency employees on the doorstep of the Agency, the CIA had been promising revenge for the victims' families. Within a day of the shooting they had known Kansi's name. Yet he had calmly boarded a flight back to Pakistan, and no one stopped him. No one from CIA was waiting for him when he arrived in Pakistan. Like the much more significant Usama bin Laden, Kansi was the black sheep of a large and wealthy family. Although troubled by what he had done, the Kansis bought protection for Mir Amal from an Afghan warlord.

For four years CIA plotted, trying various schemes to track Kansi precisely and to snatch him. Despite real creativity, none of the plans worked. What was notable about the plans, however, was that in none of them did CIA decide simply to insert a CIA or Defense Department team into the Afghan fort in which Kansi was hiding out. Once again, CIA was reluctant to put its personnel into Afghanistan. After a while, however, Kansi started to assume that CIA had forgotten about him. He began to make trips into Pakistan. People in Pakistan talked. Finally, CIA lured Kansi to a meeting, a supposed business deal about gunrunning. The CSG went over the snatch plan in detail. We agreed that the suspect should be handed over to the Fairfax, Virginia, police for prosecution by the Commonwealth's Attorney. It would be faster than the federal courts. Then we waited for the night of the meeting.

The CIA parking lot was almost empty that weekend. The front door was locked. I went around and entered by a side door with a sleepy guard. Instead of going to the Operations Center, with its War Room flat screens, I went to the Counterterrorism Center's communications room, a darkened closet filled with racks of electronics. There, a small group huddled around a radio console. It was a scene reminiscent of London calling a French underground unit in World War II.

The radio man was instead calling a Chevy Suburban that had pulled up outside a Chinese restaurant and hotel in a Pakistani city not far from the Afghan border. In the Suburban a joint CIA-FBI team was getting ready for the morning call to prayer.

Our source had placed Mir Amal Kansi on the third floor of the hotel. Kansi expected a knock on the door around 4:00 a.m., from a friend who would accompany him to the mosque. We expected something else.

The clock in the radio room rolled passed 4:00 a.m. Pakistani time. The radio remained silent. I looked around in the red-lighted room and noticed George Tenet in a sweat suit chomping a cigar. George had suffered a mild heart attack when we worked together at the White House, thus ending our occasional escapes to walk together to a nearby cigar store. Now, he just chewed on them. His deputy, General John Gordon, hovered by the door. Although Gordon had learned patience commanding a wing of MX missiles, where there never was any real action (thank God), his patience was obviously wearing thin. With tension building in the crowded, overheated room, Tenet could not take it anymore: "Where the shit are they? Ask them where they are, it's 4:15 there."

"Red Rover, Red Rover, come in, over." The radio operator tried to hail the field team.

Nothing.

By 4:30 people were pacing in the corridor outside the radio room. Finally, the radio crackled. "Base, base, this is Red Rover. The package is aloft. Repeat, the package is aloft." Instantly champagne bottles appeared from under seats and were popped amid cheers and embraces. Tenet lit the cigar, looked at me, and said, "Don't tell my wife."

Kansi had answered the knock on the door and suddenly found himself lying facedown on the floor of his small room, hearing not the call to prayer but the Miranda rights statement from the FBI. Within two minutes the Suburban was whipping through the empty city streets to the airport, where a C-12 waited, engines running.

For four years the Agency had tried everything it knew to get one man, one man who had embarrassed them by attacking their very headquarters and killing their own people. Now it had finally partially erased the embarrassment. There was a light ground fog as I left the building. As I drove out the gate onto Route 123, I saw the crosses by the road where they had died. It would be some solace to their families that the killer was now in custody and would probably die on Virginia's death row. George Tenet was calling the families now as I drove home. It had meant a lot to the Agency to get this guy, but it had taken a very long time even when the entire Agency was motivated.

THE KANSI SNATCH made the Agency feel good about itself, four years after he had attacked its headquarters. In addition to Kansi, the CSG was routinely reviewing, arranging, and implementing renditions of terrorists to the United States and elsewhere. Unfortunately, we failed in another attempted snatch, one that might have prevented 9/11. All but one of those directly involved in the World Trade Center attack in 1993 had been brought back to the U.S. The ringleader was Ramzi Yousef, who was linked to another al Qaeda operative, Khalid Sheik Muhammad. In 1996 a New York federal grand jury had indicted Muhammad for supporting that plot from overseas, and for indirect involvement in the plan to attack 747s over the Pacific. The FBI told the CSG that he was the uncle of Yousef, but they portrayed Yousef as the mastermind and Muhammad as merely the bad influence in his life. Still, we wanted Muhammad. Within a year of the indictment, we learned that Khalid Sheik Muhammad was located in Doha, Qatar, where he allegedly worked in the Water Ministry.

Having spent some time in Qatar, I was not eager to allow the local police to try to arrest him. I remembered them as a comedy act. In 1991, Qatari police cars that were escorting my motorcade managed to crash into each other in a city with almost no traffic. I also recalled their duplicity in 1990 over how they had obtained Stinger missiles (they had bought them in Afghanistan, but refused to admit it) and their later attempts to engage in diplomacy with Iran at a time when Tehran was engaged in anti-U.S. operations throughout the region. Given all of that, I wanted to know if we could perform the rendition without the knowledge of the Qatari government. Unfortunately, both the CIA and FBI claimed to have no capability to operate a covert snatch in Qatar. The Defense Department's plans for their version of a snatch, as usual, involved a force more appropriate for conquering the entire nation than for arresting one man.

Our ambassador to Qatar was a professional, and an alumnus of the CSG, Patrick Theros. I asked Theros if it would be possible for him to go to the Chamberlain, the Emir's Minister of Palace Affairs, and obtain the Emir's approval for a snatch, without that word getting to anyone else. He thought it could be done, but gave no guarantee. Nonetheless, with no other option available, the CSG agreed to try an approach in which an FBI arrest team would go in with permission, with a small number of senior Qatari security officials accompanying them to the arrest.

Despite Qatari assurances that only a few senior officials knew about our plan, Khalid Sheik Muhammad learned of it and fled the country ahead of the FBI arrest team's arrival. We were, of course, outraged at Qatari security and assumed the leak came from within the palace. One report said that Khalid Sheik Muhammad had fled the country on a passport provided by the Ministry of Religious Affairs. Unfortunately, the CSG knew much less than the full story. Khalid Sheik Muhammad was not merely a bad influence on his mastermind nephew, it was the uncle who was the terrorist mastermind. Not only did he plan the World Trade Center attack in 1993 and the 747 plot in 1995, Khalid Sheik Muhammad was a close associate of bin Laden and al Qaeda's chief operational leader. Had the CSG been told that, the NSC would have insisted on a CIA or military snatch team, despite their protestation of inability. Had we been told of Khalid Sheik Muhammad's role even after he escaped, we would have insisted on an all-out effort to find him. Instead, the role of this key al Qaeda figure did not become clear to CIA or FBI until after the September 11 attacks.

Other countries also reportedly failed to cooperate in snatches. Adam Garfinkle in the Spring 2002 *National Interest* reported that in 1997 Imad Mugniyah was the subject of a U.S. arrest attempt when he was aboard an aircraft scheduled to land in Saudi Arabia, but the Saudi government waved the aircraft off rather than cooperate with the U.S. in apprehending the Hezbollah leader."

As 1998 DAWNED, al Qaeda grew stronger thanks to a merger with Egyptian Islamic Jihad. The FBI had uncovered the role of Egyptian Sheik Abdul Rahman in plans to commit terrorism in New York in 1993. By 1996, he was sentenced to life in prison in the United States.

His friends, including Usama bin Laden and Egyptian Islamic Jihad leader Ayman Zawahiri, had planned revenge and plotted to gain his release. In 1997, they struck tourists at Luxor, Egypt, killing sixty-two. Egyptian police found bodies slit open, stuffed with leaflets demanding the release of the blind sheik. Faced with the collapse of the tourism industry, Egypt cracked down against the jihadists with even greater ferocity than it had employed after the attempt on President Mubarak's life in Ethiopia.

Weakened, Egyptian Islamic Jihad grew closer to bin Laden. The blind sheik's son attached himself to bin Laden and promised revenge on the United States. In February 1998, EIJ and al Qaeda were among several groups that jointly issued a declaration of war against Egypt, the United States, and other governments. It did not come as a shock to us. We had considered ourselves at war with al Qaeda even before we knew its name or its reach. We had been working with friendly governments for at least three years to identify and destroy sleeper cells in Europe, Africa, and the Middle East. We had arranged snatches of many al Qaeda operatives and had been planning to snatch bin Laden himself. In the spring of 1998, bin Laden was indicted by Manhattan U.S. Attorney Mary Jo White's federal grand jury. The CSG wanted to add bin Laden to our list of snatched terrorists. In early 1998, we wanted to go on the offensive against al Qaeda. We also wanted to begin a major program to protect the homeland against terrorism, whether from al Qaeda or other groups. The events of 1998 would make it easier to persuade the Congress and the media that we needed to do both.

Chapter 7

Beginning Homeland Protection

When the Situation Room called me on a Sunday night in 1995 with the word that something had happened in Tokyo, the first reports had indicated chemical weapons. First reports are usually wrong, but I drove in to the Situation Room just in case. The media accounts were pretty convincing that some chemical weapon had been released by somebody. My calls to CIA, FBI, and State told me nothing more than CNN had. So I called the Department of Health and Human Services.

I had earlier formed an interagency working group on terrorism and weapons of mass destruction. Two people had stood out as can-do activists who were as worried as I was at the possibility of Ramzi Yousef's mysterious organization getting its hands on a chemical weapon or a nuclear device. One was Lisa Gordon-Hagerty at the Department of Energy. She had linked up the scientists at the department's nuclear labs with the commandos of the Joint Special Operations Command and was conducting field exercises on what you do when you have to get a nuclear bomb away from terrorists.

The other impressive member of the group was Frank Young at the Public Health Service of HHS. The Public Health Service is a bizarre civilian-military hybrid. Part of HHS, the officers of the Public Health Service wear Navy uniforms and use Navy ranks. So Frank was not just a doctor, he was also an admiral. In his spare time, he was a Protestant minister. Frank had created a nationwide network of chemical and biological weapons experts and medical personnel to investigate whether any unusual medical reports that might come in from time to time were actually reflecting covert terrorist use of chemical or biological weapons.

On that Sunday night in March 1995, I called Frank from the Situation Room. "Admiral, Doctor, Reverend, Frank," I began. "Something funny going on in Tokyo."

"From the press reports it sounds like a nerve agent gas was released." Frank replied. "Not the kind of thing that the Japanese military has. If it's all right, I am putting together a team to fly out there as soon as possible and help the Japanese figure it out. I'm also calling my Japanese counterparts. It's Monday there now."

"Sounds good, Frank. I will tell State to get Embassy Tokyo to help your team. See what you can find out and we will have a CSG in the morning." That Monday morning was the first time Health and Human Services had ever attended a meeting of the core Counterterrorism Security Group in the Situation Room.

Frank Young, sitting at the opposite end of the table from the chair, in his admiral's uniform, had a full report ready: "The agent employed was sarin nerve gas, but apparently not at full military dose. The group responsible was a religious cult known as the Aum Shinrikyo."

By now I had enough experience with CIA and FBI to doubt that they would ever have even heard of the Aum. I was not disappointed. Except for press reports from the previous twelve hours, they had nothing in their files on the Aum. I had come to respect the new FBI representative on the CSG, John O'Neill. He had worked closely with me to coordinate the previous month's arrest of Ramzi Yousef. That arrest occurred during O'Neill's first week on the job, after arriving in Washington from an organized crime assignment in Chicago. He had worked straight through for days without going home and he had thought of every detail. O'Neill was obviously very bright and activist, but also playful. Like me, he was from a working-class background and he tended to straight talk that some found abrasive.

I decided to push a little to see how he'd respond. "How can you be so sure there are no Aum here, John, just because you don't have an FBI file on them? Did you look them up in the Manhattan phone book to see if they're there?"

"You serious?" O'Neill asked, not sure whether I was being funny. When I assured him that I meant it, he directed his deputy to leave the conference room and call FBI New York. A while later the FBI agent returned to the room and handed O'Neill a note.

O'Neill glanced at it and said, "Fuck. They're in the phone book, on East 48th Street at Fifth."

Everyone in that CSG meeting had the same thought at the same moment: sarin in the New York City subway. O'Neill called for backup. "We need some chemical weapons decon guys up there quick. Some guys who can detect and diagnose chemicals. The Army."

The Pentagon representatives at the meeting were not keen on the idea of olive green Army trucks rumbling through Midtown, disgorging troops in space suits while the lunch crowd at Rockefeller Center watched in growing panic. Besides, the nearest chemical unit was in Maryland, four hours down Interstate 95. The Pentagon guys also raised the same mantra in Latin that Defense Department representatives chanted whenever asked to do something in the United States, *posse comitatus.* The phrase refers to an 1876 law, passed at the end of Reconstruction, that prohibited federal military authorities from exercising civilian police powers inside the United States (as they had in the occupied Confederacy from 1865 to 1876). The law contains a clause allowing the President to waive it in an emergency. I had drafted a fill-in-the-blanks waiver in my desk drawer, unsigned.

I did not have to deploy the *posse comitatus* waiver. O'Neill persuaded the Pentagon to stage the unit to a National Guard armory in Manhattan, while the U.S. Attorney tried to develop enough of a story to get a search warrant. In the meantime, a "fire marshal" conducted a surprise inspection of the building. He found that the Aum were moving out, carrying boxes into a rental van. An FBI surveillance car followed the van out onto Fifth Avenue for several blocks, but then lost the truck in Midtown traffic. When that news got to us in the Situation Room, it looked like O'Neill's veins were going to pop: chemical weapons lost in Manhattan, on his watch. I thought I should go see the National Security Advisor.

While Tony Lake and I were contemplating the mechanics of evacuating large portions of New York, O'Neill called. They had the van. They had a warrant. They had found nothing but boxes of books. The office on 48th Street was clean.

We later learned that the Aum had made not only sarin nerve gas, but also an anthrax weapon. They had sprayed their homemade anthrax at a U.S. military facility in Japan, but they had the spore size wrong and the attack failed to sicken anyone. It also failed to be noticed.

I had insisted that the Presidential Decision Directive on terrorism issued in 1995 address the possibility of terrorists getting their hands on chemical, biological, or nuclear materials. It was now the President's policy that there was no higher priority than the prevention of such acquisition, or if terrorists were actually found to have such weapons, no greater priority than removing that capability. The policy also called for planning on how to handle a situation in which such weapons were used.

In 1996, however, we had no capability to deal with a chemical or biological weapon being used in the United States. The old Cold War–era Civil Defense program had withered and died even before the Cold War itself had ended. Senators Sam Nunn, Dick Lugar, and Pete Domenici had been focusing on the disposition of Soviet nuclear, chemical, and biological weapons, now that the Soviet Union had dissolved. The three senators had sponsored money to account for, secure, and destroy the weapons. They had sought to fund alternative employment for the Soviet weapons scientists. Finally, they put aside a small amount of federal dollars to begin to train emergency responders in big U.S. cities to deal with such weapons, just in case some fell into the wrong hands and ended up here.

The three senators' program, my own interest, and Bill Clinton's reading habits came together to begin to create some domestic preparedness capability.

My interest stemmed from experiences in the Cold War and the Gulf War. In the last year of the Cold War, as an Assistant Secretary of State, I was visited by a State Department Intelligence Bureau officer carrying a locked case, the kind approved by CIA for carrying the most sensitive intelligence documents. I did not know what I was about to read, only that I was to be one of five people in the State Department allowed to read it. Inside the bag was the debriefing of a senior Soviet official who had defected to the British. He told about something that the U.S. intelligence community had believed did not exist, a massive Soviet program to develop and deploy biological weapons.

The Soviet Union, the United States, and other nations had signed a treaty outlawing biological weapons in 1973. We had proceeded to destroy ours. The Soviet Union had claimed to have done the same. They had lied. Not only had they not destroyed their bioweapons program, they had expanded it and developed weapons with truly horrific capability. Their labs had worked on Marburg and Ebola, strains that made the victim bleed to death from every orifice and organ. They had perfected bombs, artillery shells, and other weapons to disperse such agents as anthrax, botulinum, smallpox, and antibiotic-resistant strains of the plague. Then they had actually filled weapons with these agents and stockpiled them. Over 100,000 Soviets were employed in the secret program at facilities throughout the Soviet Union. Moreover, the friendly senior Soviet officials with whom we were negotiating arms control treaties had known all about the illegal program and the efforts to keep it secret from us.

It was not the kind of news that any of us had wanted to hear, but it was definitely not what Secretary of State Jim Baker needed. Baker had told the Pentagon, the Congress, and the President that we could safely sign several major arms control agreements with the Soviets. He had said it was highly unlikely that these Soviet leaders would risk getting caught violating an international arms control agreement and, moreover, if they did, U.S. intelligence would catch a violation using "national technical means." Now he was faced with the reality that the same Soviets had risked getting caught in a big violation and that U.S. "national technical means" had failed to find a major nationwide program. Were it not for one senior Soviet scientist's faith in British intelligence, we would not have known about an enormous biological weapons threat.

Baker's first reaction had been to keep the knowledge about the Soviet program restricted, until he could get the Soviet leadership to admit it existed and promise to destroy the program in front of U.S. observers. Unfortunately, the Soviets were not quite so ready to cooperate when confronted. They claimed that the U.S. must have such a program too. They wanted to inspect our facilities. Discussions went on for some time until the Soviets did agree to destroy everything and permit limited reciprocal "visits," but I was never satisfied that the Soviets had given us the two things we really needed: first, a complete list of everything they had developed (and destroyed), and second, the antidotes they had developed to whatever new strains of disease had festered up in their pots.

Two years later, when the First Gulf War was looming after the Iraqi invasion of Kuwait, I had been asked to develop our policy for dealing with Iraqi chemical and other "special" weapons. The CIA knew Iraq had chemical weapons then; they had used them by the ton on the Iranians. Iraq was one of two dozen nations that the U.S. government said had nuclear, chemical, and/or biological weapons.

With my British counterparts in a joint U.K.-U.S. working group in the fall of 1990, we tried to assess how many chemical-protective suits and gas masks we needed for our troops, and for the several hundred thousand other allied troops from over thirty countries, not to mention the civilians in the region, that could be hit by Iraqi Scud missiles. It was a hopeless task. There were probably not enough protective suits in the world to cover the population at risk. We agreed to recommend that "nonessential" British and American civilians fly home. My Deputy, Bill Rope, doggedly tried to steal masks from stateside military units to send to U.S. embassies' staffs. Years before, Israel had equipped its entire population with gas masks and had hundreds of thousands of special medicine kits in the hands of its citizens. We weren't even prepared to do that for our armed forces.

The policy on inoculating U.S. and U.K. front-line troops was also problematic. There was no agreement about which diseases troops should be vaccinated against, and there were concerns about the side effects of some medicines. I asked to be briefed by the Army's experts from Fort Dietrich on the state of our vaccination supply. A colonel, who was also a medical doctor, came to the State Department with his team of experts.

"Well, Colonel, let's start with anthrax. What is the size of our supply of vaccines?"

"We have a horse," he replied with evident embarrassment. Noting my puzzlement, he continued. "We have gradually shot this poor horse up with a lot of anthrax and she is now totally immune. We could use her blood to make tens of thousands of shots."

There was only one response I thought possible. "We need you to get some more horses, Colonel."

Worse than its absence of infected horses, our Army had no modern chem-bio detection vehicles and so had borrowed some Fox armored vehicles from the German Bundeswehr for that purpose. The Foxes had the unfortunate habit of triggering false alarms with some regularity, to the point where troops were no longer responding by jumping into their heavy, sweaty, uncomfortable protective gear. The fact was we could not assemble a decent defensive capability in time for the war.

We therefore turned to deterrence and retaliation. What would we do if Iraq used chemical or biological weapons? We had one report that they were planning to scare us with a simulated nuclear weapon. The alleged plan was to set off several truckloads of high explosives, mixed with radiological material. The U.S. would detect both the major explosion and then the radioactivity and assume Iraq had just tested a nuclear weapon. That according to the reported Iraqi plan, was supposed to deter us from invading.

But could we deter Iraq? If we did not, there were few decent options for an American response. We had no biological weapons, our own chemical weapons left over from the 1960s and 1970s were immobile, leaky, and a risk to anyone who went near them. Using nuclear weapons seemed out of the question and, in any event, what would we use them on? Iraqis who had been forced to fight for Saddam Hussein?

We took the issue to the "inner cabinet" of Principals chaired by Brent Scowcroft. Seated around Scowcroft's coffee table on a couch and in wing-back chairs were Defense Secretary Dick Cheney, Chairman of the Joint Chiefs Colin Powell, and a few others. It was one of those problems Principals hate, one with no solution. Scowcroft, cracking open some peanuts, turned to Cheney. "Mr. Secretary, what would you recommend?"

Cheney then looked at Powell in a way that said they had talked and disagreed. "Go on, Colin, say what you think," Cheney urged.

Powell shrugged and, with a sheepish look on his face, said, "I just think chemical weapons are goofy."

Amused, Scowcroft, a retired Air Force general, looked at Powell, "Goofy? Is that some Army terminology?"

Growing more serious, Powell explained. "Chemical weapons will just slow us down a little. We will batten up the tanks and drive through. I don't think Saddam will use biological weapons because they are not really suited for the battlefield. They take too long. Besides all of this shit can literally blow back on you. And nuclear, I don't think he has nuclear."

Cheney jumped in, now agreeing with Powell. "Besides, we're already planning to throw the kitchen sink at them. There is not a lot more we could do, except give priority to taking out ammunition piles that may have chem or bio." He paused. "What we should do is just tell Saddam that if he uses any of this stuff, we'll go to Baghdad and hang him."

In the end, Secretary Baker carried a letter from President Bush to Iraqi Foreign Minister Tariq Aziz at a meeting in Switzerland. There has been some controversy about the exact wording of the U.S. threat in that letter. Whatever it said, Tariq Aziz handed it back after reading it. He later noted that if he had given Saddam anything that said that, Saddam would have had him shot. As far as we know, Saddam did not use chemical, biological, or nuclear weapons in the First Gulf War.

These experiences led me to worry greatly about the possibility of terrorists getting their hands on such weapons. President Clinton's concern about the same issue, however, had less to do with me than with his own reading. Clinton's reading habits had always amazed me. He was an eclectic reader, who apparently stayed up very late almost every night devouring a book. After the Tokyo attack, he began reading fictional accounts like *Rainbow Six* and *The Cobra Event* in which terrorists wield chemical and biological weapons. Some books he sent to us for our comments. Some he discussed directly with experts outside the government. The books just reinforced what he had already decided: we needed to do more to prevent terrorists from getting their hands on these weapons and we needed to be ready if they did.

Despite the 1995 Presidential Decision Directive on the subject, only the Defense Department was taking the chem-bio threat seriously, and the Pentagon's concern seemed limited to the safety of their troops from such weapons. No one took responsibility for the safety of all the other Americans who might be hit with chemical or biological, or even nuclear, weapons. The other departments were not taking my hints that they should put some serious money in their budgets for this purpose.

Sandy Berger had moved up from Deputy to become the National Security Advisor in 1997. I wanted him to have the President insert funds for the programs into what was, after all, called the President's Budget Request to Congress. Berger advised against it. "If the departments don't want the money, they'll just go around our backs to the Congress and tell them to shift the funds back to the departments' own pet rocks." It was a disappointingly realistic assessment of White House power. "What you have to do, Dick, is scare the shit out of the Cabinet members the way you have scared me with this stuff. Make them want to do something about it. Make it their idea."

That seemed like an invitation. "You assemble them. I'll scare them," I responded.

They assembled in the oddly prim and proper Blair House, a series of connected townhouses opposite the Executive Office Building on Pennsylvania Avenue. Blair House is owned by the Protocol Office of the State Department and is meant to house visiting heads of state, not to host Cabinet meetings. Nonetheless, in March 1998 the Cabinet members and other senior officials showed up, from State, Defense, CIA, Justice, FBI, Health and Human Services, FEMA, Energy, OMB, and other White House offices. Attendance was mandatory. Berger had told everyone that the President wanted them there, but he had never said the President would join them. When they showed up, Berger made me the chairman of the meeting, to the surprise of Cabinet members who might have thought that it would be the President.

It was to be a "tabletop exercise," a simulation of a Cabinet meeting during which certain events would unfold.

They assembled around a large U-shaped series of tables in a ballroom. At the open end of the table was a large screen on which we projected "facts" as the events began to happen. I stood in the middle of the U with a cordless microphone, feeling like the host of a daytime television talk show. Within the CSG, we held exercises like this for years to smoke out operational difficulties, coordination problems, and practical shortcomings. The Cabinet had never done one before.

We began with a report on the big screen of a spreading infection in the Soutwest. It could be a natural outbreak, which sometimes happened in New Mexico (what one scientist called the "land of the flea and the home of the plague"). Then another report: the infected patients were diagnosed with Marburg or Ebola, which was incurable and contagious. I walked over to Secretary Donna Shalala of Health and Human Services and asked, "This would seem to be your problem. What are you going to do? Will you quarantine the area? Do you have that authority? Who goes in to help?"

While those questions hung in the air, I moved in front of Attorney General Reno. She had never cared what anyone's rank was and had taken to calling me directly on my private line whenever she had a problem or idea that she thought was in my portfolio. I asked her "Let's say for the sake of argument that we can quarantine the area. How can we stop people who want to leave the quarantine zone? Do you order them to be shot if they resist?" No Cabinet member knew the answer. While they had views, which differed, it was clear that there was no plan.

The second scenario described a chemical weapon released in a U.S. city. The group dealt better with that, but still realized that most cities had neither the training nor the equipment to deal with such an event.

The third scenario hit close to home, literally. In that scenario a terrorist group called the FBI and announced that it had a nuclear weapon in Washington. The report went on to state that the joint Energy-Defense search team, acting on a tip from the Coast Guard, located the weapon on a cabin cruiser tied up in a yacht club less than two miles from the White House. The blast radius would take out most of downtown Washington. "FBI, do you hit the boat with a SWAT team?" I asked. They wanted to, but were then told that only the Defense Department commando team was trained in what to do with a nuclear weapon and that team was not stationed in Washington. "Do we wait?" I then asked. We agreed to wait and to call for the commando unit. Then the slide on the screen asked the question that provoked the most debate: "Do we tell the citizens of Washington?" If we told the citizens to evacuate, the terrorists might immediately explode the weapon. If we did not tell them and the weapon went off two hours later, people would needlessly die.

In the evolving scenario, the special Army commandos with nuclear weapons training arrived and set up near the boat. Then, suddenly, the commandos attacked the terrorists and soon thereafter shot the nuclear weapon to disable it. "Wasn't there some risk in that?" I asked, "What if the shot had caused the bomb to go off?" The Pentagon participants were quick to reassure everyone that no special Army commando unit would ever disobey orders in that way. "Ah, but they didn't," I contended. "We ordered them to deploy near the boat. When we did that, we gave them implicit authority to act if they saw things happening that led them to believe that the terrorists were going to detonate the weapon. And when they got on the boat and saw a timer clicking down, they had the implicit authority to take whatever action they judged best to stop it from going off. If they believe that they do not have time to ask for permission in order to save several hundred thousand lives, shouldn't they act?" Another debate ensued. I asked "If the bomb did go off, FEMA, what would you guys do? Do you have units trained in recovery operations in radioactive environments?"

At the end of the half day, a collection of black Cadillacs fanned out from Blair House carrying appropriately frightened senior officials back to their offices. Most were calling ahead to their headquarters to convene meetings. They knew now these programs would need more money, but most of all they knew their departments would need some plans.

In a few weeks it was time for more, this time with the President attending in the White House Cabinet Room. When the Cabinet members arrived, they found their natural places at the table taken by strangers. Instead, the name tags for the Cabinet were in the row of seats along the wall seats that were typically reserved for their staff, the people known as "back benchers." The strangers at the table had been assembled, at my request, by Admiral Frank Young, who had just retired from the Public Health Service. They included a Nobel Prize–winning biochemist, several other scientists and researchers on antidotes for biological weapons, and the New York City emergency services director. Together they had drafted a budget proposal for an aggressive plan for responding to a biological weapons attack. They briefed the President. Their plan would do in one year what I hoped to fund over five years. Clinton looked over to the OMB officials attending. "I think we really have to do this stuff. Let's see if we can find the money."

It had become pretty clear to Sandy Berger that terrorism and domestic preparedness were major problems, presidential priorities, and should be among the very few growing budgets in Washington. These issues could not continue to be handled by only one of the dozen Special Assistants to the President who made up the senior level of the NSC Staff. Nor could we continue to point to presidential speeches as official guidance to the departments and agencies. Berger thought we needed a "terrorism czar," and he wanted it to be me. We already had one job in Washington with the unfortunate nickname of "czar," the head of the White House Office of National Drug Control Policy. With a title that long, it was little wonder the press called him "the Drug Czar." The few people who had held that job had not acquitted themselves well. In fact, I had urged that there be a personnel switch in 1996 and argued that Army General Barry McCaffrey should be given the job. By 1998 McCaffrey was doing better than anyone had before, but there were still huge coordination and bureaucratic rivalry problems in the U.S. counter-narcotics program. I did not want to repeat that in counterterrorism and feared that the departments would see a czar as a challenge to their authority.

Nonetheless, Berger floated the idea of a "National Coordinator" for counterterrorism and proposed that we codify it with a new Presidential Decision Directive. We did need new, more detailed Presidential policy guidance. I drafted three new directives and circulated them under the tentative draft titles of PDD-X, Y, and Z.

Z updated our Continuity of Government program, which had been allowed to fall apart when the threat of a Soviet nuclear attack had gone away. If terrorists could attack Washington, particularly with weapons of mass destruction, we needed to have a robust system of command and control, with plans to devolve authority and capabilities to officials outside Washington.

Y addressed something with the clumsy name of "critical infrastructure protection and cyber security." After the Oklahoma City bombing, the President had asked the Attorney General and her Deputy, Jamie Gorelick, to conduct a quick review of the vulnerabilities of key domestic facilities. One of their conclusions surprised us: the nation was increasingly dependent on networked computers that were vulnerable to nonexplosive attack—hacking. To address that weakness, the President had appointed a large Presidential Commission on Critical Infrastructure Protection under former Air Force General Tom Marsh. The Commission had come back with a meticulously researched and lengthy report that could be boiled down to one sentence: all over the United States we have begun to rely upon vulnerable computer networks to run transportation, banking, power systems, and other "critical infrastructures." In classified documents accompanying the report, the commissioners pointed out that the U.S. intelligence and military communities could do some real damage if we faced a foe as dependent upon computers as we were. If the U.S. could do it to others, others could do it to us. PDD-Y created a program to address this new problem.

X was the overall policy document. Although most of the text detailed policies on counterterrorism, X also set up an overall management structure. There would be ten components to the U.S. policy and programs for counterterrorism and security. For each program, there would be clarity about responsibility, which department or agencies were in charge. The CSG would officially become not just a crisis response committee, but a policy formulation body with a budget and programmatic role. Moreover, the CSG would have to oversee how the ten programs were run, the same way that a congressional committee had oversight of an Administration program. The ten programs were:

1. *Apprehension, Extradition or Rendition, and Prosecution of Terrorists.* Although we did not see terrorism as primarily a law enforcement issue, there was a police component to countering terrorism. This program involved finding individual terrorists, wherever they were, and bringing them before U.S. courts. The lead was given to the Justice Department and its component, the FBI.
2. *Disruption of Terrorist Groups.* This program called for destruction of terrorist groups by means other than those used by law enforcement. The lead was given to CIA.
3. *International Cooperation against Terrorists.* This was a program of persuading other countries to fight terrorism and giving those who needed it the training and other means to do so. The lead was given to the State Department.
4. *Preventing Terrorists from Acquiring Weapons of Mass Destruction.* In this program, plans and capabilities would be developed to detect and destroy any effort by a terrorist group to develop or procure chemical, biological, or nuclear weapons. The lead was shared by CIA and Defense.
5. *Consequence Management of Terrorist Attacks.* It was in program five that all of the WMD preparedness activities were contained. The lead was shared by Health and Human Services and FEMA, with significant roles for Defense and Justice.
6. *Transportation Security.* Designed to implement the recommendations of the Gore Commission on Aviation Safety and Security, program six focused on preventing terrorism involving aircraft. The lead was assigned to the Department of Transportation.
7. *Protection of Critical Infrastructure and Cyber Systems.* To implement the Marsh Commission on critical infrastructure protection, this program was elaborated in detail in PDD-Y. The lead was shared by Justice (FBI) and, because so many of

the computer networks were owned and operated by the private sector, by Commerce. DOD was also given a major role.

8. *Continuity of Government.* This program was designed to insure that there be both a President and a functioning Federal government, even after an attempt to decapitate the U.S. government. It was detailed in the highly classified PDD-Z.
9. *Countering the Foreign Terrorist Threat in the U.S.* Although FBI officially believed that there were no sleeper cells in the U.S. we created a program to prevent such cells and find them if they existed. Justice (FBI) was given the lead, with roles for Immigration and Treasury.
10. *Protection of Americans Overseas.* Terrorists had attacked a U.S. military base overseas and had tried to attack civilians, including at our embassies. This program created missions of Force Protection, Diplomatic Security, and overall concern for the safety and welfare of Americans abroad. It was shared between DOD and the State Department.

To coordinate these efforts, there would be four committees made up of senior and midlevel managers from the departments. The Counterterrorism Security Group would continue, running programs 1–3, 6, 9, and 10. A new Critical Infrastructure Coordination Group would run program 7. A Weapons of Mass Destruction and Preparedness Group would run programs 4 and 5. The existing Continuity of Government Interagency Group would run program 8.

A new position, a "National Coordinator," was created to chair all four committees. The four committees would report to the Principals Committee. The National Coordinator would also serve as a member of the Cabinet-level Principals Committee, and would have two NSC Staff Senior Directors reporting to him, along with other NSC Staff. Predictably, most departments and agencies saw it as a White House power grab. No one, however, had a better idea. No agency wanted to see one department given all of this responsibility. In 1997 there was no support for creating a new agency because of the disruptiveness of such a move, which would shift everyone's focus from terrorists outside the government to bureaucrats within.

PDD-X went ahead, but with clear limits on the power of the National Coordinator inserted by various agencies and departments. Unlike the Drug Czar, who had a budget of several hundred million dollars, the National Coordinator would not have direct control of any funds. He could only recommend budgets to the President. The Drug Czar had several hundred staff; the National Coordinator would have twelve. Finally, just to make it clear that the National Coordinator was just a White House staff job, the directive contained language noting that he could not order law enforcement agents, troops, or spies to do anything, only their agencies could. Some czar. On balance, however, it was a slight improvement to have a National Coordinator for Security, Infrastructure Protection, and Counterterrorism. With a title that long, however, it quickly became "Terrorism Czar" to the media. It was clearly an improvement to have ten programs with clear accountability and responsibility focused in the departments and agencies, but the notion that there was a Terrorism Czar was misleading. In fact, what the departments had insisted on and the White House had acquiesced to was that there would not be a czar with a staff, budget, or operational decision making. I now had the appearance of responsibility for counterterrorism, but none of the tools or authority to get the job done.

With everyone satisfied, X, Y, and Z went to the President and became PDD-62, PDD-63, and after a few weeks, PDD-67. The President announced them in his commencement address to the Naval Academy in June 1998. The title of PDD-62 was "Counterterrorism and Protection of the Homeland," in recognition that the threat was not just overseas. Later, others would claim they began the focus on protecting the homeland. Clinton's directive began, "Because of our military superiority, potential enemies, be they nations or terrorist groups . . . are increasingly likely to attack us in unconventional ways . . . to exploit vulnerabilities . . . against civilians."

PDD-62 had come at that point in the year, June, when departments begin to prepare their proposed programs for the White House budget review process that culminates at the end of the year in presidential decisions. Those decisions, announced in January or February, then begin a second journey of eight or nine months through the Congress. It is a bit like two pregnancies in a row, lasting sixteen months, with all the potential for miscarriage.

If PDD-62 had given me anything, it was a further invitation to get funding for counterterrorism and security programs. I set to work. By January, the President was set to ask the Congress for $10 billion for counterterrorism, security, weapons of mass destruction preparedness, and infrastructure protection. Before the overall federal budget went to the Congress, however, the White House decided to have a week-long series of "Theme Days." On each day, the President would go to a location associated with one of his budget priorities and give a speech outlining how the new budget supported the priority. The week began and the first event was held. The White House Communications staff called and informed us that we would have the third day for "all that counterterrorism stuff." We had about thirty-six hours to find a venue, get an audience, move in what the Communications people called "show-and-tells," and draft a speech. This kind of unreasonable demand seemed normal in the Clinton White House. Because the White House staff always rose to these challenges and produced good events, the last-minute style lasted throughout Clinton's eight years.

We called the National Academy of Sciences, which was four blocks from the White House, had an auditorium, and could easily assemble scientists to fill it. The theme would be using science and technology to increase our security. We ordered a giant banner that said that, to hang behind the President. Our office staff then set to calling people inside and outside the government who had worked on the initiatives for counterterrorism, homeland protection, weapons of mass destruction preparedness, and cyber security. They were invited to the speech and invited to set up a display in the Academy. I specifically asked the Arlington, Virginia, Fire Department to bring a new prototype Mass Decontamination Vehicle, a truck that could be used to wash down hundreds of people who had been exposed to chemical weapons. My view was that every major city should be given at least one such MDV, so I wrote that announcement into the draft of the President's speech. Attorney General Reno took it out, arguing that cities should decide for themselves what to do with federal assistance for domestic preparedness against weapons of mass destruction. That exchange reflected a struggle over priorities that continues today, causing a waste of billions of dollars of homeland security funds, as localities buy things they do not need and ignore necessary procurement.

Reno and I had disagreed before about how to disburse money to the cities to prepare them for chemical, biological, or radiological disaster. She was concerned that we satisfy the "stakeholders," which I learned meant not people with backyard grills, but the local authorities. I was concerned that the local authorities would not know what to buy or would justify some purchase that had little to do with chem-bio defense. Moreover, I was concerned that we develop metropolitan-area plans incorporating more than just the core cities. Arlington, for example, had the first MDV and parked it three miles from the White House. Should we ignore that and buy another one for Washington, D.C. before Cleveland got its first MDV? I wanted to use the promise of federal money as a way of coercing cities and suburbs into cooperating in the development of unified disaster plans, as we had with the Metropolitan Medical Strike Teams of doctors and medical staffs. Reno, a former Dade County prosecutor, would not budge. The money was already going into her Department's budget, so she didn't have to budge.

When our Theme Day dawned, I went to the Oval Office to attempt to do a "pre-brief." For every public event on the President's schedule, there was a preceding ten-minute slot called a pre-brief in which a member of the staff would explain to the President what the event was about and what he should do at it. Although it was abundantly clear that Clinton did not need, and in any event would not accept, pre-briefs, the schedule continued to carry them. One of two things happened during the assigned time slots. Either you were left sitting outside the Oval Office waiting, or you were invited in and the President would discuss with you something other than the upcoming event. On our Theme Day it was the latter. I feared he would discuss the Impeachment, which was dominating the media and Washington chatter.

Instead, the President chose to discuss the problems facing his cousin, a woman who administered public housing in Arkansas. We continued to discuss that topic as we walked to the limousine and drove through Foggy Bottom with sirens wailing. I sat next to him with a notebook filled with PowerPoint slides and backup material to answer any conceivable question about the $10 billion budget proposal. As the motorcade drove into the basement garage of the Academy, the President acknowledged my apparent concern that we talk about the topic at hand. His mood changed from the affable Arkansas country boy to the analytical President, the duality that both charmed and frightened the White House staff close to the President.

"I read the speech, you know," he said to calm any concern I might have had that he thought this was health care theme day. "The way I see this whole problem, it's like arrows and shields . . ."

"Huh?" I asked as we sat in the car and Secret Service agents stood waiting to open the doors.

"Yeah, you know, like some guy invents the bow and arrow and he's ahead for a while until some guy invents the shield that catches all the arrows. Guy puts a wall around the town and the enemy invents the catapult to get over the wall. Offense, defense, action, reaction. Now we got new offensive weapons facing us and we need new defensive ones. Am I right?"

I acknowledged that was one way to look at the problem and we went into the Academy where a full auditorium was awaiting us. As we did, my pager beeped and carried a message: "DC police are towing away the Arlington MVD." My best show-and-tell had parked in an area that Secret Service decided to have cleared. There was never enough time to get these events done flawlessly.

Sitting in the front row of the auditorium, I noticed that Clinton seemed to be rewriting the speech during the long introductory remarks. When he spoke, however, he used the text we had given him and I followed along with my copy. Then my text ended—and the President did not. He stepped out from behind the podium and leaned on it and smiled at me. My stomach dropped because we had seen him do this before and knew what it meant: he was about to wing it, to ad-lib in a way that would either get us all in trouble or be the best part of the speech, or both.

"What we are seeing here, as any military person in the audience can tell you, goes back to the dawn of time . . . an offensive weapon is developed and it takes time to develop the defense . . ." He talked of bows, arrows, castles, moats. Then he noted how things were different, "because of the speed with which change is occurring" and technology is evolving. New offensive technologies were being developed and defenses were not yet available. The President said he had struggled to alert the nation to the dangers of terrorism without frightening people into believing that anything they saw in a new action movie might happen the next day. We were meeting terrorism "in ways I can and in ways I cannot discuss," but we needed new defensive capabilities and only scientists and engineers like those assembled could create those protections. The President appealed to the audience to use the funds he sought to get our best scientific minds to close the gap between the introduction of the new weapons of terror and the creation of new defenses.

The room erupted in applause. Clinton plunged into the audience and shook hands. When he got to me, he grabbed me and whispered in my ear, "You liked that ending, didn't you?"

He had identified a new problem and was ramming through a major initiative to deal with it, even at a time of tight federal budgets. From having had no domestic capability to deal with the effects of terrorism and weapons of mass destruction, we were funding training and equipment for public health departments, hospitals, fire departments, and emergency services units. We were buying specialized medicines and vaccines, stockpiling them secretly around the country, and arranging for on-call mass production of more. There would be research and development of new detection, diagnostic, and decontamination technologies, along with new pharmaceuticals.

There would also be even more funds for many departments to address terrorism. New agencies would be created and funded to protect the nation's cyber networks. After the speech, Attorney General Reno, Health and Human Services Secretary Donna Shalala, and I briefed the White House press corps on all of the initiatives. I knew we had made the conceptual breakthrough when Shalala began by saying, "HHS is now a key part in the fight against terrorism." Shalala would later join me and Secretary of Defense Bill Cohen on one of a five-part series of shows on *Nightline,* entitled *BioWar,* focusing on the need for homeland protection against terrorists with weapons of mass destruction.

Throughout the country exercises were held, both tabletops involving simulations in a room, and field exercises with units actually deploying. In one field exercise, hundreds of FBI, Energy, and Defense Department personnel quickly set up a temporary camp outside Norfolk when simulated intelligence reports indicated that a terrorist cell would infiltrate a nuclear weapon into the headquarters of the Navy's fleet. The CSG members went to the exercise and played our real roles, as we had done so many times in tabletops in Washington. In a field exercise, however, counterterrorism action units actually assault targets. In the Norfolk exercise, Navy SEALs hit a boat playing the terrorist mother ship, while FBI's Hostage Rescue Team crashed into a house in which the sleeper cell was waiting. A special nuclear bomb squad moved in to defuse the weapon, while staff from several agencies pretended to be reporters and peppered officials with tough questions at a simulated press conference.

As part of the Annapolis announcements, I had become the National Coordinator and began emerging from the shadows of national security and intelligence to meet with the media and brief members of Congress. As I feared, having the world's press running profiles of the new American Terrorism Czar resulted in the kind of attention I did not want. Walking into my office one morning in 1999, I sensed something was wrong. It was the way that the normally cheery Coast Guard Chief Jack Robinson greeted me. It was the look that my assistant of over ten years, Beverly Roundtree, gave me as I walked by her desk. I no sooner sat down in front of my computer than Lisa Gordon-Hagerty walked in with that "this is really serious shit" expression on her face.

"Have you read the cable?" Lisa asked. I had no idea what she was talking about. She showed me. An Arab leader had called our consul general the night before, saying he had urgent and important information to share, the consul should drive over immediately. When he did, the Arab leader gave him an "intelligence report" that had a long, detailed account. The bottom line of the report was that Usama bin Laden had put out a contract on the American Terrorism Czar, Dick Clarke. I was to be killed in Washington.

"Well, that's an interesting way to start the day," I joked, but Lisa did not see anything funny about the report. "Look, Lis, we get garbage reports all the time. That's probably what this is."

She looked daggers at me and said softly and slowly, "And what if it's not?"

"Well, as Mr. Spock said to Captain Kirk, if you die we all move up one in rank." I was still reading the details in the report, some of which looked plausible.

She was not amused. "Don't you get it, Dick, Usama is trying to get you killed."

"Well, that's not surprising, since I'm trying to get him killed," I replied as Lisa left the office with a purposeful stride. She was not going to let it go. Neither was Sandy Berger, whom I had earlier browbeaten into having a Secret Service protective detail with him twenty-four hours a day. By the end of the day at Berger's request, the President had signed a memo designating me as a "protectee," which made me eligible for the same kind of Secret Service blanket. I called the Secret Service Director. "Look, having me run around in a bulletproof Caddy with Suburbans front and back will only make it easier for someone to find me. Can't we try something else?"

After a few minutes trying to persuade me, he asked, "Well, are you willing to be a target, see if we can flush them out?" I agreed.

Being a target meant that it would appear as though nothing had changed, that I had no protection. In reality, there would be agents hiding around my neighborhood and staged along the routes that I drove. Unmarked cars would follow a few cars behind me, looking for someone looking for me. My house would be given new locks, alarms, and exterior lights. And I would go to Secret Service agent school to learn evasive driving and, more frightening for my staff, how to shoot the .357 Sig Sauer handgun. For someone who believed in greater gun control, walking around with a cannon under my coat seemed strange, but only at first.

I dined one night at a sidewalk café in Washington's Adams Morgan neighborhood with a visiting Arab cabinet minister who had said he wanted to see the real Washington. After a while of looking uncomfortable, he said, "Don't they give you protection, bodyguards?"

It had not occurred to me that he would have thought that being with me made him vulnerable too. I tried to make him feel better, telling him, "See that beggar on the sidewalk, that guy over at the bar—they are protecting us." My Arab friend looked skeptical, until his limousine returned to pick him up after dinner, only to be blocked by a Suburban that appeared from nowhere with six serious-looking Secret Service agents.

After weeks of investigation and surveillance, we concluded the threat to me was probably bogus. Some of the security went away, but some of it stayed and my hatred for bin Laden grew even more personal, even though I was "safe" because I lived in America.

Despite the unwanted attention publicity brought, explaining to the press about terrorism was necessary to achieve Clinton's goal of preparing, but not frightening, the public. As part of a campaign of press briefings and speeches, I agreed to bring Lesley Stahl of *60 Minutes* to a secret location where we had stored tons of specialized medicines and equipment for dealing with a chemical or biological attack in the mid-Atlantic region. As the CBS cameras filmed, I broke open a crate and took out an auto-injector needle of atropine, a nerve gas antidote, and demonstrated how one would drive it into one's thigh. Stahl asked whether all of this would actually do any good. I replied that were there an attack, such as the use of anthrax, these secret stockpiles could save thousands of lives. Three years later, faced with an actual anthrax attack, we ordered the stockpiled medicines distributed.

Stahl and I also discussed Usama bin Laden on that *60 Minutes* segment. I acknowledged that al Qaeda sought weapons of mass destruction. For years we had been receiving raw intelligence reports and finished CIA analyses saying that al Qaeda was seeking chemical or nuclear weapons. When we asked for further details, however, there were none. Frustrated, in early 2001 I called Charlie Allen, who had become the Assistant Director of Central Intelligence for Collection, a kind of overall coordinator of what all U.S. intelligence agencies were doing to get information. We agreed to assemble everyone from every intelligence agency who had any responsibility for collecting or analyzing information about al Qaeda and weapons of mass destruction. We met in a secret location in Virginia. There were a lot of people in attendance. Each agency briefed on what they knew. More rumors and shadows. Nothing specific, credible, or actionable.

To break the mold, Charlie Allen and I split the group into two teams. The first team was told to assume the role of al Qaeda and to develop plans for acquiring weapons of mass destruction without the Americans knowing it. They had the rest of the day to develop the plan and report back. The second team was told they were in charge of American intelligence. They were told to assume that al Qaeda did actually have chemical and nuclear activities under way and had been successful hiding them. The U.S. team could use any method or capability to find the activities, but they needed to do so quickly because, in the exercise, we knew that al Qaeda planned to use the weapons soon. Charlie asked the group: "Assume they have special weapons and they are well hidden so you can't see the weapons. What would you see? What would they be saying, doing? What are the collateral indicators?" Forcing the analysts from several agenies to work together and think differently about the problem reenergized them.

The exercise taught us three lessons: first, there had not been a coordinated U.S. intelligence effort to think creatively about how to find any al Qaeda weapons of mass destruction; second, it was easier to hide such a program than to discover it; and finally, it is impossible to prove a negative, i.e., we could not prove that al Qaeda had no weapons of mass destruction. The exercise resulted in a renewed intelligence effort. As part of that effort, a third-country national working for CIA made it into an al Qaeda camp in Afghanistan where reports said chemical weapons were being made. The agent took samples, but analysis of them showed nothing. CIA took pride in the risks that the third-country national had run in going to the camp. (Later, Judy Miller of the *New York Times* would go to Afghanistan and drive up to the gate of an al Qaeda camp reputed to have chemical weapons, as part of her preparations for a week-long series on al Qaeda.)

The U.S. analysts playing al Qaeda in our exercise had identified one area as a good place to hide. As a result, it was photographed repeatedly and its cave entrances mapped. The region was a valley in Afghanistan called Tora Bora.

Chapter 8

Delenda Est

OUR EMBASSIES IN TANZANIA AND KENYA, in East Africa, were struck almost simultaneously on August 7, 1998. Our embassy in Tanzania was badly damaged. In Kenya, there was carnage. Two hundred fifty-seven were dead and five thousand wounded. Among the fatalities were twelve Americans. Al Qaeda had now followed up a fatwa, or religious ruling, earlier in 1998 declaring war on the United States with an actual act of war.

The CSG met by secure video conference at five in the morning. I asked Gayle Smith, Special Assistant to the President for Africa, to sit on my right. On the video screen we could see that at the State Department site Gayle's predecessor and now the Assistant Secretary of State for African Affairs, Susan Rice, joined the regular counterterrorism crew. Susan Rice was one of the rare breed of hands-on and "get it done" policy makers. On my left was Lisa Gordon-Hagerty, who had just joined my NSC team from Energy. She had come to the White House to help build the homeland protection program, but her first task was going to be relief and recovery in Africa.

"Let's begin. We are going to have to triage this, sequence it," I started the meeting. "First, rescue. We need to get teams in there fast. Urban heavy search-and-rescue. We may still have people alive inside and I doubt there are local units that can handle this. FEMA, who is on deck? We need two." The Federal Emergency Management Agency had paid for some local fire departments to hire extra staff, get specialized training, and procure equipment for searching through building collapses for bodies, dead and alive. That morning the Fairfax County, Virginia, fire department was the first that could roll. "We will need

Air Force medical Nightingale flights to get our wounded out to Europe. Those hospitals can't handle this load." In Europe, the Air Force kept medical teams on standby to fly into a disaster area and evacuate the injured on flying ambulances.

"Then we are going to have to get medical help in those countries for their wounded," Rice added. "It's mainly their people who have been hurt because of an attack on us."

"Second, security. DOD, what have you got nearby that can secure the two sites and the stuff we will be sending?" The Navy had created Fleet Anti-terrorism Support Teams (FAST)—units of Marines to do specialized security at sensitive sites. The Marines got the call.

"Third, investigation. I assume FBI will want to send Evidence Recovery Teams to both locations right away before the sites get trampled. And investigators to help the local police?" John O'Neill had teams on standby in Los Angeles, Miami, New York, and Washington. The New York unit had its equipment at a nearby Air Force base in New Jersey. They went out first.

"Fourth, coordination. We have no embassies in these countries now and we are descending upon them with hundreds of staff. State, can we launch two FESTs?" The FEST was the Foreign Emergency Support Team, an interagency response group led by a senior State Department official. Their mission was to go into a country where there had been a terrorist attack and provide highly trained staff to the U.S. ambassador. Most embassies did not have the numbers or type of people they needed to handle an emergency like this. The FEST did. A customized FEST aircraft was always on four-hour or less standby. Susan Rice wanted to get people from her bureau on the two FEST flights to relieve and assist her two ambassadors.

"Fifth, lift. We just agreed on enough people and equipment to fill up a dozen C-141s or C-5s. I know we have only two or three on standby, so we are going to have to pull priority here and cancel other flights. If we can get midair refueling for them that will get us there quicker. Lisa Gordon-Hagerty is going to serve as the overall mission controller for the President." Lisa looked aghast at me and mouthed "Why me?" I continued, "She decides what goes first, how much we need. If there are problems in the flow of assets to Africa, Lisa decides.

"Sixth, stopping the next one. We can't assume this is it. There may be more attacks planned. Susan, let's shut down all embassies in Africa. Let's also button down all embassies around the world. If any ambassador thinks somebody is threatening their post, they can close it without calling Washington.

"Finally, attribution and response. CIA, let's meet in my office at 7:30 to go over the evidence. The senior officer from each CSG agency is invited. I suspect we all know what the evidence will show. We will need to give the President options."

I was pleased that we had become adept at responding to terrorist attacks, but deeply bothered that we had had to do so. FEMA, FBI, State, CIA, the Marines, and the other agencies reacted with alacrity. The Air Force did not. Pilots needed crew rest. Aircraft broke down. Aerial tankers were unavailable. The first foreign rescue team to arrive on the scene was from Israel. When my Israeli counterpart had heard about the attack, he had launched an aircraft with a heavy search-and-rescue team on a dedicated aircraft they kept loaded with equipment and on constant alert. The Israelis had not called us to ask; they knew we would be busy.

The smaller, in-person meeting of the CSG that morning revealed initial evidence that al Qaeda had launched the attacks. CIA knew there had been an al Qaeda cell in Kenya, but they had thought that, working with the Kenyan police, the U.S. government had broken it up. More troublesome, the CIA brought reports to the meeting that suggested that al Qaeda planned more attacks. An attack in Albania seemed about to happen. Another in Uganda or Rwanda was possible, although we had just closed those two embassies. From my office, the CSG members called back to their departments on secure phones. The State Department closed our embassy in Tirana, Albania. The Defense Department agreed to dispatch a heavily armed Marine FAST unit to surround the embassy in Tirana. The U.S. government was working with the Albanian police to round up the al Qaeda cell.

Because we were all pretty certain where this was going, I asked CIA and the Joint Chiefs of Staff to create a joint team to develop response options against al Qaeda. If it turned out to be somebody else that did the attacks, we would develop different plans. None of us thought that would be necessary.

That day and the next several were consumed with meetings with the President and the Principals, coordination of the "flow" to Africa, and preparation to receive the bodies of our dead. A week passed in a flash. Seven days after the attack, the Principals met again with the President. Just before going to the meeting, I read a CIA report from a source in Afghanistan that bin Laden and his top staff were planning a meeting on August 20 to review the results of their attacks and plan the next wave. Terrorist coordinators from outside Afghanistan had been summoned back for the session. As we sat down in the Cabinet Room, I slipped the report to George Tenet, who was sitting next to me. On it, I penned, "You thinking what I'm thinking?" He passed it back with a note on it, "You better believe I am." We had both come to the conclusion that this report meant we had the opportunity not merely to stage a retaliatory bombing, but also a chance to get bin Laden and his top deputies, if the President would agree to a strike now during the white-hot "Monica" scandal press coverage. At that moment, Tenet and I were the only ones in the Cabinet Room that knew about the CIA report.

In the meeting, CIA and FBI provided detailed evidence that the operation had been al Qaeda. "This one is a slam dunk, Mr. President," Tenet began. "There is no doubt that this was an al Qaeda operation. Both we and the bureau have plenty of evidence." Some arrests had already been made. Tenet described the upcoming meeting in Afghanistan for the President and the other Principals, drawing nods around the table. The Principals were resolute: if al Qaeda could issue fatwas declaring war on us, we could do the same and more to them. Although we had been going after al Qaeda for several years, now it would be the top priority to eliminate the organization. The President asked National Security Advisor Sandy Berger to coordinate all of the moving parts necessary for a military response, tentatively planned for August 20, six days later. Any targets in addition to the al Qaeda meeting place were to be nominated by CIA and the Defense Department. Military assets had to be moved into place. Pakistan would have to be dealt with in some way.

Clinton also asked Berger to pull together an overall plan to deal with al Qaeda. "Listen, retaliating for these attacks is all well and good, but we gotta get rid of these guys once and for all," Clinton said, looking seriously over his half glasses at Tenet, Cohen, and Berger, "You understand what I'm telling you?" We had been dealing with al Qaeda as one of several terrorist threats. Now, I hoped, we would gain interagency agreement that destroying al Qaeda was one of our top national security objectives, and an urgent one.

Although the Pakistanis were helping us with the investigation following the embassy attacks by looking for people who had fled Africa before and after the attack for Afghanistan, they had been less than helpful before. Al Qaeda members had moved freely through Pakistan to Afghanistan. Despite the fact that Pakistan's Inter-Services Intelligence Directorate was training, equipping, and advising the Taliban in Afghanistan, they professed no ability to influence that group to close terrorist camps and hand over bin Laden. Any U.S. military strike on Afghanistan would have to cross Pakistani airspace. If they were not told in advance, they might shoot down our aircraft or cruise missiles. If they were told in advance, some of us believed that the ISID would alert the Taliban and possibly al Qaeda. The State Department Deputy Secretary, Strobe Talbott, also feared that the Pakistanis would see the U.S. attack coming and assume it was an Indian air raid. Talbott thought that Pakistan would not hesitate to launch an attack on India, even before confirming what was going on, and that could trigger a nuclear war between the two South Asian rivals (each of which now had nuclear bombs).

All of this was taking place against the backdrop of the continuing Monica scandal. Like most of his advisors, I was beyond mad that the President had not shown enough discretion or self-control, although from what I knew of Presidential history, marital fidelity had also been a problem for several of his illustrious predecessors. I was angrier, almost incredulous, that the bitterness of Clinton's enemies knew no bounds, that they intended to hurt not just Clinton but the country by turning the President's personal problem into a global, public circus for their own political ends. Now I feared that the timing of the President's interrogation about the scandal, August 17, would get in the way of our hitting the al Qaeda meeting.

It did not. Clinton made clear that we were to give him our best national security advice, without regard to his personal problems. "Do you all recommend that we strike on the 20th? Fine. Do not give me political advice or personal advice about the timing. That's my problem. Let me worry about that." If we thought this was the best time to hit the Afghan camps, he would order it and take the heat for "Wag the Dog" criticism that we all knew would happen, for the media and congressional reaction that would say that he was using a military strike to divert attention from his deposition in the investigation. (*Wag the Dog* was a movie that had been released that year, in which fictional presidential advisors create an artificial crisis with Albania to attack it and divert attention from domestic problems. Ironically, Clinton was blamed for a "Wag the Dog" strategy in 1998 dealing with the real threat from al Qaeda but no one labeled Bush's 2003 war on Iraq as a "Wag the Dog" move even though the "crisis" was manufactured and Bush political advisor Karl Rove was telling Republicans to "run on the war.")

Clinton testified on the 17th and then flew to Martha's Vineyard. He had had one full day of vacation when Don Kerrick arrived. Kerrick was an Army general who had served several times on the NSC staff and had been a key player in the Bosnia crisis. Now, as the Deputy National Security Advisor, he was taking the final plans for the attack on al Qaeda to the little island off the Massachusetts coast.

CIA and the Joint Chiefs had nominated not just buildings at the al Qaeda camp scheduled to host the meetings, but also other al Qaeda camps in Afghanistan and facilities in Sudan that bin Laden had invested in. They recommended that the attack be conducted only with cruise missiles, not commandos or piloted aircraft, either of which could result in U.S. casualties or prisoners. Joint Chiefs Vice Chairman Joe Ralston had agreed to fly to Pakistan, stopping at the airport allegedly for refueling en route from somewhere else. He had called the head of the Pakistani military and invited him to a one-on-one dinner meeting on the 20th, at the airport, to discuss the tensions between the United States and Pakistan. The Pakistani general, a friend of Ralston's, had accepted. The cruise missiles would hit Pakistan's airspace and be detected while the dinner was going on. Ralston would explain that they were our missiles and should not be shot at. The plan called for Ralston to get on his plane and leave before dessert was served.

The U.S. military are particularly sensitive to civilians telling them how to do their job, or even asking them how they intend to do it. The officer corps have all been taught to tell civilians "Just give me the objective. I'll figure out how to do it." This response has its roots in Vietnam, when Lyndon Johnson sat in the Situation Room going over maps and pictures, ruling out bombing targets. It was this tradition that prevented us from knowing how the military would go after Aideed in Somalia—otherwise, we would have suggested that repeated daytime raids from helicopters in a city was not a good idea. It was this tradition that also meant I could not formally become involved in discussions about what platforms would be used to launch the cruise missiles. Nonetheless, I called my friends on the Joint Staff to raise the issue that the Pakistani military might detect strange U.S. Navy activity off their coast long before Joe Ralston was sipping curry soup. I was assured the missiles would be fired from submerged attack subs. There might be a destroyer employed, but there was often a U.S. destroyer passing by the Pakistani coast.

Up to this point the number of people in the U.S. government who knew that a retaliatory response was imminent was small, essentially those of us on the Principals Committee. Such a military operation, however, requires paperwork. There must be a presidential announcement, press briefings at several agencies, briefings for the Congress, a War Powers Notification to the Congress, explanations given at the U.N. and passed to our embassies for use with countries around the world, stepped-up security at U.S. facilities in Pakistan and elsewhere, and more. To do all of that before the attack, I needed the CSG members and some of their staffs to draft and approve the materials. The Principals, however, were worried about a leak getting out that an attack was imminent. The Principals finally agreed that I could pull together a meeting in the late afternoon, tell the CSG members what was about to happen, and put them to work drafting. The catch was that they could not leave the White House complex until the attack took place (or at least until after the news cycle and the next day's newspapers had gone to bed).

It was not the CSG members that anyone thought would leak word of the attack. Each of them, however, had staffs, which taken together numbered in the hundreds. Many of the staff had people in their lives that they trusted with exciting secrets like an upcoming military attack. None of the CSG members protested when I surprised them at the meeting by saying that they would be staying awhile and needed to come up with good excuses for their offices and families. Senior people like Under Secretary of State Tom Pickering (who had held eight Senate confirmation jobs in his illustrious career) merely rolled up their sleeves and asked for a computer to start drafting. One CIA officer however, protested the inclusion of targets in Sudan. I explained that it was CIA and the Defense Department that had chosen the targets, that the Principals (including George Tenet) had nominated the targets, and that the President had approved them. Nonetheless, I could sense that he felt left out of the process by his own agency and would probably complain about the targets later, to the press or congressional staff.

While the night went on, I assumed the targets were locked in. The President, however, was still wondering about one commercial facility in Sudan owned by bin Laden. At the last possible minute, he pulled that target off the list because it had no military or offensive value to al Qaeda. He left on the list the Shifa chemical plant that CIA had linked to al Qaeda and to a unique chemical weapons compound.

It turned out my friends on the Joint Staff had given me hollow assurances about the Navy's plans. In the northern Arabian Sea, U.S. destroyers were lining up, their missiles spinning in their launch tubes; it wasn't just a single ship. Sure enough, the Pakistani navy noticed and alerted Islamabad. ISID received the alert. Then the first of seventy-five missiles were launched. Some circled until others were launched, and then they all flew toward the Pakistani coast at about four hundred miles an hour. Almost two hours later, they would hit the al Qaeda camps in Afghanistan. Other Tomahawks were being fired from the Red Sea toward Shifa in Sudan.

Reports differ concerning how close the cruise missile attack came to hitting the al Qaeda leadership. Whatever the truth is, bin Laden was not killed in the raid. Apparently, however, Pakistani ISID officers were killed. The Pakistanis were reported by media sources to be present at the camp training Kashmiri terrorists. ISID had several offices around Afghanistan and was assisting the Taliban in its fight to gain control of the northern part of the country where the Northern Alliance still held out. I believed that if Pakistan's ISID wanted to capture bin Laden or tell us where he was, they could have done so with little effort. They did not cooperate with us because ISID saw al Qaeda as helpful to the Taliban. ISID also saw al Qaeda and its affiliates as helpful in pressuring India, particularly in Kashmir. Some, like General Hamid Gul, the former director of ISID, also appeared to share bin Laden's anti-Western ideology.

The American public's reaction to the U.S. retaliation over the next several days was about as adverse as we could have been imagined. According to the media and many in Congress, Clinton had launched a military strike to divert attention from the Monica scandal; CIA Chief Tenet was probably making up the story of an al Qaeda meeting because bin Laden was still alive; the Sudanese were to be believed that they had never made chemical weapons precursors at Shifa or, if they had, it was certainly just to kill weeds; the Defense Department had wasted valuable cruise missiles attacking huts and tents; and Clinton stopped the military from putting "boots on the ground" in Afghanistan and had insisted on the ineffectual cruise missiles; real men use commandos.

Our response to two deadly terrorist attacks was an attempt to wipe out al Qaeda leadership, yet it quickly became grist for the right-wing talk radio mill and part of the Get Clinton campaign. That reaction made it more difficult to get approval for follow-up attacks on al Qaeda, such as my later attempts to persuade the Principals to forget about finding bin Laden and just bomb the training camps.

What was particularly frustrating was that Clinton had pulled Joint Staff Chairman Hugh Shelton and me aside after the Cabinet

Room meeting, saying to the former Special Forces commander, "Hugh, what I think would scare the shit out of these al Qaeda guys more than any cruise missile . . . would be the sight of U.S. commandos, Ninja guys in black suits, jumping out of helicopters into their camps, spraying machine guns. Even if we don't get the big guys, it will have a good effect." Shelton looked pained. He explained that the camps were a long way away from anywhere we could launch a helicopter raid. Nonetheless, America's top military officer agreed to "look into it."

ON THE SAME DAY that we sent cruise missiles into Afghanistan, President Clinton signed Executive Order 13099, imposing sanctions against Usama bin Laden and al Qaeda. Some months later these sanctions would be extended to the Taliban, as we determined that there was effectively little difference between their leadership and that of al Qaeda. With these orders, the focus of U.S. strategy to combat al Qaeda's financial network moved from a narrow approach focused primarily on law enforcement to a wider approach that aimed to bring into the fight all the varied tools and resources of the U.S. government.

We would need to improve and coordinate intelligence, diplomatic, law enforcement, and regulatory efforts across the dozens of government departments, agencies, and offices that would have to be involved. Most of these bureaucracies had little or no experience in focusing on terrorist financing. Many approached the issue from their own limited perspective, uninterested in a unified strategy. Some were involved in longstanding turf battles against what they saw as competing parts of the government. But the President wanted answers and actions, so these constraints would need to be pushed aside.

I asked Will Wechsler of my staff to lead a new CSG Sub-Group on Terrorist financing. Will came to my office from the Pentagon, where he had been a civilian aide to General Shalikashvili, the Chairman of the Joint Chiefs of Staff. Will and I quickly came to the conclusion that the departments were generally doing a lousy job of tracking and disrupting international criminals' financial networks and had done little or nothing against terrorist financing. One of our few important victories against criminal financing had come a few years earlier when the President had invoked the International Emergency Economic Powers Act against the Cali drug cartel. Now we were going to take the same approach to al Qaeda.

Will began by meeting with Rick Newcomb, the quietly effective head of the Treasury Department's Office of Foreign Asset Control (OFAC) and the architect of the effort against the Cali cartel. Together they asked all those in the intelligence community, law enforcement agencies, and the State Department who were supposed to know about terrorist financing what they knew about al Qaeda's finances.

Will came into my office looking worried after his first round of meetings. "This is insane," he said. "FBI thinks we should just leave this to them, but they can't tell me anything I can't read in the newspapers. CIA has given us a data dump of everything they've ever come across on the subject and thinks that answers the question. There are no formal assessments at all, no understanding of the whole picture of where the money is coming from. As far as I can tell, there are only a handful of people at CIA who know anything about how bad guys move money around the world and none of them are part of the Counterterrorism Center. The general impression I get out there is that this is all a waste of time because, they keep saying, it doesn't take much money to blow something up and Usama's got all he needs from daddy."

"You need to put together a small group of people who will get the answers," I told him. "Use Rick and his staff and whoever you can find at the CIA who will be helpful. Keep the rest of the interagency involved, but don't let them slow you down. Ask the questions. I don't need precision, just some answers that can get us started. The CIA guys are crazy if they think bin Laden is doing this global network on the cheap."

As it happened, not long after this conversation I had an opportunity to raise this issue at a Principals Committee meeting on terrorism. George Tenet gave the summary version of the CIA data dump. (If you overload people with a large number of small facts, sometimes they don't notice that it doesn't add up to anything.) "George," I said, "that was a great briefing, but it didn't tell us everything about al Qaeda's finances. We still need to know how much money they have, where they get it, how they move it, and where they keep it." George was not amused, but then again neither were the other Principals, nor the President, who had ordered CIA to go after terrorists' money in PDD-39 in 1995 and PDD-63 earlier in 1998.

Wechsler came back some weeks later with what they had come to call the new "theory of the case." As too often happens in government, after they went through everything in CIA's data dump a picture emerged that was the exact opposite of the initial conventional wisdom: Although any one terrorist act might cost a little only, it took a lot of money to run everything that al Qaeda was up to. And while bin Laden's own personal fortune was undoubtedly useful in setting up al Qaeda, the organization's financial network was far beyond one man's wallet. Instead, we were looking at a vast, global fundraising machine.

This machine involved both legitimate businesses and criminal enterprises. But it was clear that the most important source of al Qaeda's money was its continuous fundraising efforts through Islamic charities and nongovernmental organizations. The terrorists moved their money though old-fashioned smuggling, but also by bank transfers through the unsuspecting (and often unregulated) holes in the global financial system, as well as the growing Islamic banking system. Some of the specifics were still uncertain, but the "theory of the case" looked very solid.

Will called my attention to reports that would vaguely reference "money exchange" offices without any real explanation of what kinds of businesses were being described. Smiling, he told me that he had found one person in the bowels of Treasury's Financial Crimes Enforcement Network who knew what the references meant. That's how we first learned all about the hawala system, an ancient underground system that offers money transfers without money movement—and virtually no paper trail.

CIA knew little about the system, but set about learning. FBI knew even less, and set about doing nothing. When I asked FBI to identify some hawalas in the United States, they at first said "What's a wala?" and, when told, came back with word that there were none.

Wechsler found several in New York City by searching the Internet. Despite our repeated requests over the following years, nobody from FBI ever could answer even our most basic questions about the number, location, and activities of major hawalas in the U.S.—much less take action. And it eventually became clear that this subject was not a priority for FinCEN either, as they eventually let go the expert who had originally briefed us on the hawala system.

Once they had developed their theory of the case, Will, Rick, and their small team then set about strategizing what to do about it. We clearly needed more intelligence, but we couldn't afford to wait to act until we knew all the details. One thing was clear: a lot of the money being raised was coming from people in Saudi Arabia. Many Saudi charities being used by al Qaeda were quasi-governmental entities that the regime used to spread its version of Islam abroad. Moreover, the Saudi government seemed to have little in the way of laws or regulations that would help them know much about the money flows inside their country—even if they mustered the political will to want to know.

We decided that we needed to have a serious talk with the Saudis as well as with a few of the financial centers in the region. We recognized that the Saudi regime had been largely uncooperative on previous law enforcement–focused investigations of terrorism, including the 1996 bombing of Khobar Towers that killed nineteen members of the U.S. Air Force. So we wanted a different approach.

First, although law enforcement issues would play a role, this would be primarily an attempt to talk with the Saudis on a political level. Our goal would be map the important "nodes" in the al Qaeda financial network and then disrupt or destroy them using any available tool of the U.S. government. We were eager to take action, but we also knew the damage we could do to our credibility if we were seen to take action on the basis of flimsy intelligence—and at this point much of our intelligence was flimsy.

Second, we would use the leverage inherent in the presidential order to block al Qaeda accounts and the accounts of anyone else later deemed to be providing "material assistance" to the terrorists—a characterization that could apply potentially to significant actors within Saudi Arabia. Third, we would need buy-in from the highest levels of the Saudi government, so we asked Vice President Gore to talk to the Crown Prince about the problem and about accepting a U.S. delegation that would meet to discuss only this subject with representatives of all relevant Saudi agencies together, so there could be no run-around. And fourth—perhaps most important—we decided to lay our cards on the table and show Saudi Arabia what we knew about al Qaeda's finances, what we didn't know, and what we suspected and ask them to fill in the blanks.

We wanted to avoid a typical pattern of Saudi behavior we had seen: achingly slow progress, broken promises, denial, and cooperation limited to specific answers to specific questions. At the same time, we thought that, as longstanding friends of the U.S., the Saudis deserved the opportunity to establish a new kind of relationship with us on counterterrorism. We were looking for a full partnership, behind the scenes, of course. We recognized that they might not have the political will to strike such a partnership, but we thought it was worth a try—keeping the threat of public sanctions against Saudi entities in reserve if it didn't work.

Some U.S. government agencies didn't seem to like this different approach we were recommending. Some at State didn't like the idea of threatening sanctions, even though that authority was implicit in the President's executive order. Some at FBI really didn't like the fact that discussions of terrorist financing with the Saudis were going to take place outside their channels and without their being in charge. Soon after we told FBI about the initiative, a leak found its way to the *New York Times,* almost forcing us to cancel the trip.

And some in the intelligence community who jealously guarded "their" channels with Saudi intelligence also didn't like this approach. Turf is a powerful thing in Washington. This objection continued even after CIA cleared every piece of information we would be discussing with the Saudis. There was even a last ditch attempt by some in CIA's operation's directorate on the day that Wechsler's meetings were to take place—to deny our ability to hand over already cleared information.

Despite the interagency obstructionists, the meetings in the region went on as planned. We got answers to some questions. We forced the regulators in Saudi Arabia to talk with the police and intelligence agencies, something that they were clearly not used to doing. Some important actions were taken, such as the denial of landing rights to Ariana Airlines by Saudi Arabia and the UAE. Ariana, Afghanistan's national airline, had been taken over by the Taliban and had, in many ways, become al Qaeda's direct lifeline to the outside world. When governments understood the leverage inherent in the Executive Order and were then faced with the possibility of having to choose between doing business with Ariana Airlines or with American Airlines—well, asking the question gave you the answer. Later we worked with Russia through the U.N. Security Council to add a multilateral aspect to these sanctions.

In the end, however, despite Saudi promises to provide additional information and support, little was forthcoming in the months after the visit, nor after a subsequent visit from Rick Newcomb to follow up. The Saudis protested our focus on continuing contacts between Usama and his wealthy, influential family, who were supposed to have broken all ties with him years before. "How can we tell a mother not to call her son?" they asked. They reacted defensively when we pointed out some weaknesses in their regulatory regime, pointedly noting that many in the U.S. Congress had recently sought to weaken aspects of the U.S. Bank Secrecy Act. And they were right about the U.S. Congress; although the Clinton administration had sought tougher money laundering provisions, only after 9/11 did Congress muster the political will to strengthen the U.S. laws to fight terrorist financing and money laundering.

So we went back to the drawing board. Mike Sheehan at the State Department sought unsuccessfully within his bureaucracy to raise the political stakes with Saudi Arabia and other countries unless we got more support in fighting terrorism financing. Rick Newcomb began to think about which entities in Saudi Arabia might deserve targeting sanctions. CIA went back to trying to map the important "nodes" in al Qaeda's financial network. This was important and extremely difficult work, but necessary if we were to take unilateral actions without real Saudi cooperation.

After Secretary Robert Rubin stepped down, it was easier to get cooperation from Treasury. Rubin had opposed our use of the International Economic Emergency Powers Act to go after terrorist financing fronts in the United States. His attitude toward strengthening international money laundering rules had been less than enthusiastic. The new Treasury Secretary, Larry Summers, was surprisingly a breath of fresh air. He asked Will Wechsler to join him for the last year of the Clinton administration in developing a multilateral approach to "name and shame" foreign money laundering havens that were providing "no questions asked" financial services for al Qaeda and other terrorists and criminals. This initiative made countries pay a price in the financial markets for their lack of cooperation and thus successfully forced over a dozen countries to rewrite their laws. Liechtenstein and the Bahamas later used those new laws after 9/11 to help us track down and freeze a key part of al Qaeda's financial network.

When the Bush administration came into office, I wanted to raise the profile of our efforts to combat terrorist financing, but found little interest. The new President's economic advisor, Larry Lindsey, had long argued for weakening U.S. anti–money laundering laws in a way that would undercut international standards. The new Secretary of the Treasury, Paul O'Neill, was lukewarm at best toward the multilateral efforts to "name and shame" foreign money laundering havens, and allowed the process to shut down before the status of Saudi Arabian cooperation was ever assessed.

In general, the Bush appointees distrusted anything invented by the Clinton administration and anything of a multilateral nature—so the international terrorist financing effort had two strikes against it. The new Bush focus in early 2001 was on confronting China, withdrawing from various multilateral obligations, and spending much more money on an antimissile defense system—not on looking into al Qaeda's financial network. Will Wechsler quit Treasury within months of the change of administration.

ALTHOUGH HE HAD APPROVED the retaliatory bombing and the sanctions after the attacks on the African embassies, Clinton had also asked Berger for an overall plan to deal with al Qaeda. My team set out to develop what we had taken to calling a "Pol-Mil Plan." A politico-military plan was something we had first invented to deal with Haiti. When General Shalikashvili, Hugh Shelton's predecessor, had presented Clinton with a military plan to invade Haiti, the President had been impressed by the detail, responsibilities being assigned, timelines, resources. Clinton asked for the civilian plan, saying, "Because the military will take over Haiti in a few hours. If they don't, we sure have been wasting billions of dollars over there at the Pentagon. But after they do—then what? We need this kind of detail on what happens after the shooting."

The Pol-Mil Plan for Haiti (and then others for Bosnia, Kosovo, Iran, and Iraq) came in the form of a thick loose-leaf notebook with tabs for every conceivable issue. It was full of advance planning, anticipation of possible contingencies, specification of goals and objectives, identification of means of achieving the goals, estimation of resources required, timelines, and assignment of responsibilities. Pol-Mil Plan Haiti went through several iterations and exercises before U.S. forces moved onto the island. For the Principals the existence of the detailed Pol-Mil Plan was a security blanket that increased their confidence. Now we drafted one for dealing with al Qaeda.

Every military operation has a codeword or phrase, such as Infinite Reach, Just Cause, El Dorado Canyon, Provide Comfort. To express the intent of the Pol-Mil Plan for al Qaeda, I borrowed a phrase from Cato the Elder, Roman Senator and famous orator who in 201 B.C.E. had encouraged war by ending every speech with the line "Carthage must be destroyed," or as Cato would have said it, "Carthago delenda est." When the Pol-Mil Plan was handed out it was labeled "Top Secret Delenda." The Under Secretaries of State and Defense, Tom Pickering and Walt Slocombe, looked up from their copies knowingly. "You're right," Pickering said. "Al Qaeda must be destroyed."

Destroying al Qaeda would require a multifaceted, detailed plan. Intelligence agencies would need to identify and break up al Qaeda's cells, find its money, train and arm its enemies, and eliminate its leaders. Law enforcement agencies had similar responsibilities, including finding sleeper cells in the U.S. The State Department would persuade other governments to assist us, would provide international approval of our actions, and would fund nations that needed help to join in our efforts. The Defense and State Departments would reduce the number of low-hanging-fruit targets by hardening facilities. Treasury would seize al Qaeda funds here and work the international banking system to freeze them elsewhere. Resources were needed and were identified. Additional legal authorities were required and plans to obtain them were detailed. Military plans were requested for additional bombing and possible commando operations.

During their review of the Pol-Mil Plan, the principals had agreed that we should stop referring publicly to Usama bin Laden (who had survived the August 20 missile strike) and focus attention on the network, al Qaeda. Unfortunately, few of the Principals then did so in their public comments. Like the media, the Principals were fixated on one man, the leader of this group that had declared war on us for no good reason. We all knew that killing bin Laden would not make al Qaeda go away. In fact, immediately after his death there would be a negative backlash against us. There was also the certainty that he would become a popular martyr, as the Latin American Communist Che Guevara had become after CIA had hunted him down in Bolivia. Nonetheless bin Laden obviously had something special. He had done what no one else had been able to do previously, he had united unconnected dissidents from dozens of countries. Maybe without him that network would fall apart over time. Thus, while we all knew we had to destroy the organization and had set out to do so, one of the first steps along that path was to eliminate its leader.

My past experience with our attempts to find rogue foreign leaders had been mixed. I had spent Christmas Eve 1989 in the State Department Operations Center as troops swept Panama looking for Manuel Noriega. From the Ops Center I had watched midnight Mass from the Vatican and looked to see the Vatican foreign minister being handed our note saying that we had trapped Noriega in the Vatican embassy in Panama. Yet despite having invaded the country and hit Noriega's known hangouts with Special Forces, he had eluded our operations for days.

From the White House, I had also helped to coordinate the effort to get Pablo Escobar, the leader of one of the Colombian drug cartels. Although we had the help of the Colombian police and military, Escobar stayed at large for years before he was shot by a special Colombian unit. I had agreed with Jonathan Howe that we should arrest Farah Aideed for killing U.N. peacekeepers, then watched as months went by and Aideed prepared for us, until finally U.S. Special Forces tried in vain to capture him and were killed in the process, along with a thousand Somalis.

Given the reluctance of the military to plan seriously for commando operations in Afghanistan and the fecklessness to date of CIA's Afghan friends, the best option to get bin Laden seemed to be to hit a building in which he was staying. For that purpose, the Defense Department was asked to keep cruise missile platforms off the Pakistani coast. This time we specified that they had to be in submarines. Aboard the submarines, the cruise missiles had multiple target options preloaded. The targets were places bin Ladin was thought to have been before, houses and villa complexes in several cities. Now all we needed was word that he was at one of those places again, and would likely stay there for a few hours.

That proved hard to get.

CIA's assets in Afghanistan could usually tell us where bin Laden had been a few days earlier. They did not know, except rarely, where he would be the next day. On a few occasions, they were able to tell us where they thought he was at that moment. When word came through that we had a contemporaneous sighting from our informants, the CSG met immediately by secure video conference. In three meetings during 1998 and 1999, the CSG requested emergency meetings of the Principals to recommend to the President a cruise missile strike on the facility in which bin Laden was believed to be at the time.

We had to act quickly. By the time the information reached the CSG, it was already getting old. By the time the Principals met and recommended action to the President, another hour or two would have passed. After presidential approval, it would take at least two hours for the missiles to hit the target. Bin Laden had to stay put throughout that time, perhaps six hours or more. Working with CIA and the Joint Chiefs, we tried to compress that time. General John Maher established a procedure whereby the attack submarines moved to their launch positions and readied their missiles for firing as soon as the CSG recommended an emergency Principals meeting, shaving off almost an hour.

On each of the three occasions when we thought we had an opportunity, however, there was reason not to fire the missiles. Twice, George Tenet admitted to the Principals that the information came from a single source that was not always right. There was a risk we would be firing on a building that did not contain bin Laden. He recommended against the attacks. "Look, I want to get this guy as much as any of you. More. But can I tell you that I have 100 percent, 90 percent confidence in these reports, no. This is one source, no corroboration, what we call 'single threaded' reporting." On the third occasion, Tenet and I carefully examined satellite photos of CIA's proposed target and determined that it looked a lot more like a luxury mobile home camp than a terrorist hideout. We feared that the target was not al Qaeda, but a falcon hunting party from a friendly Arab state. Perhaps our source was being used to cause us to attack one of our friends and drive a rift between us. Tenet and I recommended against that attack. The planned attack was canceled.

Tenet's later review of the three events, using other sources who were able to report later on, revealed that on only one of the occasions was bin Laden actually at the proposed target when we thought he was. On that occasion, the house bin Laden was in was located next to a hospital, which would have received collateral damage from a cruise missile attack. CIA was extremely sensitive to the possibility that its sources might be wrong and the Agency would take the blame when the U.S. attacked the wrong place. On May 7, 1999, U.S. bombs had fallen on the Chinese embassy in Belgrade during the NATO bombing of Serbia. An investigation showed that the aircraft had hit the building it was assigned to strike, but the CIA had erroneously thought that the building was a Serbian government compound. U.S. relations with China had been badly, if temporarily, damaged by the mistaken bombing.

On these three occasions and during the presentation of the Pol-

Mil Plan, I tried to make the case to the Principals that we should strike at known al Qaeda camps whether or not bin Laden was in them. "I know that you don't want to blow up al Qaeda facilities in Afghanistan trying to get bin Laden only to have the bastard show up the next day at a press conference saying how feckless we are. So don't say we were trying to get bin Laden; say we were trying to destroy the camps. If we get him, so much the better."

The response I received from all the other members of the Principals usually went along the lines of: "So we spend millions of dollars' worth of cruise missiles and bombs blowing up a buck fifty's worth of jungle gyms and mud huts again?" Sometimes I heard, "Look, we are bombing Iraq every week. We may have to bomb Serbia. European, Russian, Islamic press are already calling us the Mad Bomber. You want to bomb a third country?"

Several times I tried the line of argument that the camps, whatever it cost to build them, were churning out thousands of trained terrorists, who were going home and setting up cells in countries all over the world. "We have to stop this conveyor belt, this production line. Blow them up every once in a while and recruits won't want to go there."

This line of reasoning had some impact on the Principals but not enough. General Shelton noted that the regional commander, General Anthony Zinni of CENTCOM, advised against further bombings because of the negative effect they had in Pakistan. Zinni was afraid that we would cause a public outcry in Pakistan that would force that nuclear power to distance itself from us. We could lose the leverage necessary to prevent India and Pakistan from going to war, nuclear war. Both Madeleine Albright at the State Department and Bill Cohen at Defense found the routine and regular bombing of Afghanistan an unappealing concept.

I had thought that I had a special relationship with Albright and could persuade her, raising the political risk of inaction. Albright and I and a handful of others (Michael Sheehan, Jamie Rubin) had entered into a pact together in 1996 to oust Boutros-Ghali as Secretary General of the United Nations, a secret plan we had called Operation Orient Express, reflecting our hope that many nations would join us in doing in the U.N. head. In the end, the U.S. had to do it alone (with its U.N. veto) and Sheehan and I had to prevent the President from giving in to pressure from world leaders and extending Boutros-Ghali's tenure, often by our racing to the Oval Office when we were alerted that a head of state was telephoning the President. In the end Clinton was impressed that we had managed not only to oust Boutros-Ghali but to have Kofi Annan selected to replace him. (Clinton told Sheehan and me, "Get me a crow, I should eat crow, because I said you would never pull it off.") The entire operation had strengthened Albright's hand in the competition to be Secretary of State in the second Clinton administration. Our personal relationship meant I had access to Albright and could talk frankly, but she was also hearing from her Deputy Secretary, Strobe Talbott, who was adamantly opposed to making the terrorist camps in Afghanistan a free-fire zone for routine American bombing. Talbott thought it was bad enough that we had made southern Iraq such a "bomb anytime" area. He knew his Russian friends were making hay by labeling America "the Mad Bomber."

It was ironic that people had once worried whether Bill Clinton would use force and now there was criticism that he was using too much. In the Islamic world, there was criticism that Clinton was still bombing Iraq. After the start of hostilities with Belgrade, there were days when U.S. forces bombed both Serbia and Iraq. General Shelton and General Zinni looked on the idea of regular strikes against Afghanistan as another burden on an already stretched military. An aircraft carrier would have to be maintained off the Pakistani coast, tying down a major U.S. military asset.

Nonetheless, the idea of bombing all of the al Qaeda infrastructure was never ruled out. Indeed, the Joint Chiefs were instructed to prepare plans to hit the facilities not only with cruise missiles, but with B-1, B-2, and B-52 strategic bomber strikes. The targeters went to work, matching specific types of bombs and missiles to individual buildings at camps and sites across Afghanistan. They planned the choreography necessary to coordinate which aircraft and missiles went where, and in what sequence, as well as where the aerial tankers would circle and how rescue units would be stationed to get downed pilots. I waited for another opportunity to make the case.

While there was little support for a large-scale bombing campaign, there continued to be interest in eliminating the al Qaeda leadership. For years we had assumed that the Executive Order against U.S. agencies engaging in assassination was a firm ban against the use of lethal force in nonmilitary situations. The issue was not merely a legal one. There were moral issues as well as pragmatic considerations.

Israel had adopted a program to kill terrorists after the massacre of their Olympic team at Munich. Mossad, Israeli intelligence, sent hit teams around the Middle East and Europe, assassinating those involved with the Munich attack. On at least one occasion, they killed the wrong man as a result of mistaken identity. The assassinations had also done little to deter further attacks on Israelis. Indeed, Israel had become caught in a vortex of assassination and retaliation that seemed to get progressively worse.

Al Qaeda and bin Laden tested our own restraint. They seemed intent on continuing to kill innocent people, Americans and others. The U.S. military had been unable to come up with a way of attacking the al Qaeda leadership effectively. Gradually, the Principals accepted the idea that we needed to examine our policy on targeted assassination.

Beginning in the Reagan administration, U.S. policy had permitted the use of lethal force against a terrorist if the lethal act was necessary to stop an imminent attack. It was clear that there were going to be more al Qaeda attacks. What did "imminent" mean? Did we have to know the exact date and location of the next al Qaeda attack in order to use lethal force?

What seemed particularly absurd to the Principals about our policy on the use of force was that it did not apply to the U.S. military. We could fire a cruise missile into Afghanistan or ask a pilot to drop a bomb with the intention of killing al Qaeda leaders, but we could not ask an Afghan to go shoot bin Laden. If we used a bomber, the chances of collateral damage were higher. Moreover, using a B-1 meant that we had to publicly acknowledge our role and subject friendly governments like Pakistan to public criticism for their support or tolerance of it.

On the issue of the White House authorizing CIA to kill bin Laden, much has been written. Several reporters, including Barton Gellman in the *Washington Post* of December 19, 2001, have written that President Clinton approved multiple intelligence documents authorizing CIA to use lethal force against Usama bin Laden and his deputies. Sandy Berger elaborated before the Joint House-Senate Inquiry Committee, saying, "We received rulings in the Department of Justice not to prohibit our efforts to try to kill bin Laden, because [the assassination ban] did not apply to situations in which you're acting in self-defense or you're acting against command-and-control targets against an enemy, which he certainly was."

Yet bin Laden was not killed. President Clinton as reported in *USA Today* (November 12, 2001) reflected his frustration by noting, "I tried to take bin Laden out . . . the last four years I was in office."

I still to this day do not understand why it was impossible for the United States to find a competent group of Afghans, Americans, third-country nationals, or some combination who could locate bin Laden in Afghanistan and kill him. Some have claimed that the lethal authorizations were convoluted and the "people in the field" did not know what they could do. Every time such an objection was raised during those years, an additional authorization was drafted with the involvement of all the concerned agencies, and approved by the President's signature. The Principals and the President did not want to open the Pandora's box that the Israelis had found after Munich, they did not want a broad assassination policy and hit list, but the President's intent was very clear: kill bin Laden. I believe that those who in CIA who claim the authorizations were insufficient or unclear are throwing up that claim as an excuse to cover the fact that they were pathetically unable to accomplish the mission.

Chapter 9

Millennium Alert

Early in December 1999, the head of CIA's Counterterrorism Center, Cofer Black, called. "We have to go to battle stations."

"Cofer, it's not Friday," I joked. It had become something of a tradition that either Black or FBI Assistant Director Dale Watson would call on Friday afternoons with late-breaking news that would cause us to spend the weekend in the office. We called the regular Friday afternoon CSG meetings the "Friday Follies."

"No, Dick, this is the real deal," Black insisted. "Jordan infiltrated a cell, planning lots of bang-bang for New Year's. The Radisson Hotel, Christian tourist sites, lots of dead Americans. Deal is, Dick, I don't think this is it. You know bin Laden, he likes attacks in multiple locations. They're like cockroaches. You see one, but you know that means there is a whole nest of them."

Cofer Black was a hard-charging, get-it-done kind of CIA officer who had proved himself in the back alleys of unsavory places. He was what the CIA needed a lot more of, but had little of. I had urged George Tenet to find such a guy to run the Counterterrorism Center, someone who shared Tenet's view and mine that we had to go on the offensive. Unfortunately, Black reported to Tenet through the CIA's Deputy Director for Operations, Jim Pavitt, and Pavitt thought both Tenet and I were exaggerating the whole al Qaeda threat and would get CIA in trouble. Now, however, Black had proof that al Qaeda was planning attacks around the Millennium rollover.

IN THE MONTHS leading up to Cofer's phone call, much had been done to reduce our vulnerabilities at home and abroad.

We had hundreds of foreign diplomatic facilities (embassies, consulates, ambassadors' residences, and so on) in over 180 nations. A handful were built using the security guidelines adopted after Embassy Beirut was destroyed in the 1980s. Many, however, were so vulnerable that they invited attack. The institutional culture of the Department of State, however, resisted protecting the embassies. U.S. diplomats hated being housed in fortresses, walled off from the societies they were supposed to be serving. If there were new funds, the Department of State had many things it wanted to do with the money other than build more fortresses. I had found this attitude dismaying, since it was Department of State personnel who would be killed in embassy attacks. The Department should have been trying to do everything necessary to protect its own people. I knew that Madeleine Albright would understand the problem.

After one Principals meeting in the West Wing, I had asked to speak one on one and we walked together up West Executive Drive while her motorcade waited. "What do you think will happen if you lose another embassy? The Republicans in the Congress will go after you."

I had her attention. She shot back, "First of all, I didn't lose these two embassies. I inherited them in the shape they were." Then the Secretary of State, realizing that I was a friend who had tried to help her get the job, smiled coyly at me. "I know you, Dick. You have a plan. What is it you want me to approve?"

"Share the burden. These embassies don't just house State Department people, they have staff from a dozen agencies in them. Let's get them on the hook too. Let me run an interagency process to survey the embassies and identify which ones need quick fixes, which ones we may have to close. Then let me go after the money to build new ones, to put defenses around others."

With Secretary Albright's approval, the White House took on the embassy security mission. I sent teams of Diplomatic Security, Secret Service, FBI, FEMA, and Defense Department experts to cities around the world to survey our embassies the way that a terrorist would.

What streets did we need to close to prevent a truck bomb from getting too close? Were there enough local police and were they doing their job? Where did we need machine guns and fire zones? If there was a street that needed to be closed, the U.S. Ambassador was to go see the Foreign Minister personally. If that did not work in a week, the Secretary of State or National Security Advisor would be on the telephone. If we still did not get results, we would publicly announce that we were suspending diplomatic and consular services in the country and would advise U.S. citizens and businesses to stay away.

The teams came back with lists of immediate steps to harden scores of embassies. They also had embassies that could not be saved, where nothing could be done to make them safe. Those embassies were closed and the State Department sent out property buyers to find new locations.

We were able, in the wake of the embassy attacks, to persuade Congress to provide another Emergency Supplemental appropriation to cover the costs of the first wave of embassy hardening and to begin building two fortress-style embassies to replace the facilities we had lost. The CSG sat around the conference table in the Situation Room critiquing architectural plans for new embassies from Beijing to Berlin. Yet when it came time for the fiscal year 2000 budget, the State Department's submission to the White House did not include the funds to continue the embassy-hardening program. In a matter of four months from the attacks in Africa, embassy protection had slipped back to a low budget priority.

I called Josh Gottbaum, the number three person at the Office of Management and Budget and the official designated to work with me to make sure the President's terrorism and homeland protection priorities were funded. I explained the problem. Josh got it. "Well, it seems to me that it's the President's embassies and it's the President's budget . . . not the State Department's. Let me see here . . . yes, I think we will just drop several hundred million from what they want and add several hundred million of what we know the President would want. Done."

Meanwhile, the State Department had been hard at work trying to put pressure on the Taliban to close the terrorist camps in Afghanistan and hand over the terrorists. Unfortunately, we had little leverage with the Taliban. The three nations that did have leverage were Pakistan, Saudi Arabia, and the United Arab Emirates. They alone had diplomatic relations with Afghanistan. The Saudis and the Emirates also provided substantial foreign aid to that war-devastated land. All three had appealed on our behalf to the Taliban to cooperate on bin Laden. We also spoke directly to the Taliban. The answers that came back from Kandahar were transparent rejections. The Taliban had talked of their Islamic obligation as a host to take in those who sought shelter. They had spoken of convening a court of Islamic scholars to try bin Laden, if we would like to provide the evidence and accusations. They had assured us that they were preventing bin Laden from engaging in any terrorism.

In response, we had adopted a three-part strategy. First, I granted a media interview in which I stated that if there were any further al Qaeda terrorism against the United States, we would hold the Taliban responsible and retaliate against them the next time. There was some complaining that I had not obtained proper approval for that announcement, but nobody retracted it. Second, we asked the Saudis and UAE rulers to terminate diplomatic relations with Afghanistan and terminate foreign aid. The UAE agreed to cooperate fully, and did. The Saudis, too, terminated diplomatic relations. Both also sent their own emissaries to reason with the Taliban. The Saudi emissary was Intelligence Minister Prince Turki. Press reports suggested that he offered to increase aid to the Taliban if they would give up bin Laden. Turki was rebuffed, something that seldom happens in the life of a senior Saudi prince. Third, we had sought economic sanctions against the Taliban. The President ordered all Taliban assets in the United States seized. In a rare show of solidarity, the United States and Russia co-sponsored sanctions in the U.N. Security Council.

There were two problems that had prevented progress with the Taliban. The first was that the Taliban rightly believed that if they evicted bin Laden, as Sudan had done, the U.S. would then have other objections that would block aid. America would want the Taliban to insure women's rights and would insist on verifying an end to opium production. The second problem was that Taliban leaders, including

Mullah Omar, completely agreed with bin Laden and al Qaeda's goals. There were stories of intermarriage between the bin Laden and Omar families. There were also economic, military, and political ties that were inviolable. One Taliban official, speaking honestly, told Assistant Secretary of State Rick Inderfurth, "If we give you bin Laden, we will face a revolt against us."

WHILE ALL THIS WAS GOING ON, of course, al Qaeda was busy laying the groundwork for an attack against us. The Millennium was approaching, and it was a temptingly symbolic occasion upon which, as Cofer Black would help discover, they couldn't resist seizing.

From my position at the time of Cofer's phone call, not yet knowing of al Qaeda's plans, I had only limited options. I had tried to argue that the U.S. work harder to fight against the Taliban in its civil war in Afghanistan. The Northern Alliance still held sway over a third of the country but provinces switched sides as a result of combat or cash, and much of the combatants and all of the cash came from bin Laden to help the Taliban. It was only a matter of time before the Alliance crumbled. I argued that we could provide the counterweight, sending arms and funds to Massoud's northern forces. If Massoud posed a serious threat to the Taliban, bin Laden would have to devote his arms and men to the fight against the Northern Alliance rather than fighting us. Massoud had at least token support from India, Russia, and Uzbekistan. CIA had kept open contact with him, but had refused to provide him with significant assistance.

Once again, CIA's career management saw my proposal to aid the Northern Alliance as a risk to CIA. For those who had spent fifteen, twenty, or more years in CIA, there was a clear pattern: Whoever was in the White House would get worked up over the cause du jour. He would be unable to get the rest of the government to produce results, so he would turn to the CIA. He would push the CIA to do risky, potentially controversial things. Later, after things went badly, the White House people would be gone and CIA would get the blame. It was through this template that the Agency saw the Northern Alliance: Sure, Massoud was a good guy now, but later the Congress, or the media, or some other White House staff would focus on the fact that he sold opium, abused human rights, and had killed civilians. They would blame CIA. Audits of the CIA assistance would undoubtedly show that some funds had gone for questionable purposes. In the final analysis, the CIA proclaimed the Northern Alliance was feckless and no match for the Taliban.

Although CIA staff would admit their Agency's bias to me in private, in official meetings they nodded and said they would prepare to help Massoud and his Northern Alliance. Of course, they first needed their internal legal review to be complete and then there would have to be an interagency legal review. The money to help Massoud, apart from token aid that the CIA called "trinkets," would have to be given to the Agency over and above all funds already available to them.

This reluctance to fund the Northern Alliance without "found money" caused me to wonder exactly what CIA was doing with all of the counterterrorism budget increases that the White House had given them through several Emergency Supplemental budgets. Working with the Office of Management and Budget and CIA's own auditors, we discovered that almost all of the Agency's activities against al Qaeda were being paid for by the Emergency Supplementals. There were almost no baseline CIA funds going into the effort. In 2000 and in 2001 we asked CIA to identify some funds, any money, earmarked for other activities that were less important than the fight against al Qaeda, so that those funds could be transferred to the higher priority of countering bin Laden. The formal, official CIA response was that there were none. Another way to say that was that everything they were doing was more important than fighting al Qaeda.

This institutional response was in sharp contrast with George Tenet's personal fixation with al Qaeda. Tenet often called me alarmed about raw intelligence reports of al Qaeda activity. He testified before congressional committees that al Qaeda was the major threat to the United States. It was also in sharp contrast to the attitude in the Counterterrorism Center at CIA, which by 1997 was led by the hard-charging Cofer Black. Black wanted to destroy al Qaeda as much as I did, if only the Directorate of Operations would let him.

WHEN BLACK CALLED THAT DAY IN 1999, we quickly convened a CSG meeting and sent out warnings to U.S. embassies, military bases, and to the 18,000 police agencies in the United States. The message: Be advised, al Qaeda terrorists may be planning attacks around the time of the Millennium. Be on heightened alert for suspicious activity. And then we waited.

That message went overseas, but also to all federal law enforcement agents, as well as many county sheriffs, state troopers, highway patrol officers, and city cops. The break came in an unlikely location. A pleasant boat ride from British Columbia to Washington state ended with a routine screening by U.S. Customs officers. One passenger in line fidgeted, would not make eye contact. When the Customs officer, Diana Dean, went to pull him out of line, he bolted and ran off the boat, leaving his car on the ferry. Dean gave chase and called for backup. A few minutes later Ahmed Ressam was in custody. His car held explosives, and a map of Los Angeles International Airport.

If that were not enough to send us spinning, CIA had learned further details about the al Qaeda plot in Jordan. The head of the cell, who had helped assemble the bombs, had recently quit his job—as a cab driver in Boston.

The Jordanian Crown Prince, visiting the bomb factory hidden in an upper-middle-class home, had been amazed at the size of the haul. "They weren't planning terrorism, they were planning a revolution." The King immediately declared a state of emergency and flooded the streets with soldiers and armored vehicles. More than the usual suspects were swept up and interrogated. The investigation led to an al Qaeda operative in Pakistan, and to another American who had lived not far from Los Angeles International Airport.

In the fifteen months since the embassy bombings, National Security Advisor Sandy Berger had held dozens of Principals meetings on al Qaeda. He knew their names, their modus operandi, and he feared they would strike again before we could cripple their organization. He convened the Principals in crisis mode. "We have stopped two sets of attacks planned for the Millennium. You can bet your measly federal paycheck that there are more out there and we have to stop them too. I spoke with the President and he wants you all to know . . ." Berger looked at Janet Reno, Louis Freeh, George Tenet, ". . . this is it, nothing more important, all assets. We stop this fucker." (It was the sort of attention we needed in the summer of 2001, but we got only in the CSG, not in the Principals Committee.)

Following the first of these Principals meetings, we prepared, at Berger's request, a Pol-Mil Plan for the Millennium Alert, alerting units, increasing security, rounding up suspects around the world.

Berger was, in general, a cautious lawyer who had an unparalleled skill in seeing the many ways something could develop and go wrong, how people could under some circumstances blame you even if you came up with the cure for cancer. That skill kept the Administration out of a lot of hot water. He had also become, however, a true believer in the fight against al Qaeda, understanding early on the nature of the threat. Berger had a coldly cynical and accurate understanding of the flaws and weaknesses of the various departments and agencies. He did not think we could just trust that FBI, CIA, and the military would automatically do the right things to protect us.

This time, however, FBI did respond well. It did one of the things it is very good at: it threw bodies at the problem. Thousands of agents fanned out, pulling at strings. The strings from Ressam, the man on the ferry, led to a sleeper cell of Algerian mujahedeen in Montreal. How the Canadians had missed the cell was difficult to understand, but now they were cooperating. The leads the Royal Canadian Mounted Police provided went to what looked like cells in Boston and New York. By the time I called John O'Neill (by then the FBI Special Agent in Charge of National Security in New York City) to ask what he was doing, he was on a back street in Brooklyn where his agents had just arrested an al Qaeda operative connected to Ressam.

The Justice Department normally reviewed FBI requests for national security wiretaps with a skeptical eye. Justice correctly wanted to insure there were no abuses, lest the Congress restrict their ability to do any electronic surveillance under the Foreign Intelligence Surveillance Act. In the weeks before the Millennium, however, Fran Townsend and her staff at Justice brought dozens of FISA requests to the special intelligence court judges. More happened in a week than normally took place in a year.

For the next several days as Christmas and then the Millennium approached, Berger held daily Principals meetings that often sounded like the pre-watch briefings on *Hill Street Blues.* The Attorney General and FBI Director gave reports that included descriptions of suspect vans and results of search warrants. We all learned what BOLO meant in cop talk (Be on the Lookout for . . .). Tenet called his key counterparts around the world, wringing out details, cajoling security services into preemptive raids on possible cells.

In addition to coordinating the offensive, the CSG prepared for the worst. Disaster recovery units were prepositioned. All the assets we had used after the African bombings were mobilized. No one in the counterterrorism business was going to have any holidays, especially on New Year's Eve. On Christmas Day, Berger and I spent the morning at FBI headquarters with scores of agents and the afternoon at CIA's Counterterrorism Center with dozens of analysts. Again, we waited.

In Yemen, a U.S. Navy destroyer was planning a port call in Aden harbor as part of CENTCOM's effort to increase military-to-military contacts and cooperation. The destroyer, named after four brothers who had all died on the same ship in World War II, was the USS *The Sullivans.* As we later learned, Al Qaeda had it in the crosshairs. A small boat was loaded with high explosives in order to be driven right into the destroyer. Al Qaeda planned that attack to be simultaneous with others: Los Angeles Airport exploding in blood and glass; the Amman Radisson collapsing in flames and dust, Christian tourists gunned down at Mount Nebo. Perhaps the Yemen cell knew as they loaded the boat that the Los Angeles and Amman plans had been disrupted. Perhaps they knew they were the only part of the plot that the Americans had not discovered. As they pushed the boat down the landing and into the water, however, it moved off a little into the harbor, and sank. The explosives weighed too much.

In a vault just off the floor of the Y2K Coordination Center, we waited for midnight in Riyadh, then in Paris. There were no major computer failures, no explosions. I went down the list, calling each command center and monitoring post that would detect something happening. CIA noted that more than half the world had celebrated the rollover without incident. FAA said that almost no one was flying that night and airlines had canceled flights. Secret Service was ready to move the President to the Lincoln Memorial for the Washington celebration. FEMA said the disaster units were at air bases and prepositioned in cities. Coast Guard had filled New York Harbor and its rivers with armed cutters. Energy had deployed its nuclear weapons detection teams. I could hardly hear John O'Neill when I called his cell phone; he was at the New York Police Command Post in Time Square. "We've shaken every tree, but I figure if they're gonna do anything in New York, they're gonna do it here," he explained. "So I'm here."

At midnight I went to the roof to look down on the celebration at the Lincoln Memorial. Fireworks burst in the cold night sky. As the celebration ended and the President's motorcade began to return to the White House to continue the party, Sandy Berger called from the limousine. "So far, so good. Any signs of trouble?"

"No, but Los Angeles celebrates in three hours," I answered, wondering how I would stay awake until then. It had been a long three weeks.

"Well, thank everybody for the President and for me. I think we dodged the bullet, but we also learned a lot. We got a lot of work to do." Berger was right. For anyone who doubted it before, the Boston taxi driver, the Los Angeles airport, the Brooklyn connection, the Montreal cell had all said one thing: they're here.

At 3:00 a.m. we went back to the rooftop and popped open a bottle.

THE MILITARY HAVE A PRACTICE known as "Lessons Learned" or "After Action Review." Whenever a major military operation or exercise is conducted, a formal process analyzes what went right and what could have been done better. In the military tradition of not wanting to fight for the same hill twice, the U.S. military is not eager to, as Santayana said, "be condemned to repeat" something out of failure to learn the lesson the first time. After what became known as the

Millennium Terrorist Alert of December 1999, the Principals chartered the CSG to prepare a Millennium After Action Review. Each agency examined what it had learned and the group collectively looked at our shortcomings. The list of shortcomings clustered around one fact, that there were probably al Qaeda sleeper cells in the United States.

I had believed for at least five years that al Qaeda was here. I had not had much luck convincing the FBI to pay close attention. Officially, the FBI said they knew of only a handful of sympathizers who were under surveillance. There were no active cells, no indigenously based threat, according to the Bureau. John O'Neill and I believed otherwise, but O'Neill had transferred to the New York Office. It was the most important FBI office in the country and O'Neill had made it the operational arm of the FBI for going after al Qaeda overseas. Nonetheless, most field offices and much of FBI Headquarters was focused elsewhere. Louis Freeh's interest in foreign-based terrorism seemed to be almost entirely focused on investigating the Khobar attack. The National Security Division, where the terrorism account was located, was consumed with Russian and Chinese espionage, the case of FBI agent Robert Hanssen, the American spying for the Russians, and the case of Wen Ho Lee and the possible spying at the nuclear labs.

In the fifty-six Field Offices (except New York) the emphasis was on drugs, organized crime, and other issues that generated arrests and prosecutions. The managers of these offices had little time for surveillance and infiltration of possible Islamic radicals. In some cities, we had created Joint Terrorism Task Forces that brought together representatives from all the local federal law enforcement agencies with the state and local police. I had assumed that these JTTFs were hunting al Qaeda. To test that proposition, I traveled around the country visiting FBI offices and JTTFs. What I found was deeply disturbing.

In every instance, the Special Agents in Charge and their JTTF directors all professed that there was no al Qaeda presence in their region, but they had taken almost no steps to uncover any in the first place. Instead, they were following whatever terrorist organization was making itself obvious. In some cases it was the Irish Republican Army, in others it was Indian Sikhs, or domestic militias.

"Is there an al Qaeda presence in this city?" I would ask.

Often I would get the response, "What's al Qaeda? Is that that Been Layding guy? He hasn't been here."

Roger Cressey or Paul Kurtz would follow up. "What do they say about jihad at the mosques, after the services? What do they pass out? What do they collect money for?"

"Hell, we can't go to a mosque or even a church unless we have cause. Can't send in a source either," would always be the answer. Then they would add, "Listen, we go for prosecutions and the U.S. Attorney here isn't interested in some minor infraction for supporting terrorism. Shit, we don't even have any Assistant U.S. Attorneys who have top secret clearance."

They all noted that the Attorney General's Guidelines made it impossible for them to do things without already knowing about a probable crime. They could not, without someone providing them an initial lead, attend services at mosques or sit in on meetings of student groups. They were prohibited from printing organization's Web pages unless they suspected a crime was in progress. In many cities the agents did not even have Internet access.

The Attorney General's Guidelines were initially adopted in the wake of the Watergate era scandals of the early 1970s. During that period it had been revealed that the FBI had kept files on people and groups for no reason other than J. Edgar Hoover's whim. To correct that kind of abuse, the Justice Department had put the FBI in a straitjacket and they were still in it.

The lack of computer support, however, was a failure of the Bureau's leadership. Local police departments throughout the country had far more advanced data systems than the FBI. In New York I saw piles of terrorism files on the floor of the JTTF. There was only one low-paid file clerk there, and he could not keep up with the volume of paper that was being generated. There was no way for one agent to know what information another agent had collected, even in the same office. Wiretap recordings lay around for weeks because there were too few Arabic or Farsi or Pashto translators. All translations were done in the city in which the conversations were recorded.

When the FBI did uncover something interesting and report it to

Washington, no written record of it ever left the Bureau. This was in marked contrast to CIA, NSA, and the State Department, which flooded my secure e-mail with over one hundred detailed reports every day. The only way that we knew what FBI Headquarters knew was by secure telephone calls or meetings.

The volume of the reporting from other agencies became so great that we established a Threat Subgroup that tracked leads on an Excel spreadsheet called the Threat Matrix. The subgroup went through the reports, asking: what was the source of the information, was the source ever right before, is there any independent way to verify the report, what should we do to deal with the possible threat? The subgroup then followed up, going back to the report until it could be "negated," struck from the list of active threats. The subgroup had representatives from FBI, CIA, Secret Service, NSA, DOD, State, FAA, and often other agencies.

Steve Simon and later Roger Cressey chaired the Threat Subgroup. It was not unusual for them to report that whoever the FBI representative was that day, was not really participating, causing me to have to call higher levels of the Bureau. On one day I specifically remember, mild-mannered Cressey marched into my office after a Threat Subgroup meeting and announced, "That fucker is going to get some Americans killed. He just sits there like a bump on a log. Nothing to report. No comment on anybody else's work. Doesn't want to check anything out." I knew he was talking about an FBI representative.

When we would ask FBI if there were criminal violations of support to terrorism such as establishing Web sites soliciting funds or other means of terrorist financing, we would get blank stares. Rick Newcomb's office at Treasury was trying to give the FBI some guidance on where to look for terrorist money, but to little avail. When FBI said there were no Web sites in the U.S. that were recruiting jihadists for training in Afghanistan or soliciting money for terrorist front groups, I asked Steve Emerson to check. Emerson had written the book *American Jihad,* which had told me more than the FBI ever had about radical Islamic groups in the U.S. Within days, Emerson had a long list of Web sites sitting on servers in the United States. I passed the list to Justice and the FBI. Nothing appeared to happen as a result, although the Justice Department staff did note how difficult it was to prosecute "free speech" cases.

The two bright lights in the FBI were John O'Neill and Dale Watson, who replaced O'Neill in Washington when John went to the New York Office. They were a study in contrasts. O'Neill could have passed for a Boston Irish Congressman who read *GQ* magazine. Watson pretended to be a "good old boy" and actually chewed tobacco. To encourage CIA-FBI cooperation after forty years of mutual hostility, the two organizations had exchanged senior counterterrorism managers. Watson had come to the FBI Headquarters job having spent two years in the CIA Counterterrorism Center. He knew his stuff.

When Dale Watson sat down with me to develop the Millennium After Action Review he knew he had a problem. "We have to smash the FBI into bits and rebuild it to do terrorism," Dale confided. "We're off running around after crooks who rob banks when there are people planning to kill Americans right here in the USA." Hallelujah! I thought.

Watson got Freeh to approve a meeting in Tampa for all senior FBI supervisors from all fifty-six offices. He asked me to begin the meeting by telling the audience what al Qaeda was and what they wanted to do.

I began, "Al Qaeda is a worldwide political conspiracy masquerading as a religious sect. It engages in murder of innocent people to grab attention. Its goal is a fourteenth-century-style theocracy in which women have no rights, everyone is forced to be a Muslim, and the Sharia legal system is used to cut off hands and stone people to death. It also uses a global banking network and financial system to support its activities. These people are smart, many trained in our colleges, and they have a very long view. They think it may take them a century to accomplish their goals, one of which is the destruction of the United States of America. They have good spy tradecraft and employ sleeper cells and front groups that plan for years before acting. They are our number one enemy and they are amongst us, in your cities. Find them."

Watson followed me: "They are the FBI's number one priority in terrorism. You will find them. If you have to arrest them for jaywalking, do it. If the local U.S. Attorney won't prosecute them, call me. If you can't get your FISA wiretap approved by Justice, call us, don't just sit out there and sulk." People were taking notes, but some looked like they had heard this sort of "new priority" speech before.

"One more thing," Watson added. "Your bonus, your promotion, your city of assignment all depend upon how well you do on this mission." There was an uneasy shifting in seats. Everyone was staring at Dale. "I mean it, and I have Louis's backing. If you don't believe me, try me." Dale was not being a good old boy anymore.

As Watson walked me to the car, he said, "The FBI is like an aircraft carrier. It takes a long time to stop going in one direction and turn around and go in another. These Field Offices have all had their own way, little fiefdoms, for years. At least I'm starting." He was starting, but it would take years of consistent top-down management to fix. We had been throwing millions of dollars at the FBI for counterterrorism and they did not even have any data system that allowed the Joint Terrorism Task Forces to share.

The Millennium After Action Review established twenty-nine recommendations, most aimed at the threat of foreign terrorists in the United States. Among the proposals was the creation of JTTFs in every one of the fifty-six FBI offices, staffing them with Immigration officers and Internal Revenue agents. We proposed creating one central wiretap translation office and hiring more translators. There were specific proposals for joint action with Canada, in light of the discovery of the Montreal cell, including conforming our visa and asylum policies. It was clear that if you could get into Canada, you could get into the United States. In the subzero conditions of February, Roger Cressey and I went to Ottawa and gained concurrence from our Canadian counterparts on a list of joint actions. Discovery of the Montreal cell had shaken the Prime Minister's office as well.

The Principals approved the After Action proposals. Those recommendations that could be immediately implemented were. For those that would require new funds, agencies were to work with Congress to change their fiscal year 2001 budgets. The aircraft carrier was turning into the wind of foreign terrorists in the U.S. It had taken too long.

THE PRESIDENT ALSO RECEIVED a summary of the After Action Review, along with an update on the CIA's attempts to get bin Laden or, at least, to tell us where to fire cruise missiles. Clinton was not pleased with CIA's progress.

I thought we needed new eyes looking at the problem of locating the al Qaeda leadership long enough to permit us to act. Charlie Allen was managing intelligence collection priorities for the entire intelligence community. I asked him to meet with the three-star admiral who was the director of operations for the Joint Staff, Scott Frey. The two came back with a novel idea. Instead of depending on unreliable human assets to find bin Laden, why not fly an unmanned aircraft around? The new Predator had a long "dwell time" and it provided a real-time video feed, even if it was ten thousand miles away.

There were a few problems. First, we would need to get some Predators, and they were in short supply. Some were being used in Bosnia and some in Iraq. Second, we would need some money to pay for the operation. Finally, we would need to get the agencies to agree to do it.

It was the last that proved to be the biggest hurdle. Too risky. Too costly. Too not-invented-here. Usually when I hit a brick wall like that, Sandy Berger would try to persuade his counterparts of the wisdom of the idea. In this case, Berger virtually instructed that the mission be carried out. By September the satellite links and other necessary little technical issues were worked out and the first Predator flew into Afghanistan.

Roger Cressey and I made midnight trips to watch Kandahar on a giant video screen in northern Virginia. A small team sat at their consoles, not quite believing that what they were seeing was happening right then on the other side of the globe. This sort of intelligence capability was something we had seen only in Hollywood movies.

The bird flew quietly over a known terrorist camp and, as it did, a

Land Rover was headed toward the gate. "Follow that car," the mission controller called out to the "pilot" seated in front of him in the darkened Virginia room. He then turned to me and Cressey and with a big grin said, "I always wanted to say that." The pilot kept the Land Rover on-screen as it moved through market squares and in and out of a tunnel. Finally it pulled up in front of a villa and those in the vehicle went inside. "Well, we now know that villa is al Qaeda–related."

Predators flew in September and October of 2000. One Predator was damaged during takeoff, setting off a bureaucratic fight over who would pay the few hundred thousand dollars to repair it. On another flight, the Taliban's radar detected the Predator and an ancient MiG fighter was launched. The Predator's camera watched as the fighter plane lumbered into the air, climbed, and began a big circle that ended with the fighter about two miles from the Predator, aimed right at it. The image of the MiG grew from a speck to an enormous object hurtling at the camera. "Holy shit, it's going to hit us!" the controller yelled, as half the people in the control room dove under their desks. Ten thousand miles away, the MiG flew right by the Predator, apparently unable to see it.

From the camera images on three flights, I am convinced that I was looking at bin Laden. There were no submarines off the coast to fire. The Navy had been trying for months to get its submarines back and had succeeded. The seasonal winds were also picking up, making it impossible for the Predator to fly over the mountains it had to traverse. Reluctantly, we agreed that the flights would resume when the winter was over.

The Air Force had been intending to experiment with placing small rockets or missiles on the Predator, with a view to possibly having a working capability in 2004. We asked them to have it ready for the late spring of 2001.

Much has been written about the origins of the Predator unmanned aerial vehicle and about the bureaucratic battles that followed my proposal to use it as a counterterrorist weapon in the fight against al Qaeda. In their book *The Age of Sacred Terror,* Dan Benjamin and Steve Simon quote a "senior DOD official" as saying that the CIA opposed the initial use of the Predator and the White House "had to cram this down the throat of the Agency. The [CIA] Directorate of Operations, they go to cocktail parties and recruit spies, and they said this is paramilitary and can screw up my relationship with the host government."

Later in the book, on the issue of flying an armed version of the Predator to attack al Qaeda, Benjamin and Simon add that "the head of the Directorate of Operations, Jim Pavitt, was heard to say that if the Predator was used against bin Laden and the responsibility for this use of lethal force was laid at the Agency's doorstep, it would endanger the lives of CIA operatives around the world." Finally, they note that in a White House meeting a week before September 11, CIA Director George Tenet "intervened forcefully. It would be a terrible mistake, he declared, for the Director of Central Intelligence to fire a weapon like this."

The New Yorker quotes Roger Cressey as saying of the bureaucratic dispute about the use of the armed Predator prior to September 11, "It sounds terrible, but we used to say to each other that some people didn't get it . . . it was going to take body bags." It did. The armed Predator flew after al Qaeda in Afghanistan only following September 11. It proved highly successful.

DURING THE PREDATOR'S TRIAL RUN in October 2000, the al Qaeda cell that had sunk its own boat around the time of the Millenium tried once again to attack a U.S. destroyer in Aden, Yemen. This time they succeeded and killed seventeen American sailors aboard the USS *Cole.* For over three years the CSG had been concerned with security at the ports in the region that were being used by the U.S. Navy. Steve Simon had written a scathing report on security he discovered at the Navy pier near Dubai in the United Arab Emirates. Sandy Berger had sent the report to the Secretary of Defense. I had personally crawled around and climbed up into sniper positions at the U.S. Navy facility in Bahrain because of repeated reports that al Qaeda planned to attack there. The Defense Department had fixed the problems in Bahrain and the UAE, but bases weren't the only points of vulnerability. When the USS *Cole* was attacked, we were shocked to learn that the Navy was even making port calls in Yemen.

Mike Sheehan, then the State Department representative on the CSG, had summed up our feelings: "Yemen is a viper's nest of terrorists. What the fuck was the *Cole* doing there in the first place?" The system had failed. When CENTCOM decided to begin port visits in Aden, no one in the Defense Department had referred that proposal for interagency security review.

As in the case of Khobar and the East African embassy bombings, the FBI sent out a large team to collect evidence and interrogate witnesses. Ever the hands-on guy, John O'Neill led the team. He ran right into the U.S. Ambassador I would least like to deal with under those circumstances, Barbara Bodine. O'Neill could charm a corpse, but he could not find a modus vivendi with the U.S. Ambassador to Yemen. The Yemeni government also dragged its feet in the investigation, leading to President Clinton's becoming personally involved. The U.S. government left the Yemenis in no doubt about the two alternative paths that Yemeni-American relations could take.

Meanwhile in Washington neither CIA nor FBI would state the obvious: al Qaeda did it. We knew there was a large al Qaeda cell in Yemen. There was also a large cell of Egyptian Islamic Jihad, but that group had now announced its complete merger into al Qaeda, so what difference did it make which group did the attack? Lisa Gordon-Hagerty, Paul Kurtz, and Roger Cressey had worked around the clock piecing together the evidence and had made a very credible case against al Qaeda. CIA would agree only months later.

In the meantime in Principals discussions, it was difficult to gain support for a retaliatory strike when neither FBI nor CIA would say that al Qaeda did it. Once again I proposed bombing all of the al Qaeda camps in Afghanistan, without tying the operation to getting bin Laden or even to retaliating for the *Cole.* There was no support for bombing.

Mike Sheehan could not believe what took place in the Principals meeting following the attack on the *Cole.* He had grown up in the military: West Point, Korea, Special Forces school, hostage rescue team in Panama, fighting in El Salvador, Command and General Staff School, peacekeeping in Somalia and Haiti, two tours with the NSC at the White House. He had always assumed that when U.S. forces were attacked and killed, U.S. government leaders would want to avenge the attacks. Sheehan knew those leaders. Now out of the Special Forces and a civilian serving as the State Department's leading counterterrorism official, he had worked with these Principals for years. He had energized the State Department from within to use all its diplomatic assets against al Qaeda. Yet now, with seventeen dead sailors, the Principals had decided to do nothing, to wait for proof of who had committed the attack. Sheehan was particularly outraged that the highest-ranking U.S. military officer had not even suggested that the U.S. employ existing retaliation plans against al Qaeda bases in Afghanistan and against their Taliban hosts. Sheehan detested the Taliban, whose representatives had lied to his face.

On a brisk October day in 2000, Sheehan stood with me on West Executive Avenue and watch as the limousines left the White House meeting on the *Cole* attack to go back to the Pentagon. "What's it gonna take, Dick?" Sheehan demanded, "Who the shit do they think attacked the *Cole,* fuckin' Martians? The Pentagon brass won't let Delta go get bin Laden. Hell, they won't even let the Air Force carpet bomb the place. Does al Qaeda have to attack the Pentagon to get their attention?"

Time was running out on the Clinton administration. There was going to be one last major national security initiative and it was going to be a final try to achieve an Israeli-Palestinian agreement. It really looked like that long-sought goal was possible. The Israeli Prime Minister had agreed to major concessions. I would like to have tried both, Camp David and blowing up the al Qaeda camps. Nonetheless, I understood. If we could achieve a Middle East peace much of the popular support for al Qaeda and much of the hatred for America would evaporate overnight. There would be another chance to go after the camps. The Principals asked me to update the Pol-Mil Plan for the Transition, flagging the issues where there was not consensus, where decisions had not been agreed. I listed aiding the Northern Alliance, eliminating the camps, and flying armed Predators to eliminate the al Qaeda leadership.

Clinton left office with bin Laden alive, but having authorized actions to eliminate him and to step up the attacks on al Qaeda. He had defeated al Qaeda when it had attempted to take over Bosnia by having its fighters dominate the defense of the breakaway state from Serbian attacks. He had seen earlier than anyone that terrorism would be the major new threat facing America, and therefore had greatly increased funding for counterterrorism and initiated homeland protection programs. He had put an end to Iraqi and Iranian terrorism against the United States by quickly acting against the intelligence services of each nation.

Because of the intensity of the political opposition that Clinton engendered, he had been heavily criticized for bombing al Qaeda camps in Afghanistan, for engaging in "Wag the Dog" tactics to divert attention from a scandal about his personal life. For similar reasons, he could not fire the recalcitrant FBI Director who had failed to fix the Bureau or to uncover terrorists in the United States. He had given the CIA unprecedented authority to go after bin Laden personally and al Qaeda, but had not taken steps when they did little or nothing. Because Clinton was criticized as a Vietnam War opponent without a military record, he was limited in his ability to direct the military to engage in anti-terrorist commando operations they did not want to conduct. He had tried that in Somalia, and the military had made mistakes and blamed him. In the absence of a bigger provocation from al Qaeda to silence his critics, Clinton thought he could do no more. Nonetheless, he put in place the plans and programs that allowed America to respond to the big attacks when they did come, sweeping away the political barriers to action.

When Clinton left office many people, including the incoming Bush administration leadership, thought that he and his administration were overly obsessed with al Qaeda. After all, al Qaeda had killed only a few Americans, nothing like the hundreds of Marines who died at the hands of Beirut terrorists during the Reagan administration or the hundreds of Americans who were killed by Libya on Pan Am 103 during the first Bush's administration. Those two acts had not provoked U.S. military retaliation. Why was Clinton so worked up about al Qaeda and why did he talk to President-elect Bush about it and have

Sandy Berger raise it with his successor as National Security Advisor, Condi Rice? In January 2001, the new administration really thought Clinton's recommendation that eliminating al Qaeda be one of their highest priorities, well, rather odd, like so many of the Clinton administration's actions, from their perspective.

Chapter 10

Before and After September 11

AL QAEDA PLANNED ATTACKS years in advance, inserted sleeper cells, did reconnaissance. They took the long view, believing that their struggle would take decades, perhaps generations. America worked on a four-year electoral cycle and at the end of 2000, a new cycle was beginning. In the presidential campaign, terrorism had not been discussed. George Bush and Dick Cheney had mentioned the Antiballistic Missile Treaty with Russia. They had also talked about Iraq.

In January 2001, with the Florida fiasco behind us, I briefed each of my old friends and associates from the first Bush administration, Condi Rice, Steve Hadley, Dick Cheney, and Colin Powell. My message was stark: al Qaeda is at war with us, it is a highly capable organization, probably with sleeper cells in the U.S., and it is clearly planning a major series of attacks against us; we must act decisively and quickly, deciding on the issues prepared after the attack on the *Cole,* going on the offensive.

Each person reacted differently. Cheney was, as ever, quiet and calm on the surface. The wheels were spinning behind the mask. He asked an aide to arrange for a visit to CIA to learn their view of the al Qaeda threat. That was fine by me because I knew that George Tenet would be even more alarmist than I had been about what al Qaeda was planning. Cheney did make the trip up the Parkway to CIA Headquarters, one of many he would make. Most of the visits focused on Iraq and left midlevel managers and analysts wondering whether the seasoned Vice President was right about the Iraqi threat; perhaps they should adjust their own analysis. In the first weeks of the Administration, however, Cheney had heard me loud and clear about al Qaeda. Now that he was attending the NSC Principals meetings chaired by Condi Rice (something no Vice President had ever done), I hoped he would speak up about the urgency of the problem, put it on a short list for immediate action. He didn't.

Colin Powell took the unusual step during the transition of asking to meet with the CSG, the senior counterterrorism officers from NSC, State, Defense, CIA, FBI, and the military. He wanted to see us interact, respond to each other's statements. When we all agreed at the importance of the al Qaeda threat, Powell was obviously surprised at the unanimity.

Brian Sheridan, the soon departing Assistant Secretary of Defense, summed it up: "General Powell, I will be leaving when the administration changes. I am the only political appointee in the room. All these guys are career professionals. So let me give you one piece of advice, untainted by any personal interest. Keep this interagency team together and make al Qaeda your number one priority. We may all squabble about tactics and we may call each other assholes from time to time, but this is the best interagency team I have ever seen and they all want to get al Qaeda. They're comin' after us and we gotta get them first." Powell asked extensive questions about what State could do, took detailed notes, and later asked Rich Armitage (who would become Deputy Secretary) to get involved.

I met Condi Rice wandering the halls of the Executive Office Building looking for my office. She said that she had fond memories of working in the old building on the White House grounds. I escorted her to my office and gave her the same briefing on al Qaeda that I had been using with the others. Condi Rice's reaction was very polite, as she almost always is. I realized when I prepared to brief my former colleague and now boss, that she was the fourth National Security Advisor I had worked for and the seventh I had worked with.

Brent Scowcroft had been the lovable old sage, focused largely on the strategic nuclear balance until the First Gulf War came along. Brent, although a close friend of the first President Bush, suffered from the fact that the Secretary of State cut him out and talked, frequently, directly to the President. Tony Lake had been the passionate, thoughtful leader whose professorial image belied the fact that he was a master bureaucratic schemer, always several moves ahead of everyone else. Lake had always won the bureaucratic battles, but he had not won the President's heart. Their two personalities did not mesh well and Clinton shifted him to CIA Director in the second term. (Lake withdrew during a bruising confirmation fight in the Senate. Had he been CIA Director, there is no doubt in my mind that he would have relentlessly gone after bin Laden and moved out the bureaucrats who got in the way.)

Sandy Berger had been Lake's deputy, but also a long-standing friend of both Bill and Hillary Clinton. Initially the assumption on the NSC Staff was that Berger was the political commissar, but his prodigious capacity for detailed work on the tough national security issues won him the respect of the bureaucrats. As National Security Advisor, he had dominated State and the Pentagon.

Now Condi Rice was in charge. She appeared to have a closer relationship with the second President Bush than any of her predecessors had with the presidents they reported to. That should have given her some manuver room, some margin for shaping the agenda. The Vice President, however, had decided to be involved at the NSC Principals level. The Secretary of Defense also made clear that he didn't care about anyone else's relationship with the President; he was doing what he wanted to do. As I briefed Rice on al Qaeda, her facial expression gave me the impression that she had never heard the term before, so I added, "Most people think of it as Usama bin Laden's group, but it's much more than that. It's a network of affiliated terrorist organizations with cells in over fifty countries, including the U.S."

Rice looked skeptical. She focused on the fact that my office staff was large by NSC standards (twelve people) and did operational things, including domestic security issues. She said, "The NSC looks just as it did when I worked here a few years ago, except for your operation. It's all new. It does domestic things and it is not just doing policy, it seems to be worrying about operational issues. I'm not sure we will want to keep all of this in the NSC."

Rice viewed the NSC as a "foreign policy" coordination mechanism and not some place where issues such as terrorism in the U.S., or domestic preparedness for weapons of mass destruction, or computer network security should be addressed. I realized that Rice, and her deputy, Steve Hadley, were still operating with the old Cold War paradigm from when they had worked on the NSC. Condi's previous government experience had been as an NSC staffer for three years worrying about the Warsaw Pact and the Soviet Union during the Cold War. Steve Hadley had also been an NSC staffer assigned to do arms control issues with the Soviet Union. He had then been an Assistant Secretary in the Pentagon, also concerned with Soviet arms control. It struck me that neither of them had worked on the new post–Cold War security issues.

I tried to explain: "This office is new, you're right. It's post–Cold War security, not focused just on nation-state threats. The boundaries between domestic and foreign have blurred. Threats to the U.S. now are not Soviet ballistic missiles carrying bombs, they're terrorists carrying bombs. Besides, the law that established the NSC in 1947 said it should concern itself with domestic security threats too." I did not succeed entirely in making the case. Over the next several months, they suggested, I should figure out how to move some of these issues out to some other organization.

Rice decided that the position of National Coordinator for Counterterrorism would also be downgraded. No longer would the Coordinator be a member of the Principals Committee. No longer would the CSG report to the Principals, but instead to a committee of Deputy Secretaries. No longer would the National Coordinator be supported by two NSC Senior Directors or have the budget review mechanism with the Associate Director of OMB. She did, however, ask me to stay on and to keep my entire staff in place. Rice and Hadley did not seem to know anyone else whose expertise covered what they regarded as my strange portfolio. At the same time, Rice requested that I develop a reorganization plan to spin out some of the security functions to someplace outside the NSC Staff.

Within a week of the Inauguration I wrote to Rice and Hadley asking "urgently" for a Principals, or Cabinet-level, meeting to review the imminent al Qaeda threat. Rice told me that the Principals Committee, which had been the first venue for terrorism policy discussions in the Clinton administration, would not address the issue until it had been "framed" by the Deputies. I assumed that meant an opportunity for the Deputies to review the agenda. Instead, it meant months of delay. The initial Deputies meeting to review terrorism policy could not be scheduled in February. Nor could it occur in March. Finally in April, the Deputies Committee met on terrorism for the first time. The first meeting, in the small wood-paneled Situation Room conference room, did not go well.

Rice's deputy, Steve Hadley, began the meeting by asking me to brief the group. I turned immediately to the pending decisions needed to deal with al Qaeda. "We need to put pressure on both the Taliban and al Qaeda by arming the Northern Alliance and other groups in Afghanistan. Simultaneously, we need to target bin Laden and his leadership by reinitiating flights of the Predator."

Paul Wolfowitz, Donald Rumsfeld's deputy at Defense, fidgeted and scowled. Hadley asked him if he was all right. "Well, I just don't understand why we are beginning by talking about this one man bin Laden," Wolfowitz responded.

I answered as clearly and forcefully as I could: "We are talking about a network of terrorist organizations called al Qaeda, that happens to be led by bin Laden, and we are talking about that network because it and it alone poses an immediate and serious threat to the United States."

"Well, there are others that do as well, at least as much. Iraqi terrorism for example," Wolfowitz replied, looking not at me but at Hadley.

"I am unaware of any Iraqi-sponsored terrorism directed at the United States, Paul, since 1993, and I think FBI and CIA concur in that judgment, right, John?" I pointed at CIA Deputy Director John McLaughlin, who was obviously not eager to get in the middle of a debate between the White House and the Pentagon but nonetheless replied, "Yes, that is right, Dick. We have no evidence of any active Iraqi terrorist threat against the U.S."

Finally, Wolfowitz turned to me. "You give bin Laden too much credit. He could not do all these things like the 1993 attack on New York, not without a state sponsor. Just because FBI and CIA have failed to find the linkages does not mean they don't exist." I could hardly believe it but Wolfowitz was actually spouting the totally discredited Laurie Mylroie theory that Iraq was behind the 1993 truck bomb at the World Trade Center, a theory that had been investigated for years and found to be totally untrue.

It was getting a little too heated for the kind of meeting Steve Hadley liked to chair, but I thought it was important to get the extent of the disagreement out on the table: "Al Qaeda plans major acts of terrorism against the U.S. It plans to overthrow Islamic governments and set up a radical multination Caliphate, and then go to war with non-Muslim states." Then I said something I regretted as soon as I said it: "They have published all of this and sometimes, as with Hitler in *Mein Kampf,* you have to believe that these people will actually do what they say they will do."

Immediately Wolfowitz seized on the Hitler reference. "I resent any comparison between the Holocaust and this little terrorist in Afghanistan."

"I wasn't comparing the Holocaust to anything." I spoke slowly. "I was saying that like Hitler, bin Laden has told us in advance what he plans to do and we would make a big mistake to ignore it."

To my surprise, Deputy Secretary of State Rich Armitage came to my rescue. "We agree with Dick. We see al Qaeda as a major threat and countering it as an urgent priority." The briefings of Colin Powell had worked.

Hadley suggested a compromise. We would begin by focusing on al Qaeda and then later look at other terrorism, including any Iraqi terrorism. Because dealing with al Qaeda involved its Afghan sanctuary, however, Hadley suggested that we needed policy on Afghanistan in general and on the related issue of U.S.-Pakistani relations, including the return of democracy in that country and arms control with India. All of these issues were a "cluster" that had to be decided together. Hadley proposed that several more papers be written and several more meetings be scheduled over the next few months.

I WASN'T THE ONLY ONE asserting an al Qaeda threat whom Wolfowitz belittled. Our Ambassador to Indonesia, Robert Gelbard, was putting pressure on the Jakarta government to do something about al Qaeda and its offshoot, Jemmah Islamiyah (JI). Gelbard had closed the U.S. embassy in Jakarta when he received credible reports that a six-person al Qaeda hit team had been dispatched from Yemen. He had publicly criticized the Indonesian government for turning a blind eye to al Qaeda infiltration and subversion. Then on Christmas Day 2000, the JI launched an offensive against Christians, bombing twenty churches. Gelbard stepped up his pressure privately and publicly.

Bob Gelbard had been a star in the Foreign Service for three decades, had been Ambassador to Bolivia, Assistant Secretary of State for International Law Enforcement and Narcotics, Special Presidential Envoy to the Balkans. He was not the kind of diplomat who worried about place settings, but instead knew about armed helicopters and communications intercepts. He had fought drug lords and Serbian thugs. Now he saw what was taking place in Indonesia: al Qaeda was targeting the largest Islamic nation in the world as its next battlefield.

Arriving in the Pentagon early in 2001, Paul Wolfowitz began calling old acquaintances in Indonesia, where he had earlier been ambassador. What he heard from them was that Gelbard was making things uncomfortable, making too much noise about al Qaeda, being paranoid. Wolfowitz reportedly urged Gelbard's removal. Bob Gelbard came home and retired from the Foreign Service. In October 2002, al Qaeda's local front attacked nightclubs in Bali, killing 202, mainly Australians. Ten months later, they attacked the Marriott Hotel in Jakarta, killing 13. The investigations that followed revealed an extensive network of al Qaeda operatives in Indonesia, the Philippines, and Malaysia led by those whom Gelbard had suspected and had demanded be stopped.

THE DELAY IN THE DEPUTIES COMMITTEE continued in the spring of 2001, in part because of Hadley's methodical, lawyerly style. It was his idea to slowly build a consensus that action was required, "to educate the Deputies." The truth was also that the Principals Committee was meeting with a full agenda and a backlog of Bush priority issues: the Antiballistic Missile Treaty, the Kyoto environment agreement, and Iraq. There was no time for terrorism.

Winter had turned to spring. The daily NSC Staff meetings were filled with detailed discussion about the ABM Treaty and other issues that I thought were vestigial Cold War concerns. One day I saw an editorial cartoon of Uncle Sam sitting on a throne reading the ABM Treaty, while a fuse ran down on a bomb beneath his seat and a terrorist ran away behind him. The cartoon hit me hard. My frustration was boiling over. I asked to be reassigned.

I had completed the review of the organizational options for homeland defense and critical infrastructure protection that Rice had asked me to conduct. There was agreement to create a separate, senior White House position for Critical Infrastructure Protection and Cyber Security, outside of the NSC Staff. Condi Rice and Steve Hadley assumed that I would continue on the NSC focusing on terrorism and asked whom I had in mind for the new job that would be created outside the NSC. I requested that I be given that assignment, to the apparent surprise of Condi Rice and Steve Hadley. "Perhaps," I suggested, "I have become too close to the terrorism issue. I have worked it for ten years and to me it seems like a very important issue, but maybe I'm becoming like Captain Ahab with bin Laden as the White Whale. Maybe you need someone less obsessive about it." I assume that my message was clear enough: you obviously do not think that terrorism is as important as I do since you are taking months to do anything; so get somebody else to do it who can be happy working at it at your pace. We agreed that I would start the new critical infrastructure and cyber job at the beginning of the new fiscal year, October 1.

In the remaining four months, however, I was intent on pushing hard to get an Administration policy in place go after al Qaeda. Roger Cressey and I rewrote the Pol-Mil Plan as a draft National Security Presidential Decision document for the President's signature. Its goal:

eliminate al Qaeda. Some in the Deputies Committee suggested that we say instead "significantly erode al Qaeda."

George Tenet had also been asked to stay on from Clinton to Bush. He and I regularly commiserated that al Qaeda was not being addressed more seriously by the new administration. Sometimes I would walk into my office and find the Director of Central Intelligence sitting at my desk or the desk of my assistant, Beverly Roundtree, waiting to vent his frustration. We agreed that Tenet would insure that the President's daily briefings would continue to be replete with threat information on al Qaeda. President Bush, reading the intelligence every day and noticing that there was a lot about al Qaeda, asked Condi Rice why it was that we couldn't stop "swatting flies" and eliminate al Qaeda. Rice told me about the conversation and asked how the plan to get al Qaeda was coming in the Deputies Committee. "It can be presented to the Principals in two days, whenever we can get a meeting," I pressed. Rice promised to get to it soon. Time passed.

For years George Tenet had called me directly when he read a piece of raw intelligence about a threat. Often when I checked out these reports with CIA experts, they would point out that the source was untrustworthy or the report was contradicted by more reliable information. Now Tenet's calls to me about threatening intelligence reports became more frequent and the information was good. There were a growing number of reports that al Qaeda's operational pace was picking up. Cells were discovered and rounded up by security services in Italy, France, and Germany. There were reliable reports of a threat to the U.S. Navy in Bahrain, causing me to call the Bahraini Crown Prince on a yacht in the Mediterranean to ask for increased security for our Navy base and access to recently arrested al Qaeda prisoners. The Italians had credible reports that there would be an attempt to attack the G-7 Summit in Genoa, causing the CSG to review plans for that meeting with Secret Service and DOD.

By late June, Tenet and I were convinced that a major series of attacks was about to come. "It's my sixth sense, but I feel it coming. This is going to be the big one," Tenet told me. No one could have been more concerned about the al Qaeda threat than George, but he had been unable over several years to get his agency to find a way to go after the heart of al Qaeda inside Afghanistan. Now CIA's analysis said the attacks were most likely going to be in Israel or Saudi Arabia. I kept thinking about the Millennium After Action Report's message: they're here.

During the spring as initial policy debates in the Administration began, I e-mailed Condi Rice and NSC Staff colleagues that al Qaeda was trying to kill Americans, to have hundreds of dead in the streets of America. During the first week in July I convened the CSG and asked each agency to consider itself on full alert. I asked the CSG agencies to cancel summer vacations and official travel for the counterterrorism response staffs. Each agency should report anything unusual, even if a sparrow should fall from a tree. I asked FBI to send another warning to the 18,000 police departments, State to alert the embassies, and the Defense Department to go to Threat Condition Delta. The Navy moved ships out of Bahrain.

The next day I asked the senior security officials at FAA, Immigration, Secret Service, Coast Guard, Customs, and the Federal Protective Service to meet at the White House. I asked FAA to send another security warning to the airlines and airports and requested special scrutiny at the ports of entry. We considered a broad public warning, but we had no proof or specificity. What would it say? "A terrorist group you have never heard of may be planning to do something somewhere"?

FBI joined us as well as a senior CIA counterterrorism expert who explained that CIA believed al Qaeda was preparing something. When he was done, I added what I had already told the CSG agencies: "You've just heard that CIA thinks al Qaeda is planning a major attack on us. So do I. You heard CIA say it would probably be in Israel or Saudi Arabia. Maybe. But maybe it will be here. Just because there is no evidence that says that it will be here, does not mean it will be overseas. They may try to hit us at home. You have to assume that is what they are going to try to do. Cancel summer vacations, schedule overtime, have your terrorist reaction teams on alert to move fast. Tell me, tell each other, about anything unusual."

Somewhere in CIA there was information that two known al Qaeda terrorists had come into the United States. Somewhere in FBI there was information that strange things had been going on at flight schools in the United States. I had asked to know if a sparrow fell from a tree that summer. What was buried in CIA and FBI was not a matter of one sparrow falling from a tree, red lights and bells should have been going off. They had specific information about individual terrorists from which one could have deduced what was about to happen. None of that information got to me or the White House. It apparently did not even make it up the FBI chain to Dale Watson, the Executive Assistant Director in charge of counterterrorism. I certainly know what I would have done, for we had done it at the Millennium: a nationwide manhunt, rousting anyone suspected of maybe, possibly, having the slightest connection.

On September 4, 2001, the Principals Committee meeting on al Qaeda that I had called for "urgently" on January 25 finally met. In preparation for that meeting I urged Condi Rice to see the issue cleanly, the Administration could decide that al Qaeda was just a nuisance, a cost of doing business for a superpower (as Reagan and the first President Bush had apparently decided about Hezbollah and Libya when those groups had killed hundreds of Americans), and act accordingly, as it had been doing. Or it could decide that the al Qaeda terrorist group and its affiliates posed an existential threat to the American way of life, in which case we should do everything that might be required to eliminate the threat. There was no in-between. I concluded by noting that before choosing from these alternatives, it would be well for Rice to put herself in her own shoes when in the very near future al Qaeda had killed hundreds of Americans: "What will you wish then that you had already done?"

The Principals meeting, when it finally took place, was largely a nonevent. Tenet and I spoke passionately about the urgency and seriousness of the al Qaeda threat. No one disagreed.

Powell laid out an aggressive strategy for putting pressure on Pakistan to side with us against the Taliban and al Qaeda. Money might be needed, he noted, but there was no plan to find the funds.

Rumsfeld, who looked distracted throughout the session, took the Wolfowitz line that there were other terrorist concerns, like Iraq, and whatever we did on this al Qaeda business, we had to deal with the other sources of terrorism.

Tenet agreed to a series of things that CIA could do to be more aggressive, but the details would be worked offline: what would be the new authorities given CIA, how much money would be spent, where would the money come from. I doubted that process would be fruitful anytime soon. CIA had said it could not find a single dollar in any other program to transfer to the anti–al Qaeda effort. It demanded additional funds from the Congress.

The only heated disagreement came over whether to fly the armed Predator over Afghanistan to attack al Qaeda. Neither CIA nor the Defense Department would agree to run that program. Rice ended the discussion without a solution. She asked that I finalize the broad policy document, a National Security Presidential Directive, on al Qaeda and send it to her for Presidential signature.

COULD WE HAVE STOPPED the September 11 attack? It would be facile to say yes. What is clear is that there were failures in the organizations that we trusted to protect us, failures to get information to the right place at the right time, earlier failures to act boldly to reduce or eliminate the threat.

Had we had any chance of stopping it, had we the knowledge we needed to prevent that day, those of us sitting as members of the CSG would literally have given our lives to do so; many of those around the CSG table had already put their lives at risk for their country. But it must be said in truth that if we had stopped those nineteen deluded fools who acted on September 11, as we should have done, there would have been more later. At some point there would probably still have been a horrific attack that would have required the United States to respond massively and systematically to eliminate al Qaeda and its network. Al Qaeda had emerged from the soil after the Cold War like some long dormant plague, it was on a path of its own, and it would not be swayed. And America, alas, seems only to respond well to disasters, to be undistracted by warnings. Our country seems unable to do all that must be done until there has been some awful calamity that validates the importance of the threat.

After September 11, I thought that the arguments would be over, that finally everyone would see what had to be done and go about doing it. The right war was to fight for the elimination of al Qaeda, to stabilize nations threatened by radical Islamic terrorists, to offer a clear alternative to counter the radical "theology" and ideology of the terrorists, and to reduce our own vulnerabilities at home. It was an obvious agenda.

Roger Cressey, my deputy at the NSC Staff, came to me in early October, after the time that I had intended to switch from the terrorism job to Critical Infrastructure Protection and Cyber Security. The switch had been delayed by September 11. He and I, and the others in our little office, had been working eighteen-hour days and more every day since the attacks. At age thirty-six, Cressey had often been mistaken for a graduate student ten years younger. Not anymore. His worry showed and now his concern was that I would want to stay on in the NSC terrorism job to implement our plans. "You're not gonna move now, are you? Finally, they're paying attention to yah, so you wanna hang around and get your White Whale, huh?" Cressey had grown up near the fish piers in Gloucester, Massachusetts. He knew about obsessive fishing boat captains. He had wanted me to move to the new Critical Infrastructure and Cyber job. His frustration with our NSC colleagues and bosses had been getting dangerously high before the attacks.

I was exhausted, from the ten years in the White House, from the marathon since the attacks, from the sleepless nights going over what I might have done to prevent the attacks. I looked at Cressey. "Well, Rog, as I said before: counterterrorism from now on will be a self-licking ice cream cone. It won't need anybody like me running it. Everybody will know what to do now. There won't be disagreements over policy or any need for a ramrod to get things done. It's obvious stuff now. We gave them the game plan. Hell, we gave it to them in January." Cressey was beginning to smile back at me; he saw where I was going. "Cyber security is a virgin issue where we can make a real impact." I went on. "It's the next threat, the next vulnerability, but people do not understand that yet. Let's go do that for a year and see what we can get done."*

A month later, after a six-hour trip from Washington, we walked into a bar in Silicon Valley. I had just become the Special Advisor to the President for Cyberspace Security and was going to spend two weeks getting to know the leaders of the high-tech industry in California. There was a jazz combo playing and I ordered my first alcoholic drink since the night of September 10. People were laughing and having a good time. Cressey and I had spent the weeks since the attacks holed up in a fortresslike White House, going to our homes for a few hours a day, carrying our gas masks, expecting another wave of attacks. In Palo Alto, as in most of America, life was going on. The people trusted, as I did, that the mechanisms of government, now awakened, would deal with the terrorist threat completely and systematically. We were wrong.

Replacing me as the senior NSC counterterrorism official was Wayne Downing, the retired four-star Army general who had led Special Operations Command. Wayne and I had first met twenty-eight years earlier when he was a young Major and I was an even younger Pentagon analyst, thrown together to share a windowless office in the bowels of the Pentagon. As soon as the terrorist attack on Khobar Towers had occurred in 1995, I asked Wayne to lead an investigation of whether there had been lax U.S. security at that Air Force facility. There had been and he said so, much to the Pentagon's chagrin. He was a no-nonsense kind of general, the perfect man for the job of coordinating the post–September 11 response. Within months of replacing me, Wayne Downing quit the White House in frustration at the Administration's continued bureaucratic response to the threat.

Wayne was replaced by two people, John Gordon and Randy Beers. As with Downing, I had known Beers and Gordon for a long time, having started working with them in 1979 and 1981, respectively. Beers was a young Foreign Service officer then and Gordon was an Air Force

*Cressey and I did spend over a year working on the cyber security problem, producing Bush's National Strategy to Secure Cyberspace, and then quit the Administration altogether.

Major. John Gordon went on to command a wing of nuclear armed missiles in Wyoming, be George Tenet's deputy at CIA, and then be the first Director of the new National Nuclear Security Administration. Randy Beers and I would spend the next twenty-three years working together in the White House and State Department, as Deputy Assistant Secretaries, NSC Directors, Assistant Secretaries of State, and Special Assistants to the President. When Randy Beers went to the terrorism job in the NSC in 2002, he began working for his fourth president in the White House (having previously worked there for Reagan, Bush, and Clinton). Beers had enormous experience working on intelligence policy and operations, terrorism, foreign military operations, and law enforcement. He was the perfect man for the job.

Beers called from the White House months later and asked if he could stop by my house for a drink and some advice. "Randy, since when have you started calling before you dropped by? See you in a few minutes." We had been giving each other advice and counsel for years, but I sensed that there was something wrong, maybe there was new information about another planned al Qaeda attack. I sat on the stoop of my old Sears catalogue house and thought back to the night twelve years earlier when I had been sitting there drinking Lagavulin and cursing the CIA for saying that Iraq would not invade Kuwait. Older now and off Scotch, I opened a bottle of Pinot Noir from a small winery I had found along the Russian River. When Beers sat down next to me his first words were, "I think I have to quit."

I thought I knew why, but I asked. His answer flowed like a river at flood: "They still don't get it. Insteada goin' all out against al Qaeda and eliminating our vulnerabilities at home, they wanna fuckin' invade Iraq again. We have a token U.S. military force in Afghanistan, the Taliban are regrouping, we haven't caught bin Laden, or his deputy, or the head of the Taliban. And they aren't going to send more troops to Afghanistan to catch them or to help the government in Kabul secure the country. No, they're holding back, waiting to invade Iraq. Do you know how much it will strengthen al Qaeda and groups like that if we occupy Iraq? There's no threat to us now from Iraq, but 70 percent of the American people think Iraq attacked the Pentagon and the World Trade Center. You wanna know why? Because that's what the Administration wants them to think!" I could see that there was some considerable built-up anxiety with the Bush administration. I got another bottle of the Pinot Noir.

Randy continued. "Worse yet, they're using the War on Terror politically. You know that document from Karl Rove's office that someone found in the park? Remember how it said the Republicans should run for election on the war issue? Well, they did. They are doing 'Wag the Dog'! They ran against Max Cleland, saying he wasn't patriotic because he didn't agree 100 percent with Bush on how to do homeland security. Max Cleland, who lost three of his four limbs for this country in Vietnam!" Beers had lost hearing in one ear in Vietnam, where he had served two tours as a Marine. "I can't work for these people, I'm sorry I just can't."

Beers resigned. He was right about Karl Rove's strategy against not just Max Cleland, but against all Democrats. From within the White House, a decision had been made that in the 2002 congressional elections and in the 2004 reelection, the Republicans would wrap themselves in the flag, saying a vote for them was a vote against the terrorists. "Run on the war" was the direction in 2002. Then Rove meant the War on Terror, but they also had in mind another war that they would gin up.

The churn of senior counterterrorism officials continued. John Gordon was transferred shortly thereafter to the position vacated by Tom Ridge, as Homeland Security Advisor. Fran Townsend, who had worked for Janet Reno and played such a key role in getting court orders during the Millennium Terrorist Alert, took over the NSC counterterrorism coordinator job in 2003.

Looking at this revolving door in the counterterrorism job after my departure, and thinking back to the ten months that I had served President Bush as his National Coordinator for Counterterrorism and Infrastructure Protection, I am still amazed that I had never been given the chance to talk with him about terrorism until September 11. In fact, during that time I had only three meetings where I developed the agenda and briefed him on issues, but each time on subjects other than terrorism. My proposal to brief the President on terrorism was deferred until "after the Deputies Committee and Principals Committee completed their review." In this regard the second Bush administration was like his father's: NSC Staff saw the President infrequently and always with a chaperon. That style stood in sharp contrast with two terms of Clinton's presidency in which NSC Staff members regularly interacted with the Chief Executive, often telling him things that his National Security Advisor might not have said.

From the interactions I did have with Bush it was clear that the critique of him as a dumb, lazy rich kid were somewhat off the mark. When he focused, he asked the kind of questions that revealed a results-oriented mind, but he looked for the simple solution, the bumper sticker description of the problem. Once he had that, he could put energy behind a drive to achieve his goal. The problem was that many of the important issues, like terrorism, like Iraq, were laced with important subtlety and nuance. These issues needed analysis and Bush and his inner circle had no real interest in complicated analyses; on the issues that they cared about, they already knew the answers, it was received wisdom.

Bush was informed by talking with a small set of senior advisors. Early on we were told that "the President is not a big reader" and goes to bed by 10:00. Clinton, by contrast, would be plowing through an in-box filled with staff memos while watching cable television news well after midnight. He would exhaust the White House staff's and departmental staff's expertise and then reach out to university and other sources. More often than not, we would discover he had read the latest book or magazine articles on the subject at hand. Clinton stopped me in the hall one day to say "Good job on that speech in Philadelphia." Wondering how he knew what I had said, I asked, "How the hell did you see that speech?" The President gave me a sheepish grin and admitted: "I had C-SPAN on while I was reading last night." Checking the C-SPAN schedule, I discovered that my Philadelphia speech on the Middle East peace process had run at 2:00 a.m. On another occasion Clinton told me he had read a new book by Gabriel García Márquez the night before. When I tried to get a copy of the book, I learned that it had not yet been published. Clinton was reading the galleys.

There were clearly innumerable differences between Clinton and

Bush, most of them obvious, but the most telling for me was how the two sought and processed information. Bush wanted to get to the bottom line and move on. Clinton sought to hold every issue before him like a Rubik's Cube, examining it from every angle to the point of total distraction for his staff. Many times since September 11 I have wondered what difference it made that George Bush was President when we were attacked. What if it had happened with Clinton still in office or what if the Florida voting procedures had been otherwise?

Although Bush had heard about al Qaeda in intelligence reports before the attack he had spent little time learning about the sources and nature of the movement. His immediate instinct after the attacks was, naturally, to hit back. His framework, however, was summed up by his famous line "you are either with us or against us" and his early focus on dealing with Iraq as a way of demonstrating America's power. I doubt that anyone ever had the chance to make the case to him that attacking Iraq would actually make America less secure and strengthen the broader radical Islamic terrorist movement. Certainly he did not hear that from the small circle of advisors who alone are the people whose views he respects and trusts.

Any leader whom one can imagine as President on September 11 would have declared a "war on terrorism" and would have ended the Afghan sanctuary by invading. Almost any President would have stepped up domestic security and preparedness measures. Exactly what did George Bush do after September 11 that any other President one can imagine wouldn't have done after such attacks? In the end, what was unique about George Bush's reaction to terrorism was his selection as an object lesson for potential state sponsors of terrorism, not a country that had been engaging in anti-U.S. terrorism but one that had not been, Iraq. It is hard to imagine another President making that choice.

Others (Clinton, the first Bush, Carter, Ford) might have tried to understand the phenomenon of terrorism, what led fifteen Saudis and four others to commit suicide to kill Americans. Others might have tried to build a world consensus to address the root causes, while using the moment to force what had been lethargic or doubting governments to arrest known terrorists and close front organizations.

One can imagine Clinton trying one more time to force an Israeli-Palestinian settlement, going to Saudi Arabia and addressing the Muslim people in a moving appeal for religious tolerance, pushing hard for a security arrangement between India and Pakistan to create a nuclear-free zone, and stabilizing Pakistan. Such efforts may or may not have succeeded, but one thing we know they would not have done is inflame Islamic opinion and further radicalize Muslim youth into heightened hatred of America in the way that invading Iraq has done.

It was plainly obvious when four aircraft were hijacked that airline security had to be improved, but Bush resisted calls for making the airport security screeners federal employees. Then, when he lost that battle to Congress, he placed an old family friend, John McGaw, as head of the new agency to run the security screeners. Within months, McGaw had to be replaced under congressional criticism. It was to become a pattern. Bush and his prep school roommate Clay Johnson (the White House Personnel Director) looked first to family loyalists and political cronies to staff key positions. As one Republican columnist told me, "These guys are more inbred, secretive, and vindictive than the Mafia."

It was also plainly obvious after September 11 that al Qaeda's sanctuary in Taliban-run Afghanistan had to be occupied by U.S. forces and the al Qaeda leaders killed. Unfortunately, Bush's efforts were slow and small. He began by again offering the Taliban a chance to avoid U.S. occupation of their country and, when that failed, he initially sent in only a handful of Special Forces. When the Taliban and al Qaeda leaders escaped, he dispatched additional forces but less than one full division equivalent, fewer U.S. troops for all of Afghanistan than the number of NYPD assigned to Manhattan.

One would have thought that it was equally obvious after September 11 that high on the priority list would have been improving U.S. relations with the Islamic world, in order to dry up support for the deviant variant of Islam that is al Qaeda. After all, al Qaeda, the enemy that attacked us, was engaged in its own highly successful propaganda campaign to influence millions of Muslims to act against America, as a first step in a campaign to replace existing governments around the world with Taliban-like regimes. To defeat that enemy and prevent it from achieving its objectives, we needed to do more than just arrest and kill people. We and our values needed to be more appealing to Muslims than al Qaeda is. By all measures, however, al Qaeda and similar groups were increasing in support from Morocco to Indonesia. If that trend continues, the radical imams and their madrassas schools will (as Donald Rumsfeld finally understood in 2003, as reflected in his leaked internal memo that painted a far more bleak assessment of the war on terrorism than his public statements) produce more terrorists than we jail or shoot. Far from addressing the popular appeal of the enemy that attacked us, Bush handed that enemy precisely what it wanted and needed, proof that America was at war with Islam, that we were the new Crusaders come to occupy Muslim land.

Nothing America could have done would have provided al Qaeda and its new generation of cloned groups a better recruitment device than our unprovoked invasion of an oil-rich Arab country. Nothing else could have so well negated all our other positive acts and so closed Muslim eyes and ears to our subsequent calls for reform in their region. It was as if Usama bin Laden, hidden in some high mountain redoubt, were engaging in long-range mind control of George Bush, chanting "invade Iraq, you must invade Iraq."

Chapter 11

Right War, Wrong War

IT DID NOT HAVE TO BE THIS WAY. We did not have to go after Iraq after September 11. Imagine an alternative scenario in which a President mobilized the country to deal with the fundamental problems revealed by the terrorist attacks. What would a successful and comprehensive counterterrorism effort have looked like after September 11?

It would have consisted of three key agenda items. First, the President would have engaged in a massive effort to eliminate our vulnerabilities to terrorism at home and strengthen homeland security. Second, he would have launched a concerted effort globally to counter the ideology of al Qaeda and the larger radical Islamic terrorist movement with a partnership to promote the real Islam, to win support for common American and Islamic values, and to shape an alternative to the popular fundamentalist approach. Third, he would have been active with key countries not just to round up terrorists, end the sanctuaries, dry up the money, but also to strengthen open governments and make it possible politically, economically, and socially for them to go after the roots of al Qaeda–like terrorism. (The priority countries are Afghanistan, Iran, Saudi Arabia, and Pakistan.) Nowhere on the list of things that should have been done after September 11 is invading Iraq. The things that we had to do would have required enormous attention and resources. They were not available because they were devoted to Iraq. Let's look at what was done and what should have been done on these major agenda items.

PRIORITY NUMBER ONE would have been eliminating vulnerabilities to terrorism at home and strengthening homeland security. In the days after the September 11 attack the White House realized that the President needed to make a more comprehensive statement to the American people about what had happened and what we were going to do about it. Something easily understandable had to be said about preventing attacks in the U.S. The President chose in his speech before a joint session of Congress to announce a person, the Governor of Pennsylvania, Tom Ridge. Sitting in the balcony of the House in which he once also served, Ridge looked like he was from central casting. Tall, square-jawed, a wounded Vietnam veteran, Ridge had been a successful governor of a big state. Bush had asked Ridge to come to the White House to "run homeland security." There were no more details in the offer, but in the days after September 11 one did not say no to the President.

A few days later I drove to the Governor's Mansion in Harrisburg, along with General Wayne Downing. We found Ridge packing, since he had just resigned to go to Washington. When we briefed him on the homeland protection activities that had been under way for five years, he seemed somewhat relieved. "This is great. I thought I was going to have to start from scratch."

In one way, however, Ridge did have to start from scratch. The decision had been made and handed to Ridge that he would head up an organization parallel to the National Security Council, i.e., a White House Homeland Security staff of about fifty professionals to lead, coordinate, and perform oversight on the many federal programs relevant to domestic security and disaster prevention, mitigation, and recovery. It had taken the NSC decades to become effective and its efficacy was still largely dependent upon its leadership and key staff appointments. Ridge, who had never served in the Executive Branch in Washington, had to fashion a new entity quickly.

Tom Ridge had bought a pig in a poke when he agreed to come to Washington to help on homeland security. He assumed that he would have real authority as Assistant to the President for Homeland Security, but he soon found that he could do nothing without first clearing it with White House Chief of Staff Andy Card. Although Ridge opposed the idea of creating a new department and loathed the idea of becoming its Secretary, he was forced to do so by Bush and Card. Being Governor of Pennsylvania was not like actually running a nationwide department with almost 200,000 employees doing sensitive and critical security functions. Ridge was, at root, a politician, not a manager nor a security expert.

After the Clinton Administration had made terrorism and homeland protection a growing budgetary priority, a series of panels and commissions had come into existence to offer their views on the problems. Many had sought what I called a "wiring diagram" fix, the movement and consolidation of agencies and departments. Many in the Congress and the panels were unable to reconcile themselves to the fact that a lot of federal agencies could contribute to addressing a problem as big as domestic security and preparedness; it was not neat. I believed that adept White House coordination and leadership could get the many agencies all working on components of a consistent overall program. As a career civil servant with almost thirty years' experience in Washington headquarters, I believed that the alternative method, rewiring the organizational boxes, would make us less able to deal with domestic security and preparedness for years to come. The smaller mergers that created the Energy Department and the Transportation Department had taken years to jell. Ridge agreed and told me, "The last thing we need to do now is reorganize and create a new department."

Congress thought otherwise. Senator Joe Lieberman, who wanted to do more to improve domestic security, had taken the recommendation of an outside panel led by Warren Rudman and Gary Hart and turned it into draft legislation. It would create a new department. The agencies that would be merged had, among other roles, responsibility for fisheries, river floods, computer crime, citizenship training, tariffs on imports, drug smuggling, and reliability of telephone networks. They also had more obviously security-related functions. The President opposed the bill and pointed to Tom Ridge's new office. Many Members of Congress, of both parties, thought Ridge's office was not enough. Their confidence in the office was weakened early on when anthrax began appearing in the U.S. mail and the Bush administration's response seemed confused.

It was confused. Ridge and Attorney General John Ashcroft competed over who should coordinate the response, while Health Secretary Tommy Thompson's television appearances left many Americans less reassured and more alarmed. Fortunately, there was the National Pharmaceutical Stockpile created in 1998, so the needed drugs were available and procedures were in place for getting more fast. State public health labs had also been brought back from near morbidity by federal funds in 1999 and could respond to the thousands of anthrax sightings, many of which turned out to be instances of Cremora.

Republicans and Democrats in Congress objected to the White House's unwillingness to let Ridge appear before congressional committees because "White House staff do not do that." Some in Congress noted that as National Coordinator, I had appeared before nine congressional committees to brief them on counterterrorism and domestic preparedness.

The White House legislative affairs office began to take a head count on Capitol Hill. The Lieberman Bill would pass both houses, creating two disasters for President Bush: first, an unmanageable new department created just at the time its agencies and staff needed to be working on increasing domestic security, and second, the major new piece of legislation in response to September 11 would be named after the man whom the majority of voters had wanted to be Vice President just twenty months earlier. For the political analysts in the Bush White House, it was better to have one of those two outcomes than both. Thus, President Bush completely changed his position and announced the urgent need for the Lieberman Bill, except he did not call it that. He called it the Homeland Security Act.

The Bush proposal actually added more agencies into the brew than Lieberman's legislation had, including Secret Service. The White House then launched a nationwide road show to whip up support for the new Department of Homeland Security. Those who opposed the legislation, the Administration's supporters implied, were unpatriotic (few raised the question of whether the White House had been unpatriotic when it had opposed the same bill a few weeks earlier). Although delayed by the Administration's insistence that civil servants' job rights be limited, the Homeland Security Act passed and the Department was created.

The outcome, as the *Washington Post* revealed in a major review in September 2003, has been a disappointing and disorganized mess. Much of the leadership was chosen for political loyalties, not Executive Branch experience. There were inadequate resources to effect a smooth merger. The White House–led Transition Planning Office produced few useful plans. Many key career staff left in disgust. Those who stayed often complain that they are actually less able to work on the substantive programs to increase security because the new department is poorly run, there are so few institutional support mechanisms to help them, and they need to spend so much time on the administrative challenges of reorganization.

For those who have not worked in the federal government but are familiar with the business world, the best way to understand what has happened to key security organizations is to think of the Time Warner–AOL merger and then multiply it by several orders of magnitude. Twenty-two agencies were simultaneously merged into the new Department, into an organization that itself did not exist prior to the merger.

The first few initiatives of the new Department, rather than make us feel more secure, became material for late night comics. The Color Code System initially caused state and local authorities to spend millions of dollars that they did not have to respond to changes in the color, changes that were unaccompanied by any detailed threat information shared with local authorities. States and cities began to announce that they would no longer respond to changes in the color code. Then came the announcement that all American homes should have duct tape, which quickly caused fearful Americans to clean out their hardware stores of a variety of types of 3M tapes.

The good career staff who remain in some agencies have tried relatively successfully to insulate themselves from their own Department, notably Secret Service, Coast Guard, and Transportation Security. Even Secret Service, however, has been damaged by the new

Department agreeing (without consulting with Secret Service) that the service's experienced experts in financial crimes should be subordinated on terrorist financing to FBI. The FBI is not in the new domestic security department. Transportation Security Administration has also been underfunded to the point where the Department proposed that it would have to reduce the number of Federal Air Marshals on aircraft, only to withdraw the proposal just days later because of public criticism.

The Congress changed the Administration's proposed legislation creating the Department, adding detail and specificity about roles and missions. One mission about which the Congress was very clear was the need for a new center in the Department to see and analyze all information available to the government on terrorist threats and be a "second opinion." FBI and CIA both saw this congressional mandate as a challenge to their authority. Although often at odds and unwilling to share information about terrorism, CIA and FBI can make common cause when faced with the same bureaucratic enemy. Thus, they proposed the creation of a CIA-FBI entity to analyze terrorist information. President Bush proposed this new entity in his 2003 State of the Union message and it soon thereafter had offices, people, and computers. The congressionally mandated "second opinion" consists largely of unfilled federal jobs in the Department of Homeland Security.

In addition to making the Department of Homeland Security capable of giving a "second opinion" on intelligence issues related to domestic security, it is increasingly clear that we need to improve the accuracy of the "first opinion" on all intelligence issues, the analysis offered by CIA. The list of important analytical failures by CIA is now too long for us to conclude that the current system is acceptable. It is time now to do what so many veteran observers of the intelligence community have recommended: remove the intelligence analysis function from CIA and establish a small, independent bureau with a staff of career professionals and outside experts. This new Intelligence and Research Bureau should have a status somewhat like the Federal Reserve Board, with a respected chairman who has a limited term appointment, other respected Board members, and an elite staff. Their analysis should be subjected to regular independent audits for accuracy.

As to the behemoth Department of Homeland Security, it is too late now to do a phased-in implementation of the Department, as should have been done, but not too late to make the Department work. The Homeland Security mission is too important to wait the decade or two that it has typically taken new federal departments to become effective. Turning DHS from an object of ridicule within the Washington Beltway to being an organization that epitomizes smart government will require creating a management cadre throughout the Department from the best in the civil service, former military, and the private sector. It must become the place where senior managers want to work, the GE of the government. To bring about this metamorphosis, senior personnel and facilities may have to be moved from other, more established departments. Hiring bonuses may be needed. Creating a "halo effect" costs money. Regrettably, the Administration sought to do homeland security on the cheap, telling Ridge that creating the new department had to be "revenue neutral," jargon for no new money to implement the largest government reorganization in history.

Among the things that could have been done instead of, or even as part of or in addition to, the Department of Homeland Security was the creation of an agency that actually did only domestic security. Many in Washington were taken with the idea of creating in the United States what was known in Britain as MI5. Military Intelligence branch five during World War II was the group that so successfully hunted down Nazi sleepers in the United Kingdom. It later became civilian and is now known as the British Security Service. Many other successful democracies have something like the BSS. In several countries the security service has the task of finding terrorist sleeper cells and enemy spies. They do not, in some countries, have arrest powers and can only develop information to be given to police such as Scotland Yard or the Royal Canadian Mounted Police. While these security services have not been without problems, they have often been effective in rooting out particular terrorist groups and have not destroyed their democracies along the way.

Before and after September 11, the security service mission in the United States has belonged to the FBI. It was the FBI that sought out

Nazi infiltrators in World War II and went after Communists during the McCarthy era and later. Because of J. Edgar Hoover's excesses and abuse of civil liberties, however, Congress restricted the FBI's domestic security role beginning in the 1970s. Nonetheless, the FBI did continue in its counterintelligence role looking for Soviet, then Russian, and Chinese agents. There were, unfortunately, several embarrassing cases in which spies were not uncovered (in FBI and CIA) for years. There were other bureaucratic black eyes in which spies were allowed to escape or people were accused of spying and no charges were ever filed. FBI also had responsibility for finding terrorists and often seemed unable to find al Qaeda in the U.S. prior to September 11 or even to find the right-wing domestic terrorist who bomber the Atlanta Olympics and several other targets.

Bob Mueller, a federal prosecutor, arrived as the new head of the FBI just days before September 11. He cannot be blamed for the failure of the Bureau to find al Qaeda or even to have a computer network prior to then. Much of that responsibility belongs to his predecessor. Since September 11 Mueller has tried to reorient the organization from post-crime investigation to prevention, from drugs and bank robbery to terrorism. In 2002, Dale Watson, the FBI's leading counterterrorism official, retired. Months later, Watson's replacement asked to be reassigned and a third person became the Executive Assistant Director for counterterrorism. Within two months, the next incumbent retired and the post was vacant again. Without steady top leadership in charge of counterterrorism, the Bureau has not been fully able to make the transition from post-crime investigation to prevention and analysis.

As Dale Watson discovered in 2000, it is hard to turn around a bureaucracy that has been heading in another direction for years. Watson's attempts prior to September 11 met with resistance even from the Attorney General. John Ashcroft had denied Watson's requests for more counterterrorism funds because counterterrorism was not one of the three priorities of the Ashcroft Justice Department.

Would creating an MI5, a British Security Service, make America more safe? It is tempting to say yes. A lean, modern, specialized organization of terrorism analysts and agents might be better able to attract "the best and the brightest," people who would be creative at ferreting out terrorists but do not want to become gun-carrying federal policemen. The best counterterrorism agents from FBI, Customs, Immigration, Secret Service, Treasury's Bureau of Alcohol, Tobacco, and Firearms, and city police could be seconded and deputized in a new MI5. There would be none of the distractions that the FBI now has. Alternatively, if FBI keeps the terrorism mission and diminishes its focus on organized crime, drugs, and bank robberies, who will fill those roles? Already there are signs that the shift of FBI from those missions is making life easier for criminals.

The reality in America is that there are two big hurdles to the creation of a new, effective security service. The first is the right-left political alliance against security measures and the second is the FBI itself. The right-left political alliance is the phenomenon in which organizations like the National Rifle Association and the American Civil Liberties Union come together, usually with congressmen like Dick Armey, to express concern at efforts to strengthen the hand of domestic security officials. Any legislation proposing a security service will be met by a barrage of critics before they even read the bill. The FBI, which does not want to lose the domestic security mission to some new agency, will also work hard in the media and the Congress to scuttle any legislation. Were the legislation to pass, many FBI personnel will display passive-aggressive behavior rather than assist or cooperate with the security service.

These hurdles do not mean that the security service should not be pursued. If there is another major terrorist incident in this country, it most certainly will be. There is, however, little desire in the Congress now to create another new agency in light of what even Republican Members of Congress working on homeland security now admit is the demonstrable failure of the Department of Homeland Security. Thus, the best path at the present is to create the security service within the FBI, a service within a service, with a new spirit. For the security service to be effective in the FBI, however, it must have its own budget, computer network, regional offices (within FBI buildings), and personnel system. It must be able to hire and pay well civilian analysts, federal law enforcement agents from other agencies, security agents from other countries, and the best local police on counterterrorism. It must train large numbers of staff in key languages and in the philosophy, ideology, and culture of the likely terrorists. Finally, it must have routine access to all information available to the FBI and any government-held information.

To insure that the security service does not fall into the abuses of the J. Edgar Hoover era, there must be active oversight by a board of Americans all of whom inspire trust and confidence from the vast majority of our citizens. A Civil Liberties and Security Board must be more than just a civilian police complaint committee; it must actively shape the work of the security service to insure that it acts in accordance with what we believe in as Americans: civil rights and civil liberties.

John Ashcroft before September 11 had refused to increase counterterrorism funds and had not placed terrorism in the top-priority issues for the Justice Department. When I and one of my staff met with Ashcroft early in the Administration, we were left wondering if his discussion with us had been an act. My associate asked me on the drive back to the White House, "He can't really be that slow, can he? I mean, you can't get to be the Attorney General of the United States and be like that, right?"

I wasn't sure. "I don't know," I said. "Maybe he's just cagey, but after all, he did lose a Senate reelection to a dead man."

After the attacks and armed with the USA Patriot Act, Ashcroft so mismanaged the important perceptions component of the war on terrorism at home that he became a symbol to millions of Americans of someone attacking rather than protecting our civil liberties. The way in which Ashcroft has approached sensitive issues having to do with security and civil liberties has caused many Americans to trust their government even less.

There is an obvious tension between domestic security and civil liberties. We know that al Qaeda and similar groups have figured that out and use our system against us, applying for refugee status or political asylum, hiding in religious and charitable institutions, communicating on the Internet. To protect our civil liberties and defeat the terrorists, we need to be careful not to do things that create a popular backlash against security measures. As the widespread opposition to the unfortunately named Patriot Act proves, Attorney General Ashcroft has not managed that balancing act.

The most egregious example is the case of José Padilla. Whatever else he is, Padilla is apparently an American citizen. He was arrested not on a foreign combat field like the misguided John Lindh, but in Chicago. The Bush administration then denied him his rights because the Secretary of Defense, Donald Rumsfeld, determined (no doubt after long personal involvement in the review) that Padilla was an enemy. There are probably days when Donald Rumsfeld thinks lots of Americans in America are enemies (including, perhaps, on trying days for him, half the Pentagon press corps), but that should not give him the authority to lock them up without recourse. In the case of José Padilla, the Bush administration crossed a very important line that was created by the Founding Fathers to protect Americans from the possibility of some future government in this country violating their basic rights.

What Ashcroft and others did in the case of Padilla, and in proposing to amend the Patriot Act to allow for actions without judicial review, was to fundamentally shake the confidence of many Americans in the government's ability to safeguard our rights. At a time when we need greater citizen trust in the government so that we can adapt to the terrorist threat, Ashcroft is doing such things as engaging in a war of words with America's librarians over whether the FBI can scan reading records. The probability of the FBI ever needing to do that is so remote that this controversy should never have been allowed to develop. The Battle with the Librarians, the case of José Padilla, and the request for Patriot Act II make it very difficult to gain consensus to do the things that are needed to improve security, because trust in government's sensitivity to civil liberties is eroded.

Critics of all methods of improving domestic security must, however, also be cautious. If our domestic security organizations do not have the appropriate skills, staff, technology, and authorities they need, there may be more terrorist disasters in this country. The congressional and popular response to another round of major terrorist disasters in the U.S. could seriously threaten our civil liberties. Israel,

Britain, France, Italy, and other democracies have demonstrated how willing citizens can be to yield up their rights in the face of a steady assault by terrorists. Thus, those of us who most cherish America's civil liberties should be in the forefront of advocacy for effective, appropriate security measures with meaningful oversight and review mechanisms, such as a Civil Liberties and Security Board.

Because the Department of Homeland Security was not given the role of a domestic security service nor allowed to do the congressionally mandated task of a "second opinion" on terrorism analysis, one would have thought that at least it would assist the nation's cities to become prepared to deal with a major terrorist attack, particularly one involving chemical, biological, or radioactive/nuclear weapons. Just as the Administration shortchanged the creation of the new Department, it sought to keep aid to police, fire, and other emergency responders as constrained as possible under the circumstances.

In 2000, I asked DOD and FEMA to determine what units would be needed to deal with a small nuclear weapon going off in a midsize U.S. city. Both agencies said I had to be more specific, so I chose Cincinnati because I had just been there. The kind of federal plan and units needed to help metropolitan Cincinnati officials deal with such a calamity simply did not exist. Nonetheless, many city officials assumed that there were federal units somewhere that would come to help them in an extreme emergency. They also noted that it is the first twenty-four hours in which the injured can be saved, and most local officials I spoke with doubted that the U.S. Cavalry would appear that fast. In fact, many of the kinds of federal units that city officials assume will help them will never show up. Large MASH-style military field hospitals are no longer in the force structure. Military Police are in short supply and stretched with overseas deployments. (Now, because of Iraq, many National Guard units are also overseas, taking with them mobilized police and fire personnel from cities and towns. The new Northern Command created to assist in homeland emergencies has not developed a single new field unit to meet domestic requirements; it merely has the ability to plan to call on units that already happen to exist and are still in the homeland.)

So when former Senator Warren Rudman asked me, following my

departure from the White House, to join him in worrying about how we train and equip our first responders to deal with weapons of mass destruction attacks, I eagerly agreed to do so. Rudman has been dedicated to preparing the nation for dealing with terrorism both during his illustrious career in the Senate and subsequently as a private citizen. He and I disagreed about creating the Department of Homeland Security, but concurred in the need to train and equip the police, fire, emergency services, public health, and hospital staffs of our major cities. Rudman and I began to look at the state of first responders in 2003, working with a young Harvard lawyer and triathlete, Jamie Metzl, who had earlier done outstanding work for me as a White House Fellow. What we uncovered was disturbing. The program to train and equip first responders, which had started in the late 1990s, had not grown sufficiently even after the disasters of September 11. Our estimates indicate that only 25 percent of the needed funds were being requested by the Administration.

A survey of 168 cities showed that 90 percent of them had not received any significant additional federal assistance since the September 11 attacks. Emergency services organizations were understaffed and utilizing archaic equipment. Few had detailed or realistic plans to deal with a major terrorist attack using chemical, biological, or radiological devices. Emergency 911 systems, fire-police radio units, public health departments, emergency hospitals, and other first responders all had long lists of unmet requirements.

The federal government was providing first responder assistance to states based upon a formula that resulted in eight times more funds per capita for Wyoming than for California. Because of the economic downturn and its effects on state and city tax revenues, cities and states were actually dismissing fire and police personnel in 2003. Federal funds for community police under the COPS program were cut by the Bush administration. A year after September 11, the New York City Police had been cut by four thousand officers from the number on the rolls on the day of the attack.

We traveled to cities across the country and heard from every local official we talked to (mayors, police chiefs, fire chiefs, emergency services directors) that they were not receiving the funds they needed for secure and reliable communications, breathing apparatus, heavy search-and-rescue teams, personnel, or planning to deal with a major terrorist attack involving chemical, biological, or radiological weapons. Journalists loved to ask me when I was in the White House, "What keeps you up at night? What are the worst things that could happen to us?" The worst are, thankfully, not the most likely. Nonetheless, the two worst things that could happen are, first, the outbreak of a highly contagious epidemic as a result of a biological weapon, and, second, a nuclear weapon going off in an American city. Yet what Warren Rudman and I confirmed is that no city has the plan, trained staff, equipment, or facilities to handle a major, contagious biological attack requiring isolation hospitals. None was remotely prepared to deal with an incident in which a radiological or nuclear device was utilized.

When our report, "Emergency Responders: Drastically Underfunded, Dangerously Unprepared," was released, an Administration spokesman dismissed it as probably calling for "gold-plated telephones." The signatories to the report included former Chairmen of the Joint Chiefs of Staff Admiral William Crowe and General John Vessey, Nobel Laureate Joshua Lederberg, former Secretary of State George Shultz, former U.S. Attorney Mary Jo White, and former CIA and FBI Director William Webster. Warren Rudman responded to the criticism by telling a House committee, "We don't want gold-plated telephones, we just want reliable communications devices so that we never again lose hundreds of firefighters because they couldn't hear the evacuation order, as happened in the World Trade Center."

We called for $98 billion over five years, plus an unquantified amount for assisting local police, over and above the Administration's requests. More important, however, we called for a requirements process that specifies what level of capability enhancements we are trying to achieve. As Warren Rudman put it to me, "We need a transparent process that says you can get this much done for this much money over these many years. If you think more metropolitan areas need more capability sooner, fine, this is how much it will cost. Without that, these guys in the White House are just pulling the homeland security budget level out of their ass."

The simple truth is that the Administration does not have any idea how much money is needed for first responders and related state and local homeland security capability, because it has never tried to find out. It has never engaged in a requirements process. It fears that a requirements process will show how it has shortchanged those defending us. Rather than being derived from needs, the Administration's funding proposal was backed into by figuring out how much the overall federal budget would be and how much would be given to everything else within that budget.

Equipped or not, when the call comes our first responders around the country will answer it. They are our first line of defense against terrorists. The Bush administration contends that the additional resources we sought for aiding our first responders "simply do not exist." Yet, in the "war on terrorism" we are spending in Iraq in the first year of war and occupation six times what the Rudman study called for as an annual supplement to equip our defenders here at home. The resources for Iraq did not exist either. The Administration chose to run up the national debt to pay for Iraq, but not to pay for what our police and fire personnel need to defend us here at home.

Despite the Administration's rhetoric, the resources needed to secure the homeland have been denied and no system has been put in place to determine the real funding requirements. Regulations to deal with securing chemical plants and other critical assets have been slow-rolled. Many proposals have been made to employ new technology in homeland defense, but few systems have been deployed at airports, harbors, border crossings, or on our telecommunications and data networks. The public's faith and trust in the sensitivity to civil liberties by federal officials engaged in domestic security has been eroded by several dubious decisions.

Ideologically, the Bush administration is opposed to increasing domestic spending (although it has no problem with immense DOD budgets), hiring more civil servants, or regulating the private sector. While in the abstract all of those may seem things to be avoided, it is impossible to increase homeland security without doing more on every one of those three measures than the Administration has been willing to do.

America usually waits for a disaster before it responds to a threat. We have had that disaster. There is no longer any excuse for the failure of the Administration, Congress, and local governments to improve our domestic security and preparedness. Dealing with domestic protection, or homeland security, means identifying and reducing major vulnerabilities to attack. And it means coming up with a set of national requirements for response capabilities and then funding them systematically over several years. We have not done either, nor have we done well on organization, technology, resources, or sensitivity to protection of civil liberties. Defending America against terrorism at home must depend as much on reducing vulnerabilities as it does on catching "the evil-doers," for we will never catch them all and this year's crop of America's enemies will be replaced by tomorrow's. As long as we have major vulnerabilities, someone someday will utilize one of those vulnerabilities against us. Every day that we continue to have porous borders or unprotected chemical plants is another day that we are at risk. Prioritizing the vulnerabilities to be reduced and figuring out a way of paying for the effort would be a major national challenge on a par with the Space Race or the rearming for the Cold War. It should have been the focus of a great national debate and mobilization. It wasn't. And despite the "Global War on Terrorism" and despite (or because of) the "War on Iraq" we are also still highly vulnerable to terrorism.

THE SECOND AGENDA ITEM post–September 11 should have been the creation of a counterweight ideology to the al Qaeda, fundamentalist, radical version of Islam because much of the threat we face is ideological, a perversion of a religion. Bombs and bullets, handcuffs and jail bars will not address the source of that ideological challenge. We must work with our Islamic friends to craft an ideological and cultural response over many years, just as we fought Communism for almost half a century, in scores of countries, not just with wars and weapons, but with a more powerful and more attractive ideology. Unfortunately, there is often silence or at best a weak and incoherent voice countering the apparently attractive appeals of the radical mullahs.

The new leader of Central Command understands. General John Abizaid told the *New York Times* that Pakistan and Saudi Arabia are "involved in a fight against extremists that is crucial to their ability to maintain control . . . It's a battle of ideas as much as it is a military battle . . . not the type of fight that you're going to send the 82nd Airborne" in to handle. Yet Abizaid's bosses in the Pentagon and the White House do not seem to understand how to fight the battle of ideas or the limits on the ability of our shooters to defeat the al Qaeda ideology.

It will be difficult for the U.S. government to participate in formulating a subtle and successful message about religion, but we have been here before. When America realized that Communism was having an appeal, we faced the new issue of how to sell America, democracy, and capitalism. The United States found ways of assisting Christian Democratic parties in Europe and Latin America and, ironically, Islamic movements in places like Afghanistan. We found or created spokesmen, leaders, heroes, schools, books, films, development programs. That effort did as much to win the Cold War as did the U.S. Army tanks in West Germany.

When colleagues in the White House asked me what to read to understand the problem after September 11, I urged them instead to get an old black and white French film, *The Battle of Algiers.* In it, French counterterrorism authorities round up all the "known terrorist managers" and leaders (sound familiar?) but lose the war with the terrorists because they did not address the ideological underpinnings. After the known terrorist leaders were arrested, time passed, and new, unknown terrorists emerged. We are likely to face the same situation with al Qaeda. The only way to stop it is to work with leaders of Islamic nations to insure that tolerance of other religions is taught again, that their people believe they have fair opportunities to participate in government and the economy, that the social and cultural conditions that breed hatred are bred out.

Rather than seeking to work with the majority in the Islamic world to mold Muslim opinion against the radicals' values, we did exactly what al Qaeda said we would do. We invaded and occupied an oil-rich Arab country that posed no threat to us, while paying scant time and attention to the Israeli-Palestinian problem. We delivered to al Qaeda the greatest recruitment propaganda imaginable and made it difficult for friendly Islamic governments to be seen working closely with us.

I was no fan of Saddam Hussein; indeed, I had urged limiting his access to weapons of mass destruction technology as early as 1989, had been one of the first advocating confronting Iraq militarily in 1990, conceived of the U.N. program to eliminate his weapons of mass destruction in 1991, tried to reinitiate hostilities after the First Gulf War, advocated a large bombing campaign of Iraq in 1993. I know that in one sense the world is better off without him in power, but not the way it was done, not at the cost we have paid and will pay for it; not by diverting us from eliminating al Qaeda and its clones; not by using the funds we needed to eliminate our vulnerabilities to terrorism at home; not at the incredibly high price of increasing Muslim hatred of America and strengthening al Qaeda.

Former Treasury Secretary Paul O'Neill has written that the Administration planned early on to eliminate Saddam Hussein. From everything I saw and heard, he is right. The Bush administration reply to O'Neill was something like: Of course we were. Clinton signed a law making regime change in Iraq the American policy. That's true too, but neither the Congress nor Clinton had in mind regime change at the point of an American gun, a U.S. invasion of Iraq.

The administration of the second George Bush did begin with Iraq on its agenda. So many of those who had made the decisions in the first Iraq War were back: Cheney, Powell, Wolfowitz. Some of them had made clear in writings and speeches while out of office that they believed the United States should unseat Saddam, finish what they failed to do the first time. In the new administration's discussions of terrorism, Paul Wolfowitz had urged a focus on Iraqi-sponsored terrorism against the U.S. even though there was no such thing. In 2001 more and more the talk was of Iraq, of CENTCOM being asked to plan to invade. It disturbed me greatly.

President Bush has said that September 11 was a turning point in his thinking about Iraq. There was also a supposed decision point when the President decided to go to the U.N. and another when he decided not to wait further for the U.N., but all along it seemed inevitable that we would invade. Iraq was portrayed as the most dangerous thing in national security. It was an idée fixe, a rigid belief, received wisdom, a decision already made and one that no fact or event could derail.

There is seldom in history a single reason why two nations go to war against each other. The reasons given by the Bush administration for its war with Iraq have shifted from terrorism to weapons of mass destruction to the suffering of the Iraqi people. In addition to those publicly articulated rationales, there were others reportedly discussed in Washington's bureaucracy.

Five rationales are attributed to three senior advisors (Cheney, Rumsfeld, and Wolfowitz) and to President Bush:

- To clean up the mess left by the first Bush administration when, in 1991, it let Saddam Hussein consolidate power and slaughter opponents after the first U.S.-Iraq war;
- To improve Israel's strategic position by eliminating a large, hostile military;
- To create an Arab democracy that could serve as a model to other friendly Arab states now threatened with internal dissent, notably Egypt and Saudi Arabia;
- To permit the withdrawal of U.S. forces from Saudi Arabia (after twelve years), where they were stationed to counter the Iraqi military and were a source of anti-Americanism threatening to the regime;
- To create another friendly source of oil for the U.S. market and reduce dependency upon oil from Saudi Arabia, which might suffer overthrow someday.

I believe all of these motivations were at work. Most of them reflect a concern with the long-term stability of the House of Saud. In addition, particularly for President Bush, I think there was a felt need to "do something big" to respond to the events of September 11. Of course, he could have responded by investing seriously in domestic preparedness, stabilizing Afghanistan, and helping other nations deal with the sources and manifestations of fundamentalist Islamic terrorism. Those actions would have been "something big." None of those were, however, the big, fast, bold, simple move that would send a signal at home and abroad, a signal that said "don't mess with Texas, or America." Unfortunately, invading Iraq turned out to be something other than what President Bush and his inner circle had hoped it would be. The decision to invade Iraqi, largely unilaterally, in 2003 was both mistaken and costly. The costs were in lives, in money, but even more important, in opportunities lost, and in future problems created or aggravated.

The clearest indication of the depth of President Bush's understanding and of his own motivations came in Diane Sawyer's interview with Bush on ABC Television. Sawyer asked Bush about the "hard fact that there were weapons of mass destruction, as opposed to the possibility that [Saddam] might move to acquire those weapons." The President's considered response was, "What's the difference?" Then he added, "The possibility that he could acquire weapons. If he were to acquire weapons, he would be the danger."

Sawyer pressed on, noting that in addition to the weapons issue there was a "failure to establish proof of elaborate terrorism contacts" and that this was at best a lack of precision and "misleading at worst." The President replied, "Yeah. Look—what—what we based our evidence on was a very sound National Intelligence Estimate." Could it not have been more precise, Sawyer wondered. "What—I, I made my decision based upon enough intelligence to tell me this country was threatened with Saddam Hussein in power." Valiantly Sawyer asked again, what would it take to convince you that there were no weapons of mass destruction. Again Bush replied with his mantra, "America is a safer country." Finally in exasperation, the President said, "I'm telling you I made the right decision for America because Saddam Hussein used weapons of mass destruction and invaded Kuwait."

And so Bush invaded Iraq in 2003 because Saddam had used weapons of mass destruction in the 1980s and invaded Kuwait in 1990.

Bush concluded on the subject with Diane Sawyer, saying again that his invasion of Iraq "means America's a more secure country." In fact, with our Army stretched to the breaking point, our international credibility at an all-time low, Muslims further radicalized against us, our relations with key Allies damaged, and our soldiers in a shooting gallery, it is as hard to believe that America is safer for the invasion as it is to believe that President Bush had good intelligence on weapons of mass destruction or that "this country was threatened with Saddam Hussein in power."

Time and again the Administration claimed that there was an urgency to act against Iraq because there was a growing threat to the United States. They were generally vague about the details of the threat, but left the impression that it stemmed from weapons of mass destruction, i.e., chemical, biological, or nuclear weapons about to be used against us by Iraq. Like most national security bureaucrats, I believed Iraq had chemical and/or biological weapons in 2003. We knew that Iraq had them in 1992 and later because we had seen them. Iraq gave every indication that they were hiding some in 1998, but there was no reliable intelligence on what had happened to them since 1998. Charles Duelfer was the leading American expert on the issue, having spent over a decade working on Iraqi WMD analysis for the U.S. and the U.N. Duelfer thought in 2002 that there was no remaining large and threatening stockpile. He was ignored before the invasion and for months after and only asked by the Administration to go to Iraq to lead the investigation in 2004.

As studies by the Senate Intelligence Committee and the Carnegie Endowment have made clear, both the CIA and the President failed to tell the Congress and the American people that they were making judgments about the Iraqi WMD threat based on dated information. As WMD inspector David Kay was forced to admit, "we were all wrong, probably."

Even if Iraq still had WMD stockpiles, possession of weapons of mass destruction is not in and of itself a threat to the United States. Over two dozen nations possess WMD, according to unclassified CIA testimony to Congress. Never did I think the Iraqi chemical or biological weapons were an imminent threat to the United States in 2002.

Saddam had ample opportunity to use them on the U.S. for over a decade and did not. As to nuclear weapons, Iraq had demonstrated its ability to create a large, covert nuclear weapons development program in 1991. CIA had demonstrated its inability to notice such a large program. Together, those two facts were a legitimate source of concern. The means to deal with that risk were present, however, in intrusive inspections by the International Atomic Energy Agency, active control of Iraqi imports related to nuclear development, and the use of other nations' intelligence services. Indeed, those methods may have been successful because (as we now know) there was no active nuclear weapons program in 2002. Nothing in 2002 indicated Saddam intended to build nukes, much less use them, and certainly not imminently. Indeed CIA's publicly released analysis concluded that there was little risk of Iraq's WMD against the U.S. unless we attacked them.

Both the White House and the CIA must have known there was no "imminent threat" to the U.S., but one claimed the opposite, and the other allowed them to do so uncorrected.

In his famous "Top Gun" moment on the deck of the USS *Abraham Lincoln,* the President claimed that the invasion of Iraq was just one battle "in the War on Terrorism that began on September 11." It is not hard to understand why, after repeatedly hearing remarks like that, 70 percent of the American people believed that Saddam Hussein had attacked the Pentagon and the World Trade Center. I suspect that many of the heroic U.S. troops who risked their lives fighting in Iraq thought, because of misleading statements from the White House, that they were avenging the 3,000 dead from September 11. What a horrible thing it was to give such a false impression to our people and our troops. Only in September 2003, only after occupying Iraq, only after Vice President Cheney had stretched credulity on *Meet the Press,* did the President clearly state that there was "no evidence that Iraq was involved in the September 11 attacks." That new clarity might have come as a disappointing shock to American troops being targeted by snipers and blown up by landmines in Iraq.

After President Bush was forced to admit publicly that there was no connection between the al Qaeda attack of September 11 and Saddam Hussein's government in Iraq, advocates of the Iraq War began to shift their argument. They began to emphasize the "connections" and "linkages" between Iraq and al Qaeda in general, no longer specifically mentioning September 11. When challenged in congressional testimony, Under Secretary of Defense Doug Feith promised to produce the intelligence that demonstrated the link. Not only did he send a memo to a congressional committee with a précis of dozens of such intelligence reports, someone leaked the highly classified memo to a neoconservative magazine, which promptly printed the secret information. Neoconservative commentators then pointed to the illegally leaked document as conclusive proof of the al Qaeda–Iraq nexus.

For those uninitiated in how to read raw intelligence reports, the Feith memo might have been persuasive. For those who have read thousands of such reports over many years, the Feith memo proved little. The *Washington Post* quoted longtime Defense Intelligence Agency expert Pat Lang as saying the memo was "a listing of a mass of unconfirmed reports," many of which actually proved that al Qaeda and Iraq had not succeeded in establishing a modus vivendi.

The *Post* went on to quote another senior intelligence officer as saying it was merely "data points . . . among the millions of holdings of the intelligence community, many of which are simply not thought likely to be true." Indeed, the Pentagon itself issued a statement in the wake of the Feith memo leak, saying that news reports that the Defense Department had confirmed new information about an al Qaeda–Iraq link before the war are "inaccurate" and went on to describe the Feith memo as "not an analysis of the substantive issue of the relationship between Iraq and al Qaeda . . . and drew no conclusions."

The simple fact is that lots of people, particularly in the Middle East, pass along many rumors and they end up being recorded and filed by U.S. intelligence agencies in raw reports. That does not make them "intelligence." Intelligence involves analysis of raw reports, not merely their enumeration or weighing them by the pound. Analysis, in turn, involves finding independent means of corroborating the reports. Did al Qaeda agents ever talk to Iraqi agents? I would be startled if they had not. I would also be startled if American, Israeli, Iranian, British, or Jordanian agents had somehow failed to talk to al Qaeda or Iraqi agents. Talking to each other is what intelligence agents do, often under assumed identities or "false flags," looking for information or possible defectors.

It is certainly possible that Iraqi agents dangled the possibility of asylum in Iraq before bin Laden at some point when everyone knew that the U.S. was pressuring the Taliban to arrest him. If that dangle happened, bin Laden's accepting that asylum clearly did not. Was there an al Qaeda affiliate group, complete with terrorist training camp, in Iraq? Yes, in the area outside the control of Saddam Hussein, in the north of the country controlled by Saddam's opponents. This terrorist camp was known to the Bush administration, which chose not to bomb it after September 11, but rather to wait eighteen months. The group and its camp must not have been much of a threat. Now, however, there is an al Qaeda–Iraq connection, as al Qaeda fighters move to Iraq in response to Bush's invitation to "bring 'em on."

If there were evidence of Iraq giving funds or safe haven to al Qaeda before the invasion, the Administration would have produced it. There is, of course, evidence that Iran provided al Qaeda safe haven before and after September 11. There is also evidence that Saudis provided al Qaeda with funds, and that Saudi "charities" were used by al Qaeda for cover. Any Iraqi "link" to al Qaeda is a minor footnote when compared to the links with other regimes, and none of the possible "links" between Iraq and al Qaeda rise to the level of noteworthy assistance and support.

Several sources have reported that internal Pentagon plans assumed a U.S. occupation force of about thirty thousand troops, or one division plus its support units. Army Chief of Staff Eric Shinseki had, of course, candidly told a congressional committee that a realistic number was 200,000. His estimate was publicly rejected by Secretary of Defense Rumsfeld. For most of 2003, the actual number of U.S. troops in the Iraqi theater, which includes support units in Kuwait, was about 150,000. Many military analysts believed that number was too small. This difference of opinion is more than a numbers game. If there are too few U.S. troops to secure convoy routes or spot snipers, then U.S. military personnel are killed and wounded by Iraqi bombs, landmines, and bullets. It is worth recalling that Secretary of Defense Les Aspin was driven from office in 1993 because, it was charged, he had not provided U.S. troops in Somalia with what they needed to protect themselves, and seventeen soldiers were killed. In the months of the Iraqi occupation, hundreds of U.S. military personnel have been killed and many others wounded in part because there were not enough U.S. military assets to spot snipers and landmines.

There are additional costs of getting the occupation force estimate wrong. Producing the 150,000 U.S. forces in the Iraqi theater has badly stretched the Army. Most of the maneuver brigades in the Army are deployed overseas. Those left in the U.S. are too few to maintain the contingency reserve or the training base necessary. National Guard and Reserve personnel have been mobilized for extended service, disrupting the lives of tens of thousands who counted on their civilian salaries to pay mortgages and other family expenses. The irony is that during the 2000 presidential campaign, the Bush team charged that peacekeeping missions had overstretched the U.S. Army. They noted that battalions that had engaged in peacekeeping were not passing inspections because they had not been able to keep up with training proficiency and testing. By those measures, the Bush administration has now far more badly damaged the United States Army. As Army National Guard and Reserve reenlistments plummet, the damage will grow. The condition of the Army is of concern because unlike Iraq, which showed no sign of attacking us, North Korea regularly threatens us with war. If that were to happen with the Army tied down in Iraq and our reserves stretched, the outcome might not be favorable.

Before the war the Administration gave the impression to Iraqis who were closely watching that we only had a problem with Saddam and his sons, plus a handful of others. If they were to go peacefully (or with a bullet), we would be satisfied. The message sent to Iraqi commanders through a variety of creative means was "Don't Fight," just let us get rid of Saddam. Because of those messages, many Iraqi commanders did not fight and actually sent their troops home. Yet after Jerry Bremer was appointed pro-consul of Iraq, the U.S. had another message: "You're all fired." Not only did the United States announce it was dismissing the Iraqi army officer corps, it went on to relieve anyone who was a member of the Baath Party from any job they might hold. The hundreds of thousands of people affected by this bait and switch were then told that the pensions they had planned on when hitting retirement age would not be there. It is little wonder that U.S. popularity plummeted and critical infrastructures and services in Iraq stopped working.

The firing of the army and de-Baathification apparently came as a surprise to the American who had been charged with planning the postwar occupation, retired General Jay Gardner. Months after his replacement by Bremer, Gardner admitted publicly that his plans had included recalling the Iraqi army to their posts, vetting them, and reassigning most of them to duty doing the kinds of jobs that American forces have been required to perform.

In Saddam Hussein's Iraq, one had to join the Baath Party to gain promotion to managerial positions throughout the economy. By dismissing them all (and canceling their retirement), there were suddenly no experienced managers. Russians and others who suffered under the Communist Party would be familiar with the party membership requirement. After the fall of the Soviet Union, however, former Communist Party members were permitted to continue in some positions. Indeed, the first two presidents of Russia (Boris Yeltsin and Vladimir Putin) were former members of the Communist Party. After protests, riots, and attacks, the U.S. occupation authority said it would pay Iraqi army officers' retirement and permit some to be involved in the new army or at least be trainers for it. By then, no doubt, some Iraqi army officers were plotting attacks on U.S. forces.

It is difficult for the world's sole superpower to be popular, but it is not impossible. A superpower has different responsibilities and perspectives than other nations, but many other nations' governments and peoples will understand and sympathize if they believe that the superpower is a good global citizen that respects the rights and opinions of other nations. I thought this was the concept behind candidate Bush's call for a "more humble" U.S. foreign policy (presumably one more humble than the Clinton foreign policy). That thought seemed to be lost quickly after candidate Bush became President Bush. It was not just that the United States objected to the Kyoto Treaty on the environment, or the International Criminal Court (both things to which we should object), it was the arrogance in the way we objected. At a meeting with my staff in the summer of 2001, I suggested, "If these guys in this Administration are going to want an international coalition to invade Iraq next year, they are sure not making a lot of friends."

The invasion, when it came in 2003, lost us many friends. Polling data had already suggested that the U.S. was not trusted or liked by majorities in Islamic countries. After the invasion, those numbers hit all-time highs not only in Muslim countries but around the world. In Muslim countries, the U.S. invasion of Iraq increased support for al Qaeda and radical anti-Americanism. Elsewhere, we were now seen as a super-bully more than a superpower, not just for what we did but for the way we did it, disdaining international mechanisms that we would later need.

When the United States next needs international support, when we need people around the world to believe that action is required to deal with Iranian or Korean nuclear weapons, who will join us, who will believe us? When prime ministers wonder in the future if they should risk domestic opposition to support us, they will reflect on Tony Blair in the U.K. and how he lost popularity and credibility by allying himself so closely to the U.S. administration and its claims.

Even more damaging is the loss of credibility the national security institutions have suffered among our own people. Americans now know that Saddam Hussein had nothing to do with September 11, that there was no imminent threat from Iraqi weapons of mass destruction, that there was a secret sticker shock about the costs of the war in lives and dollars. It is important that the trust in America's word be restored, essential that we return to dealing with the real threats, because there are real threats still out there and real vulnerabilities here at home. Unless we address these real problems, we will suffer again.

As an analysis by the Army War College's Strategic Studies Institute, written by Jeffrey Record, argues, the Iraq war was "a strategic error of the first magnitude." Instead of energetically pursuing the priority of creating an ideological counterweight for al Qaeda, we invaded Iraq and gave al Qaeda exactly the propaganda fuel it needed. So much for the second of the three priorities that we should have been pursuing after September 11. Our third priority should have been to strengthen several key governments that are risk to al Qaeda or, in the case of Iran, are already in the hands of terrorists that have supported al Qaeda.

THE FIRST COUNTRY to require our attention would have been, and was, Afghanistan, the al Qaeda sanctuary then run by the Taliban. Following the al Qaeda attacks on America, the Bush administration adopted the goal that had been written months before and had sat waiting for Deputies meetings, Principals meetings, Presidential review: to eliminate al Qaeda. The nation demanded it. No longer could the U.S. military leadership recommend against sending troops into Afghanistan to eliminate the sanctuary. No longer could CIA quibble about aiding the "feckless" Northern Alliance in Afghanistan. Yet right from the start, we made crucial mistakes. The war that the U.S. fought in Afghanistan was not the rapid, no-holds-barred operation that one might have expected. We did not immediately send U.S. forces to capture al Qaeda and Taliban leadership. The Bush administration decided to continue appeals to the Taliban to turn over bin Laden and his followers, and then, when we attacked, we treated the war as a regime change rather than a search-and-destroy against terrorists.

In the Clinton administration the State Department had argued that the Taliban faction ruling most of Afghanistan could perhaps be separated from their al Qaeda allies. State Department officers had tried to negotiate with the Taliban, to no avail. The Clinton administration did, however, put the Taliban on notice that it would hold it responsible for further al Qaeda terrorism. In a role reversal, the State Department leadership in the Bush administration, notably Deputy Secretary Rich Armitage, argued before and after September 11 that al Qaeda and the Taliban were inseparable and should be seen as one entity. Oddly, it was the White House and Pentagon that sought to give the Taliban another chance after September 11. Even four days after initiating bombing of al Qaeda facilities on October 7, 2001, President Bush again publicly appealed to the Taliban to cooperate and turn over bin Laden. When they did not, he later said the U.S. would get bin Laden "dead or alive."

The U.S. military campaign against Afghanistan began on October 7 by implementing the bombing plans of al Qaeda camps and Taliban military facilities that had been prepared but unused during the Clinton administration. Usama bin Laden, unscathed by the bombing and not snatched by any CIA or Special Forces operation, released a videotape condemning the bombing.

Except for a Ranger raid lasting a few hours on an airstrip and camp well outside Kandahar, U.S. ground force units were not initially inserted into Afghanistan. (The Rangers were ordered not to hold the airfield and were helicoptered back out to an aircraft carrier.) On the ground, the U.S. relied upon the Afghan Northern Alliance to attack the Taliban. Joined by a handful of U.S. and British Special Forces who called in air support, the Northern Alliance advanced. The United States appealed to the Northern Alliance to slow down, not to take the capital of Kabul. They kept going anyway.

More than a month after the U.S. opened the military operation, the Taliban leader, Mullah Omar, still alive and well, ordered his forces to pull out of Kabul and move to the mountains. No U.S. troops gave chase.

Not until November 25, seven weeks after starting the operation, did the United States insert a ground force unit (Marines) to take and hold a former al Qaeda and Taliban facility, near Kandahar. The Taliban kept control of the city, however, until December 7. Not surprisingly, when the Marines entered the city, they found neither bin Laden nor Mullah Omar. The late-November operation did not include any effort by U.S. forces to seal the border with Pakistan, snatch the al Qaeda leadership, or cut off the al Qaeda escape.

The Northern Alliance continued to bear most of the burden of the fighting for the U.S. in November. While they attempted for two weeks to capture al Qaeda forces in Kunduz, aircraft reportedly slipped in and out with escaping al Qaeda personnel. Other al Qaeda and Taliban units withdrew into the high valley at Tora Bora, near the

Pakistan border. Not until mid-December did the U.S. persuade its new Afghan allies to venture into Tora Bora, with U.S. Special Forces advisors and close air support. They soon withdrew, empty-handed. Under growing criticism that the Pentagon was bungling the job of getting bin Laden and the al Qaeda leadership, Secretary Rumsfeld said just before Christmas that in the future U.S. forces would do the job, rather than continuing to rely upon Afghans.

By March 2002, U.S. ground forces had arrived in unit strength and, almost five months after the U.S. initiated combat, began a sweep of mountainous areas to capture al Qaeda personnel. Although Operation Anaconda ran into serious resistance, it too failed to capture al Qaeda leaders.

Two years after the U.S. began military operations against Afghanistan, U.S. forces, CIA officers, and pro-U.S. Afghans had still not found Usama bin Laden or his deputy Ayman Zawahiri. Nor had they found Taliban leader Mullah Omar. Indeed, long before the two-year mark the U.S. military had shifted its focus to Iraq. The U.S. Special Forces who were trained to speak Arabic, the language of al Qaeda, had been pulled out of Afghanistan and sent to Iraq. Intelligence platforms supporting the military were also redirected. American forces and those of its NATO allies still controlled a limited area of Afghanistan. In fact, of the combined U.S. forces fighting the "war on terrorism" in the Afghan and Iraqi theaters, only about 5 percent were in Afghanistan.

CIA was less tentative. As then CIA Counterterrorism Director Cofer Black explained to a Senate committee, "After September 11, the gloves came off." He did not explain why they were on before then. It could be argued that they were waiting for the Bush administration to determine its policy on al Qaeda and the priority it would give to that policy. What CIA did so readily after September 11, however, was what the Clinton White House had been pressing them to do for years, certainly since the African embassy bombings in 1998: insert CIA personnel into Afghanistan, aid the Northern Alliance, fly the Predator, and work with other security services to identify and break up cells in Europe, the Middle East, and elsewhere. There was no reputational risk to the Agency of acting in Afghanistan after the al

Qaeda attacks in America. The only risk to the U.S. intelligence institution after September 11 was if it did not act, if questions were asked of why it had not acted before, why they did not know the attacks on New York and Washington were coming.

CIA had not acted before because the career managers of its Directorate of Operations were risk-averse. The risks they sought to avoid were risks to them, to the reputation of the CIA, and, more important, to the DO itself. Inserting CIA personnel into Afghanistan might have resulted in their becoming prisoners of al Qaeda, with all the attendant embarrassing publicity. Helping the Northern Alliance might have ended up with the managers of the DO hauled before congressional oversight committees having to answer whether the money had been used for heroin traffic or for the abuse of Taliban prisoners. CIA had been subject to criticism before when past White House staffs had gotten them involved in the civil war in Lebanon, in trading arms for hostages with Iran, in supporting Latin American militaries fighting Communists and trampling human rights. Secretary Albright, reflecting on the history of the CIA, said to me that it was easy to understand why it was risk-averse: it acts in a passive-aggressive way, she said, as if "it has battered child syndrome."

George Tenet was as much concerned with the threat from al Qaeda as anyone in the government prior to September 11, but he was also trying to rebuild the CIA and in particular the Directorate of Operations. First on the Senate Intelligence Committee staff and then in the White House, he had watched as a series of CIA Directors had quickly come and gone. He knew that the revolving door of ineffective Directors had hurt morale at CIA and had failed to address the CIA's major weakness, its inability to put spies in critical positions. Tenet was reluctant to disagree with the DO on major intelligence policy issues.

What should the Administration have done about Afghanistan after September 11? The United States should have inserted forces into Afghanistan to cut off bin Laden's escape routes and to find and arrest or kill him and his deputies. After the U.S. finally introduced ground force units into Afghanistan and began sweep operations looking for al Qaeda and the Taliban, America and its coalition partners (including France and Germany) should have established a security presence throughout the country. They did not. As a result, the new Afghan government of President Hamid Kharzi was given little authority outside the capital city of Kabul. There was an opportunity to end the factional fighting and impose an integrated national government. Yet after initial efforts to unite the country, American interest waned and the warlords returned to their old ways. Afghanistan was a nation raped by war and factional fighting for twenty years. It needed everything rebuilt, but in contrast to funds sought for Iraq, U.S. economic and development aid to Afghanistan was inadequate and slowly delivered.

I had worked with Jim Dobbins since 1981 on issues ranging from basing cruise missiles in Europe to stabilizing Haiti. Dobbins was a career diplomat and expert on military and security issues. He worked on rebuilding Somalia, Haiti, Kosovo, and Bosnia. In 2001, he began similar work on Afghanistan. He was frustrated by the lack of resources and attention given the effort by the Bush administration. As Dobbins has pointed out, in the first two years of the Bosnia and Kosovo rebuilding efforts, funds available totaled $1,390 and $814 per capita. For Afghanistan, the per capita funds assigned were only $52.

Dobbins had worked on creating new national police and security services in several failed states. He hoped to do so in Afghanistan, but the Bush administration seemed uninterested in a serious effort. The goal the Pentagon approved was only a 4,800-man Afghan national army by 2004. Some regional warlords count their strength at ten thousand men under arms. The initial units of the new force were trained by the U.S., but we soon stopped support and supervision. Many of the new recruits departed the force, taking their equipment with them. Meanwhile, Mullah Omar, leader of the Taliban, was still at large and reorganizing his forces on both sides of the Pakistani border. Despite two years of U.S. forces in Afghanistan, we have not eliminated the Taliban. Afghanistan was supposed to be an example of Rumsfeld's theories that small amounts of special forces and airpower could combine to do what large Army units had been called on to do in the past. Dobbins and others who examined the Afghan security issue closely have no doubt that the United States could have brought true stability to Afghanistan with a larger force, could have made the return of the Taliban and the terrorists virtually impossible. Instead, the larger force was held back for Iraq. Because of a lack of attention and resources, Afghanistan is still a potential sanctuary for terrorists.

———

THE SECOND COUNTRY in need of significant US help to prevent its fall to al Qaeda–like groups is Pakistan. Pakistan had been tentative and bifurcated before September 11. The military's Inter-Services Intelligence Directorate had provided the Taliban with arms, men, and information. ISID personnel had trained Kashmiri terrorists at al Qaeda camps and worked with al Qaeda–related terrorists to put pressure on India. Pakistani police and security services, on the other hand, had arrested al Qaeda personnel transiting en route to Afghanistan, when given specific information by U.S. authorities. After the attacks on America, and despite the popularity of al Qaeda in parts of Pakistan, General Musharraf courageously pressed his agencies to help the U.S. find any al Qaeda presence in the country. Two of al Qaeda's top operational managers, Khalid Sheik Muhammad and Abu Zubayda, were among those found and arrested in joint Pakistani-American actions. CIA and FBI had determined Khalid Sheik Muhammad's importance in al Qaeda, his leadership in the September 11 operation, only after the attacks in America. Abu Zubayda, however, had been identified as a key target for CIA action after the Millennium threats.

For weeks in 2000, National Security Advisor Sandy Berger's checklist for talking to Tenet had included the question, "Have you found Zubayda in Pakistan yet?" On several occasions in 2000 I would tell Berger to expect a call during the night because CIA was getting close to Zubayda. I never got to make that call. When he was finally arrested in 2002, he reportedly provided his interrogators with useful information. Had CIA snatched him in 2000 as directed, he might have told of his plot with Khalid Sheik Muhammad to stage aircraft attacks in America.

To this day, Usama bin Laden is a popular icon in Pakistan.

Mosques and affiliated madrassas schools in Pakistan teach hatred of America and all that is not Islam. Large areas of Pakistan along the Afghan border are still not controlled by the central government and offer sanctuary to the Taliban and al Qaeda. All of this is true about a country that also has nuclear weapons.

More disturbing are reports that some scientists who had worked on Pakistan's nuclear program are also al Qaeda sympathizers and have discussed their expertise with al Qaeda, Libya, Iran, North Korea, and others. Nothing, and certainly not Iraq, can be more important than stopping al Qaeda from getting its hands on a nuclear weapon.

Pakistan is ruled by General Musharraf and the army. Democracy is temporarily suspended, as it has often been in Pakistan's turbulent history. Musharraf now appears to genuinely want to eradicate al Qaeda and the support for its beliefs in Pakistan. To do that, however, he must demonstrate that the government and the economy can deliver for the people of Pakistan. He must create public schools that teach tolerance to replace the madrassas that teach hate. The ideological battle for the hearts and minds of Pakistanis will only be won by the secular modernists if they can be seen to be improving the standard of living for the many poor, uneducated Pakistanis where al Qaeda derives much of its support.

Few issues demand attention and resources more than Pakistan. Once an example of an Islamic democracy with a high-tech future, Pakistan could become what bin Laden dreams of: an Islamic nation controlled by radicals, with popular support for fundamentalism and terrorism, armed with nuclear weapons. Such a state could use those nuclear weapons in a war of hatred with neighboring India or it could provide them to terrorists. For now, under General Musharraf, the nuclear weapons are reportedly under tight control. Musharraf, however, needs help to turn the popular attitude in his country from supporting al Qaeda's view of the future to supporting a modern, democratic, peaceful view of the future. Although the U.S. increased assistance to Pakistan in 2001, it is inadequate to make the difference needed, to turn the tide in Pakistan and return it to stability. On a 2003 visit to the United States, General Musharraf complained that the U.S. was offering him military assistance funds which he did not need and not providing the economic development help he desperately required.

SAUDI ARABIA IS THE THIRD of the priority nations. For several years prior to September 11, the United States government provided the Saudis with information about al Qaeda members in the Kingdom. That information seemed to disappear into a black box. Seldom were we told the results, if any, of investigations into the information we provided. The same was true of U.S. appeals for the Saudis to investigate al Qaeda fund-raising and money laundering in the Kingdom, or the use of Saudi charities and nongovernmental organizations by al Qaeda operatives. There was some greater cooperation after September 11, but discernible and serious Saudi efforts to root out al Qaeda in the Kingdom seemed to start only after al Qaeda staged truck bomb attacks in Riyadh in 2003. Why the lethargy, the reluctance, the denial?

For Americans to understand the Saudi government's attitude over the last few years, it may be easiest to explain by analogy. What might Washington's attitude be if some country alleged that the Opus Dei religious sect of Roman Catholicism were engaged in terrorism around the world and had to be destroyed, its leaders killed or arrested? Without even looking at the evidence offered by the foreign government, some in the government in Washington would say that they agreed with the basic beliefs of Opus Dei. Some in sensitive government jobs might even be members of Opus Dei (as FBI Director Louis Freeh was alleged to be), and thus reluctant to arrest their co-believers. The analogy is imprecise. Opus Dei is not engaged in terrorism. But it is certainly true that the core al Qaeda beliefs are not very different from those of many leading Saudis, whose Wahhabist version of Islam teaches intolerance of other religions and support for expanding the realm of Islam. As Keeper of the Two Holy Mosques (the Saudi King's official title), the House of Saud has seen itself as both protector of Muslims everywhere and supporter of Wahhabist evangelism everywhere. They did, therefore, use Saudi government funds to support the jihad in Afghanistan. Saudi funds, whether officially governmental or not, almost certainly funded jihadist activities in Bosnia and, as the Russian government has charged, in Chechnya. Saudi government funds established Wahhabist mosques and schools not only in the jihad countries, but in Europe and the United States. Saudi government funds and those of concerned wealthy Saudis flowed to a series of charities and nongovernmental organizations, which in turn provided support for al Qaeda operatives.

Did the Saudi government knowingly provide funding and support for al Qaeda? It is a large and wealthy government not known for transparency or exacting audits. I doubt any Minister or senior member of the royal family supported the attacks on the United States; indeed there is evidence that there were ineffectual efforts to control bin Laden. But it must also be said that Ministers and members of the royal family did knowingly support the global spread of Wahhabist Islam, jihads, and anti-Israeli activities. They ignored anti-American teaching in and around mosques and schools where intolerance was indoctrinated. They replaced a technical, Western-styled curriculum in Saudi schools with a Wahhabist religion-focused education. As long as the royal family and its rule were not the obvious targets, some undoubtedly turned a blind eye to a host of things that made al Qaeda's life easier.

After the truck bomb attacks in Riyadh in 2003, the Saudi security services appear to have been ordered to root out al Qaeda in the Kingdom. Not surprisingly to American counterterrorist experts, the Saudi security services have become involved in gun battles and street chases. They have uncovered large arms caches, not intended for jihad elsewhere or attacks on U.S. facilities in the Kingdom, but almost certainly intended for guerrilla war in Saudi Arabia, a war intended to replace the House of Saud.

The fall of the House of Saud would not come as a shock to many senior American officials who have followed the Middle East for years. Many have long feared, without being able to prove it, that that House and its military and security services are riddled with termites. Stung by the fall of the Shah of Iran in 1979 and its replacement with an anti-American theocracy, many American officials have feared a repeat performance of that tragedy across the Gulf in Saudi Arabia. This fear probably played a role in the thinking of some in the Bush administration, including Dick Cheney, who wanted to go to war with Iraq. With Saddam gone, they believed, the U.S. could reduce its dependence on Saudi Arabia, could pull forces out of the Kingdom, and could open up an alternative source of oil.

Former CIA Director Jim Woolsey has talked publicly about the need for a new government in Riyadh. The risk that the United States runs is of creating a self-fulfilling prophecy, removing the American "mandate of heaven" from the House of Saud without a plan or any influence about what would happen next. Yet the U.S. military intervention in Iraq has, ironically, further reduced support for both the U.S. and the House of Saud among many of the discontented in the Kingdom. We are securing the wrong country, and making its neighbor more unstable in the process.

The future and stability of Saudi Arabia is of paramount importance to the United States; our policy cannot just be one of reducing our dependence upon it. The American government should be engaging at several levels to develop sources of information about what is really going on inside the Kingdom and to create the means of influencing the nation's future. Instead, President Bush has chosen to deliver a lecture in Washington about the importance of democracy for Arab states. Coming as it did from a President widely hated in the Arab world for his invasion to impose a U.S.-styled democracy in Iraq, the words of the President's lecture did little to stimulate a positive response. Indeed, because the U.S. apparently believes in imposing its ideology through the violence of war, many in the Arab world wonder how the United States can criticize the fundamentalists who also seek to impose their ideology through violence.

IRAN, THE FOURTH OF THE PRIORITY COUNTRIES, is as important as the others in the war on terrorism. When the Bush administration talked about Iraq as a nation that supported terrorism, including al Qaeda, and was developing weapons of mass destruction, those comments perfectly suited Iran, not Iraq. It was Tehran that had funded and directed Hezbollah since its inception. It was Hezbollah that had killed hundreds of Americans in Lebanon (the Marine barracks) and Saudi Arabia (Khobar Towers). Hezbollah, with Iranian support, has also killed hundreds of Israelis. While the "ties" and "links" between Saddam and al Qaeda were minimal, al Qaeda regularly used Iranian territory for transit and sanctuary prior to September 11. Al Qaeda's Egyptian branch, Egyptian Islamic Jihad, operated openly in Tehran. It is no coincidence that many of the al Qaeda management team, or Shura Council, moved across the border into Iran after U.S. forces finally invaded Afghanistan.

While Iraq's weapons of mass destruction proved elusive to U.N. inspectors (and later to U.S. troops), the U.N.'s International Atomic Energy Agency found evidence that Iran was secretly engaged in a nuclear weapons program. Iran was much more actively engaged with terrorism and weapons of mass destruction than Iraq. Any objective observer looking at the evidence in 2002 and 2003 would have said that the U.S. should spend more time and attention dealing with the security threats from Tehran than those from Baghdad. That is not meant as an argument for invading Iran. Having once looked at that option in detail in 1996, I have no desire to revisit it. It is, however, an argument for paying attention to real threats. Many of these threats, like Iran, require thoughtful, imaginative, and careful responses. There are strong, active democratic forces in Iran. Without destroying their credibility by making them agents of the CIA, the United States, working with other nations, should be able to strengthen these democratic forces in Iran to the point where they can take control of the national security apparatus from the ideologues. It will not be an easy task and it will require the persistent devotion of high-level U.S. attention, not unlike what is being devoted to Iraq.

IF WE DO NOT SHIFT ATTENTION back to where it should have been after September 11, we face the prospect of the following scenario by 2007: a Taliban-like government in Pakistan armed with nuclear weapons, supporting a similar satellite nation next door in Afghanistan and promoting al Qaeda–like ideology and terror throughout the world; in the Gulf, a nuclear-armed Iran, promoting its own version of Hezbollah-styled ideology, and Saudi Arabia after the fall of the House of Saud, creating its own version of a fourteenth-century theocratic republic. Under those circumstances, even if we had created a Jeffersonian democracy in Iraq, America and the world would still be vastly less secure. Moreover, it appeared early in 2004 that Iraq would be shaped more by the thoughts of Shi'a leader Ayatollah Sistani than by Jefferson.

September 11 brought both tragedy all too painful and an opportunity unexpected. You could see it on the streets of Tehran, as tens of thousands rallied spontaneously to show their solidarity with America. You could see it on the streets of America, where flags sprouted from almost every house. There was an opportunity to unite people around the world around a set of shared values: religious tolerance, diversity, freedom, and security. With globalism rushing upon us, such a restatement of basic beliefs, akin to the U.N. Declarations after World War II, was much needed. It did not happen. We squandered the opportunity.

Many around the world also feared that the world's only remaining superpower would lash out, destabilizing nations and regions. America, after all, spends more money on its weapons and military than the next seven nations combined. Would a system that tolerated such spending act like a muscle-bound cowboy or, as the French feared, a hyper-power? Many in the Muslim world feared that America would, despite its promises, strike out against Islamic regimes and make Professor Sam Huntington's Clash of Cultures theory a self-fulfilling prophecy. They feared that America would give only lip service to the Palestinian problem that was a litmus test for so many Muslims. Many in America sought ways of demonstrating patriotism. We knew there would be heightened security measures and greater expenditures, but we put aside our fears of Big Brother and were prepared to unite as one people in the face of irrational hatred and unspeakable violence. Our leadership fell into the trap, fulfilling all of the worst fears of many around the world and here at home. Rather than seek to cultivate a unified global consensus to destroy the ideological roots of terrorism, we did in fact lash out in a largely unilateral and entirely irrelevant military adventure against a Muslim nation. Just as many nations thought we would, America pointedly snubbed the counsel of Arab friends and NATO allies, and sought security through the use of military muscle. It has left us less secure.

After September 11, Americans were asked to shop, not to sacrifice. Far from being asked to pay additional taxes to fund the war on terrorism, Americans were told that they would pay fewer taxes and we would pay for the war and additional security by passing on the costs to our grandchildren. The consensus against terrorism was shattered by such overreaching as the arrest of American citizens in the United States and their designation as "enemies" to be denied lawyers and due process. The Attorney General, rather than bringing us together, managed to persuade much of the country that the needed reforms of the Patriot Act were actually the beginning of fascism. Rather than seriously and systematically addressing the real security vulnerabilities in this country, the Administration succumbed to political pressure to reorganize agencies amid the "war on terrorism" and created an unwieldy bureaucracy. Unwilling to fund security upgrades at necessary levels, the Administration funded pork barrel procurement of high-tech weapons for small towns while police and fire personnel were laid off in high-threat cities.

September 11 erased memories of the unique process whereby George Bush had been selected as President a few months earlier. Now, as he stood with an arm around a New York fireman promising to get those who had destroyed the World Trade Center, he was every American's President. His polls soared. He had a unique opportunity to unite America, to bring the United States together with allies around the world to fight terrorism and hate, to eliminate al Qaeda, to eliminate our vulnerabilities, to strengthen important nations threatened by radicalism. He did none of those things. He invaded Iraq.

There were no longer any excuses after September 11 for failing to eliminate the threat posed by al Qaeda and its clones, for failing to reduce America's vulnerabilities to attack. Instead of addressing that threat with all the necessary attention it required, we went off on a tangent, off after Iraq, off on a path that weakened us and strengthened the next generation of al Qaedas. For even as we have been attriting the core al Qaeda organization, it has metastasized. It was like a Hydra, growing new heads. There have been far more major terrorist attacks by al Qaeda and its regional clones in the thirty months since September 11 than there were in the thirty months prior to that momentous event. I wonder if bin Laden and his deputies actually planned for September 11 to be like smashing a pod of seeds that spread around the world, allowing them to step back out of the picture and have the regional organizations they created take their generation-long struggle to the next level.

President Bush asked us soon after September 11 for cards or charts of the "senior al Qaeda managers," as though dealing with them would be like a Harvard Business School exercise in a hostile takeover. He announced his intentions to measure progress in the war on terrorism by crossing through the pictures of those caught or killed. I have a disturbing image of him sitting by a warm White House fireplace drawing a dozen red Xs on the faces of the former al Qaeda corporate board, and soon perhaps on Usama bin Laden, while the new clones of al Qaeda are working the back alleys and dark warrens of Baghdad, Cairo, Jakarta, Karachi, Detroit, and Newark, using the scenes from Iraq to stoke the hatred of America even further, recruiting thousands whose names we will never know, whose faces will never be on President Bush's little charts, not until it is again too late.

The nation needed thoughtful leadership to deal with the underlying problems September 11 reflected: a radical deviant Islamist ideology on the rise, real security vulnerabilities in the highly integrated global civilization. Instead, America got unthinking reactions, ham-handed responses, and a rejection of analysis in favor of received wisdom. It has left us less secure. We will pay the price for a long time.

Epilogue

THIS BOOK IS, as I said in the Preface, my story, from my memory. It has helped me to tell it. I needed to tell you that we tried, tried hard to stop the big al Qaeda attack, that the professionals who sat at the Counterterrorism Security Group table cared, and would have given our own lives if that could have stopped the attacks. I had to admit that, strident as I was about the al Qaeda threat, I did not resign in protest when my recommendations to bomb the al Qaeda infrastructure were deferred by the Clinton administration or my appeals for "urgent" action were ignored by the Bush administration. Perhaps I should have. I needed to tell you why I think we failed and why I think America is still failing to deal with the threat posed by terrorists distorting Islam.

That threat is not something that we can defeat with arrests and detentions alone. We must work with our Islamic friends to create an active alternative to the popular terrorist perversion of Islam. It is not something that we can do in a year or even a decade. We cannot be lulled into thinking we are succeeding because we have dealt with "the majority of the known al Qaeda leaders," or because there has been no major attack for some time. Their recruitment goes on, aided by our invasion and occupation of Iraq. Time is slipping by in which the new, follow-on al Qaedas are gaining in strength in scores of countries. Time is passing, but yet our vulnerabilities to attacks at home remain.

Terrorism, which never once was addressed by the presidential candidates in 2000, will be a major topic in the 2004 campaign. Already, as I write before the candidates have been nominated, President Bush is telling fund-raisers, illogically, that he deserves money for his reelection because he is "fighting the terrorists in Iraq so that we don't have to fight them in the streets of America." He never points out that our being in Iraq does nothing to prevent terrorists from coming to

America, but does divert funds from addressing our domestic vulnerabilities and does make terrorist recruitment easier. Nonetheless, the Las Vegas oddsmakers and Washington pundits think that Bush will easily be reelected. One shudders to think what additional errors he will make in the next four years to strengthen the al Qaeda follow-ons: attacking Syria or Iran, undermining the Saudi regime without a plan for a successor state?

A week before September 11, I wrote that the decision the Administration had to make was whether al Qaeda and its network was just a nuisance to the great superpower or whether it represented an existential threat; if it was the latter, then we had to act like it was. Despite September 11 and the many al Qaeda network attacks around the world since then, most Americans and most in the American government still think that the great superpower cannot be defeated by a gang of religious zealots who want a global theocracy, a fourteenth-century Caliphate.

Never underestimate the enemy. Our current enemy is in it for the long haul. They are smart and they are patient. Defeating them will take creativity and imagination, as well as energy. It will be the struggle of the friends of freedom and civil liberties around the world.

What happened to that team that tried to get the Bush White House to pay attention to al Qaeda before September 11 and then stayed in the Situation Room on that day holding things together, even though they thought the White House was about to be hit by a hijacked aircraft? Where are Lisa Gordon-Hagerty and Roger Cressey and Paul Kurtz? They all left the Administration, frustrated. They were never formally thanked by the President, never recognized for what they did before or on September 11. Lisa is working on the safety of nuclear materials in the United States. Paul is busy promoting cyber security. Roger and I are consulting with private sector companies concerned with security and with information assurance; we appear regularly on television, still trying to warn about al Qaeda.

And the others? Mike Sheehan gave up a cushy job to go to work for the NYPD as Deputy Commissioner for Counterterrorism, to try personally to protect the city he loves. You may see him on Wall

Street, or on the Brooklyn Bridge, or at the Lincoln Tunnel checking the defenses. Randy Beers became the national security coordinator for the John Kerry campaign.

Cressey, Beers, and I are also teaching graduate students, hoping that we can help the next generation of national security managers to understand the dangers of simplistic and unilateral approaches to counterterrorism. Some in our classes may have to make tough decisions for our country in the fight against terrorism someday, because it is going to be a generation-long struggle.

As Americans, it is up to all of us to be well informed and thoughtful, to help our country make the right decisions in this time of testing. We all need to recommit ourselves to that ancient pledge "to preserve, protect, and defend the Constitution of the United States of America, Against All Enemies . . ."

Index

ABOUT THE AUTHOR

RICHARD A. CLARKE served the last three presidents on the National Security Council Staff, establishing a record for continuous service in White House national security policy positions. Until March 2003 he was a career member of the Senior Executive Service, having begun his federal service in 1973 in the Office of the Secretary of Defense as an analyst on nuclear weapons and European security issues. In the administration of Ronald Reagan, Mr. Clarke was the Deputy Assistant Secretary of State for Intelligence. In the George H.W. Bush administration, he was the Assistant Secretary of State of Politico-Military Affairs and then a member of his NSC Staff. He served for eight years as a Special Assistant to President Clinton and served as National Coordinator for Security and Counterterrorism for both President Clinton and President George W. Bush. From 2001 to 2003, he was the Special Advisor to the President for Cyberspace Security and Chairman of the President's Critical Infrastructure Protection Board. He is now chairman of Good Harbor Consulting.